Advance Praise for
Nurturing Your Teenager's Soul

"Yet again a talented writer helps all of us to consider ways of encouraging our young people morally and spiritually and does so in a wonderfully thoughtful, accessible way! A great gift to us readers!"
—Robert Coles, author of *The Spiritual Lives of Children*

"At what time in our history could it be more fortunate that parents now have in their hands a guidebook to raising teens of character? Mimi Doe writes beautiful, practical books, and *Nurturing Your Teenager's Soul* is perhaps her·best. Filled with insights and great advice, this book helps us both reclaim our teens and let them flourish with purpose and dignity."
—Michael Gurian, author of *The Wonder of Children: Nurturing the Souls of Our Sons and Daughters*

"Mimi Doe's new book *Nurturing Your Teenager's Soul* is a treasure. Mimi Doe captures what is truly important in the parenting process. Her ideas are refreshingly down-to-earth and she writes in a style that reflects her respect for and knowledge of the challenges of being both a teenager and the parent of a teenager. I believe this book will be read and reread by parents and each reading will enrich the emotional and spiritual life of the family."
—Robert Brooks, coauthor of *Raising Resilient Children*

"Every parent who wants to help their teen to navigate these tumultuous years with a sense of self, family, and community should read this book. Mimi Doe provides practical, real guidance for parents to tap into their own spiritual strength and in turn help their adolescents achieve their full potential."
—Judith Orloff, M.D., author of *Positive Energy*

NURTURING
YOUR TEENAGER'S
SOUL

A Practical Approach to Raising a
Kind, Honorable, Compassionate Teen

Mimi Doe

Most Perigee Books are available at special quantity discounts for bulk purchases for sales promotions, premiums, fund-raising or educational use. Special books, or book excerpts, can also be created to fit specific needs.

For details, write: Special Markets, The Berkley Publishing Group, 375 Hudson Street, New York, New York 10014.

A Perigee Book
Published by the Penguin Group
Penguin Group (USA) Inc.
375 Hudson Street, New York, New York 10014, USA
Penguin Group (Canada), 10 Alcorn Avenue, Toronto, Ontario M4V 3B2, Canada
(a division of Pearson Penguin Canada Inc.)
Penguin Books Ltd., 80 Strand, London WC2R 0RL, England
Penguin Group Ireland, 25 St. Stephen's Green, Dublin 2, Ireland (a division of Penguin Books Ltd)
Penguin Group (Australia), 250 Camberwell Road, Camberwell, Victoria 3124, Australia
(a division of Pearson Australia Group Pty. Ltd.)
Penguin Books India Pvt. Ltd. 11 Community Centre, Panchsheel Park, New Delhi—110 017, India
Penguin Group (NZ), Cnr. Airborne and Rosedale Roads, Albany, Auckland 1310, New Zealand
(a division of Pearson New Zealand Ltd.)
Penguin Books (South Africa) (Pty.) Ltd., 24 Sturdee Avenue, Rosebank, Johannesburg 2196,
South Africa
Penguin Books Ltd., Registered Offices: 80 Strand, London WC2R 0RL, England

Copyright © 2004 by Mimi Doe
Text design by Tiffany Estreicher
Cover design by Wendy Bass
Cover photo © Getty Images

PRINTING HISTORY
Perigee trade paperback edition / November 2004

This book has been cataloged by the Library of Congress
Doe, Mimi.
    Nurturing your teenager's soul : a practical approach to raising a kind, honorable, compassionate teen / Mimi Doe.—Perigee trade pbk. ed.
        p.   cm.
    Includes bibliographical references and index.
    ISBN 0-399-53028-2
    1. Parent and teenager.   2. Parenting.   3. Parenting—Religious aspects.
    4. Teenagers—Religious life.   I. Title.

HQ799.15.D65 2004
649'.125—dc22
                                                     2004053497

PRINTED IN THE UNITED STATES OF AMERICA

10 9 8 7 6 5 4 3 2 1

This book is dedicated to my daughters, Whitney and Elizabeth, without whom it never would have been conceived.

Acknowledgments

I wish to acknowledge my incredible husband Tom Doe who is my ideal partner in life. Profound thanks to Tom and our daughters for filling my world with joy. There is no greater pleasure for me than spending time with these three spectacular human beings.

I wish to thank Sheila Curry Oakes, Adrienne Ianniello Schultz, Marian Lizzi, Carol Mann, and Jenni Green for their help in crafting this guide as well as my friend and fellow author Stacy DeBroff, whose humor, insight, and Pad Thai lunch dates kept me on track. My terrific brother Tim Walch is a living example of kindness in action and I thank him for his constant support. Brenna McDonough is the kind of friend that doesn't come around often in life and I am so grateful for her generous spirit. I thank all those parents who are part of the Spiritual Parenting community. Your quest to parent in the light continues to inspire me. Finally, I want to stand up and cheer for the wonderful teenagers I know and love as well as those whom I've met over the past few years. Your futures are as wide open as your bountiful spirits. Enjoy the journey.

CONTENTS

NURTURING
YOUR TEENAGER'S
SOUL

Introduction

"Spirituality keeps me focused and aware of a bigger picture. Life as a teen is full of details and I need this bigger view or I'd go crazy." **—Thomas, sixteen**

. . .

All teens—not just Thomas—are spiritual beings. Despite increased contact with a world that often tells them otherwise, their nature is divine. They crave a connection to something greater than themselves while questioning the adults with whom they live. Teenagers need, as we all do, to experience a sacred connection with Spirit that provides meaning and direction to life. They also desperately want to maintain an open, loving relationship with us, their parents, even when it appears that they are pushing us away.

The challenges of the years from twelve to nineteen can distract teens and their parents from a Divine Presence and from each other. And yet, adolescence is a time when we experience a spiritual hunger which is often misunderstood as restlessness, frustration, or anger. When we acknowledge this ripe sacred yearning, the teen years can be seen as a time of possibilities and expansion. Our sons and daughters are on the brink of discovering their vast potential and feel this calling, although it is often blurred and confused by the pull of the culture in which they live and the bodies that house their spirits.

Daily pressures can seem overwhelming: peer influences, the hazards of substance abuse and sexual activity, the risks and freedoms of driving and dating, the pressure to succeed in school and get into a good college. We want to help our teens meet these challenges and enter the world as successful, confident young adults. We advise, warn, help with algebra, turn over our car keys, wait up into the wee hours, and travel to college campuses. However, we may be missing the core component for helping our teens develop into healthy and competent adults—nurturing their spirituality.

Spirituality can be thought of as a positive sense of life purpose and a feeling of hope for one's future. Spirituality is a connection with a power greater than ourselves and with all creation. The process we follow as we quest for more knowledge of what is inside and outside of ourselves is our "spiritual journey." Jamie, a fifteen-year-old ripe with a soulful curiosity says it well: "What I'm figuring out is: How do I *do* my life?"

You are able to contribute to your teenage children's spirituality in ways more profound than you ever imagined. It's as simple as choosing to love them more deeply in the midst of the ordinary: replacing irritation with understanding, suggesting options rather than insisting upon specific solutions, and focusing on their beautiful inner light rather than on annoying behaviors. Nurturing a teenager's spirituality should become as integral a part of parenting as setting a curfew and requiring the use of seat belts.

Two questions consume teens: "Who am I?" and "Where do I fit in?" Although they may look for answers in decidedly nonspiritual places, their search for an identity and home in this world is a spiritual quest. Spirituality provides meaning to life. It fuels self-worth, a sense of purpose and guides us toward behaviors that honor the Divine spark in others and ourselves.

Spirituality can thrive inside churches, mosques, and synagogues—and far from them. Many people find a direct connection to God in nature through creative expression or in moments of human sharing. Spirit can have many names: Goddess, Higher Power, the I Am, Allah, Mother/Father

God, or as the shirt worn by Max, a seventeen-year-old skateboarder reads, "God's my Home Boy." Whatever you are comfortable calling it, the Divine Essence at the center of the universe connects every living thing and calls each of us, especially our teenagers, to be all that we can be.

Adolescents are fluid beings moving between Gandhi and Eminem as quickly as they change classes. They are ready for meaningful philosophical exploration and discussions one minute—then blast the car horn and flip their finger to a slow driver the next. They numb out in front of questionable television programming on Friday night and awaken at dawn to plant in the local food bank's garden. A teenager might come home from school weeping over lunchroom cliques and social injustice within her peer group and just when you are about to set up a meeting with her guidance counselor, she mentions plans for a sleep over with the gang after Friday's game.

We are programmed to believe these are mood swings and rampaging hormones rather than seeing a connection between their desire for more control over their lives, a hunger for meaning, and limited time for reflection on the sweeping insights washing over them. Teen's lives move very quickly and it can be during this motion that they are encouraged toward spiritual intimacy. In fact, even with constant activity, life can be deeply lonely for teenagers when they lack a deep personal connection with their spirituality.

Our kids experience more changes in their daily rhythms than most adults. In a typical day a fifteen-year-old girl might experience: the jarring dash from bed to the bus, utter boredom in English class, loneliness after being "dissed" at lunch, anger over the unfair sports call during her soccer match, jubilation when returning home to find an article she wrote printed in the local paper, and frustration at her parent's harsh words over her too frequent Internet usage. This is a great deal of emotion to feel in one day. When kids are comfortable in their communion with Spirit, they have a ready resource to ground them as their emotional life takes flight.

Spirituality seeps between the cracks of busy days to wrap teenagers in the web of understanding, joy, acceptance, and belonging. Spiritual parenting bolsters our kids' inner lives and becomes the salve for raw emotions and fragile psyches—ours and our teens'.

It's never too late to uncover new ways to be in a relationship with your son or daughter so that you each might experience more joy and a deeper, more magnificent connection with one another and with God.

Spiritual parenting offers the everyday spirituality that nourishes your teen's soul. By adopting the principles of spiritual parenting, you create a framework for adjusting, reacting, and calmly embracing the new terrain that comes with parenting an adolescent. Spiritual parenting feeds your soul while you care for those of your children. In this way you find compassionate energy and loving acceptance to embrace this phase of your life as a sacred journey rather than a swaying roller coaster ride on a rainy day.

My daughters—Whitney, sixteen, and Elizabeth, thirteen—are exploring their spiritual convictions and in so doing continue to teach me how to be a spiritual parent.

I've learned that spiritual parenting a teenager is less about doing than being. It's not a system for teaching your son or daughter about religion. In fact, many of us who parent teens have found that trying to teach religion at this age only invites struggle. As our children pass through adolescence, their ability to hear us often vanishes along with their security blankies. However, our behavior toward them speaks volumes.

Parenting teens spiritually is a way of consistently and quietly shining light into their lives. Not a probing flashlight of inquisition, but rather a gentle beacon of soulful nurturing. Spiritual parenting involves mirroring the Divine light radiating through our teen and reflecting it back. It means waiting patiently for moments of connection and using these moments mindfully.

Teenagers are the sector of the population most looked at, and yet least listened to or understood. Spiritual parenting asks us to listen to and honor our sons and daughters. Compassionate and understanding parents are spiritual parents. Parents who are present with a teenager who is angry, in pain, or rejoicing are spiritual parents. When we set loving limits, coach rather than control, consistently communicate, expect mistakes, and suspend judgment we are able to find soulfullness in the path of loving our child. Our journey as spiritual parents isn't to impose esoteric teachings on our teens in between trips to the grocery store and the orthodontist, but rather to open the lid to what's already there, within both of us, and allow it to flow constantly as spiritual energy does.

Parenting an adolescent need not be the dark, frightening, tumultuous scenario that is so vividly portrayed in parenting books, radio talk shows, and daily conversations. Yes, we have to adjust and adapt to our evolving adolescent's needs and honor our own comfort zones, but there is no biological mandate that states, "All teens are at all times rude, unkind, trouble-making monsters." What we say is what we get, and how we envision our lives with our teenage sons and daughters is a powerful influence not to be overlooked.

Choosing to parent from a spiritual perspective doesn't guarantee that you will have a serene relationship with your teen. It doesn't mean you will eat tofu and levitate all day or that your child will give up his Walkman and feed the hungry. It doesn't mean you won't lose your temper, feel disappointment, or that you'll have a ready response to every challenging situation or snide comment. It's not possible for adolescence to be a perpetually happy time. Our teens are supposed to be shedding elements of their childlike selves to emerge into the complexities of adulthood and the enormous energy of a mature spiritual being. In this tremendous task, there will inevitably come periods of conflict and discontent for both of you.

Spiritual parenting simply and profoundly orients you to what is most important during this time of change. The Ten Principles in this book are meant to guide and ground you as you respond to and support your teenagers through their evolution into happy, spiritually fulfilled beings.

How to Use the Ten Principles

The Principles of Spiritual Parenting remind you that you are not alone as a parent, even if you're the only adult in your household. They encourage you to cultivate peace of mind and compassion, trust Divine guidance, act on inspiration, seek and savor the positive in your daily rhythms, and loosen your grip. The Principles support you as you mentor your teenager, create room for nonjudgmental conversation, articulate clear expectations,

Ten Principles of Spiritual Parenting

PRINCIPLE ONE: You Are Part of Something Bigger

PRINCIPLE TWO: Understand That All Life Is Connected and Has Meaning

PRINCIPLE THREE: Words Can Profoundly Change Lives

PRINCIPLE FOUR: Listen Fully, Acknowledge Deeply

PRINCIPLE FIVE: Supported Dreams Manifest Miracles

PRINCIPLE SIX: Be What You Want to See

PRINCIPLE SEVEN: Remain Flexibly Firm

PRINCIPLE EIGHT: Awaken Wonder and Spirit Flows

PRINCIPLE NINE: Let Go and Trust

PRINCIPLE TEN: Each Day Offers Renewal

boldly demonstrate your values, and live as a model for how spirituality and daily life merge. Spiritual parenting turns what could be the daily tedium of parenting into a profoundly meaningful partnership between you, your teenager, and God.

Terri, a mother of two teens, says, "Knowing that God is with me inspires me to make sometimes unpopular choices as a parent. Every time, the positive results are far beyond what I imagined. I'm deeply grateful that I don't have to rely solely on myself. I have an amazing Source of inspiration, strength, and peace. Without, it all our lives would be vastly different."

The ideas presented here are meant to encourage you to look beyond chameleonlike changes in interests, clothing, behavior, and attitude to your child's deeper Divine nature. Not only is your teenager developing a more mature body and a more complex ability to organize abstract thinking, but he is also attempting to merge that with a profound esoteric realm. The teenage years are a ripe time to create a conscious union with the Infinite.

In the following pages, you will find ideas to choose from so you might create more meaningful relationships with each of your children while nourishing their rich, vast, wise inner selves. After all, such is the wondrous core of these people who came to the world to express something irreplaceable and unique.

In *Modern Man in Search of a Soul,* Carl Jung observed that among his patients over the age of thirty-five, not one had a problem that did not have a spiritual source. When we foster our teenager's connection with spirituality, we lessen the chance that they will face the breathtaking void that may manifest as problems in their adult lives. We also strengthen their lifeline during the transition to their adult selves.

Unfortunately, most parents of teens have not developed a frame of reference that informs their daily interactions with their sons and daughters. Our kids seem to grow up faster than our ability to adapt. The families who *do* live and parent with a clear set of articulated principles or intentions seem to enjoy their teenagers the most, and their teens flourish.

I encourage you to use the Ten Principles in this book as your "parenting intentions" so that you might create a wider panorama of possibilities in the relationships with your teenagers. Referring to the Principles as a basis for your everyday actions will free you from the often overwhelming sensation of indecision.

The suggestions that follow have worked for many teens and their families. Some of the kids would describe themselves as spiritual, others would not. Some parents would say they are religious, while others prefer to worship at home or in their hearts. Some of the tips, conversation starters, resources, and stories may appeal to you; others will not. Adapt these ideas to make them your own and think of this book as an ongoing buffet from which you can pick and choose, go back for seconds, or skip a course all together.

I use the word "God" because it is a useful term for my experience of the Divine. Please substitute a word that is comfortable for you and your family. Spiritual energy bundled into a word is frustratingly limiting as is the spiritual electricity surging through our children's maturing bodies.

In this book, I've shared many stories and quotes from parents and teenagers. The names are fictitious, but the circumstances are quite real.

Each Principle will include a **Parents' Insight-Building Exercise.** These are tools to help you access the wonderful wisdom you already have. The meditations will allow you to pause your frantic life and gain clarity on the principle presented. Often we aren't able to hear our guidance until we carve out time and force ourselves to sit quietly and listen. The Insight Exercises give you a format and framework for asking and receiving guidance. I encourage you to keep a journal so you might keep track of the thoughts, inspirations, ideas, and solutions that arise as you journey within. I find that the most effective way of using these meditations is to record yourself reading them. Play them back whenever you set aside the time. Or simply read the directions, then put aside the book and begin.

I've also provided **Parents' Check-In Questions.** Use these questions to get a clear picture of where you are with each Principle. Often reading the questions will prompt a rush of feelings. Again, use your journal or notebook to jot down your responses. Don't feel as if this is another chore to add to your long "to do" list but rather an available tool to craft and hone your parenting. Many parents find enormous guidance comes when they are willing and open enough to ask themselves these questions. Their own spiritual lives deepen and answers begin to show up as if by magic.

Conversation Starters are provided in each chapter if you find yourself at a loss for how to dive in to the Principle with your teen. Again, these are simply ideas and topical prompts to guide you as you make conversation a time to grow a deeper relationship with your son or daughter. These prompts can get you out of the "How was your day at school?" rut.

I've gathered the best resources I could find for you and your teen and listed them in the **Resources** section. I will update these resources on my Web site: www.SpiritualParenting.com.

Enjoy these vibrant fleeting years with your son or daughter. Your own joy and spirituality will be deepened as you honor this young adult life you are nurturing into fruition.

You Are Part of Something Bigger

"God is like the internet. Both are always there for me to tap into and both are my access to possibilities. It's my choice."   **—Alie, sixteen**

"You can't have conviction unless your beliefs get tested."   **—Mark, eighteen**

"God is something weak people need."   **—Ken, sixteen**

• • •

Every teen has a unique relationship with God during the tumultuous years between twelve and nineteen. Some teens reject the notion of God outright, no matter what they thought a few years earlier or what their parents believe. To find their adult selves, teens often need to camp out for a little while in value territory that lies 180 degrees away from where the family tent is pitched.

Some teens see God as a power figure, not understanding that Divine goodness and love encompass their ultimate well-being. Not surprisingly, they may reject the presence of another authority figure and the idea of depending upon God. Other teenagers begin to question God when not even the Higher Power can keep middle school heartache from hurting. Two or three years later, tough questions spring from high school friends' betrayals and bad choices. Teens may struggle to find the Divine handprint amid tragedies such as acts of violence, death, and life-altering injuries that occur within their circle of acquaintances.

Still others find support and solace in God during the often puzzling teen years. Buoyed through the tossing seas of peer pressure, dating, driving, and academics, they repeatedly align with the true north that guides us all. They embrace the idea that God respects them and that their journey to self-discovery is a part of God's plan. These teens seem to understand, on some level, that the spark of the Divine within is their unique human potential. They feel a sense of something "more" that often eludes their peers.

I've spoken with many teens who have not been exposed to religion or have been brought up with watered-down faith or atheism. Their response is to seek out the opposite. They knock on the doors of churches, synagogues, and mosques searching for God. They devour books on philosophy and religion while scanning their environment for spiritual clues and cues.

Teens yearn for meaning, and I've heard from those who, regardless of their success at a young age in sports and school, are hungry for a personal, intentional relationship with God that gives them value beyond their secular achievements.

This connection with God can sustain a teenager throughout their transition into adulthood. In fact, spirituality is occupying a growing place in the scientific study of the prevention of drug abuse. One recent study run from the psychology department of the University of Kentucky focused on the link between religious coping and drug use. The results showed that a reliance on God has the strongest effect on reducing drug use in adolescent boys.

Tom, a sixteen-year-old, sent an e-mail response to an article I had written. He wrote, "I found that smoking weed didn't give me what I wanted. It took me a while but I realized I was disillusioned with the God I loved as a kid. Weed became my religion for a while but the magic felt pretty hollow. So, I'm back looking for God. . . ."

I was with a group of teens Tom's age recently as they grappled with the death of a friend. They wondered how God could do this to someone so young. They questioned what this boy might have done wrong or how God might be trying to teach them a lesson. I was shocked to hear that these smart, compassionate teenagers thought that God would kill someone in an automobile accident to teach his friends a lesson. As I spoke with these sad kids, many described God as a white-bearded old man watching their every move, tallying up wrongdoings only to seek vengeance. It would be pretty hard to sustain a loving relationship with or seek comfort from such an image. I tried to help them move through their pain and loss by forging a more personal union with an approachable, loving God. At the end of our time together, I felt a shift. The kids seemed relieved to release the idea that their "screwups" might be the cause of their friend's death. I have hope that this tragedy will prompt them to forge a new understanding of and relationship with God.

For every teen, childish notions about God must give way to more adult thinking. As children mature, they hopefully stop viewing God as a wish-fulfilling cousin to Santa Claus and begin to appreciate the wondrous mystery of the Divine power in whose infinite heart we all live.

Our role in nurturing our child's spiritual life often becomes less direct during the teen years. We can find ourselves more hesitant to point out the magical sparkle in a crimson tree against a sapphire sky or make direct suggestions about prayer. We lack the words that will motivate a teen who's feeling alone and adrift to turn to God. In fact, the more we talk about it now, the more resistance we may engender. Teens are beginning to do their own spiritual thinking. We've lead them to the water, now they choose how to drink.

Rebecca, a seventeen-year-old high school junior, says, "You can't make somebody else believe in God. There's no hard evidence to point to. The only evidence of God is in your own life, and people don't have to see it if they don't want to."

However, as parents we can influence whether our kids feel close to God or doubt the existence of a Higher Power. We can *be* what we want our teens to experience and know the truth of our connection to God so wholeheartedly that it fills our household. In our energy and actions, our teens can find the evidence of the anchor that sustains us.

A nineteen-year-old girl whose family moved in and out of financial crisis said, "My parents never forced me to believe anything, but showed me the truth with their lives. They didn't just idly believe in something, they lived it. I saw how God helped us through very tough times, and saw how blessed I was. My family truly focused on the positive and that made me choose a spiritual path. I haven't regretted it since."

Cultivating and nourishing a spiritual connection during our children's teen years is an important way for us to reflect the essential goodness of the universe to them. It is also a lifesaver for us. Adolescence can be a time when a parent's relationship to God might be tested. The teen years have the potential to be a wild ride. Sometimes, parents get bounced around so much on the road of adolescence that we're tempted to reach over and grab the wheel, instead of trusting God to navigate.

As parents, a sense of something much larger than ourselves helps us keep our bearings from day to day and maintain a long-term perspective. This belief is a resource upon which we may draw in difficult moments. We find solace, too, in the knowledge that our children travel with God as their boundaries expand. Spiritual connection allows us to be fully present for the sweet moments, rejoicing wholeheartedly when it's time for celebration.

"During the years my oldest daughter was sixteen and seventeen, her life was such a mess that I doubted she'd finish high school. I had to coparent with God, because I didn't have the courage and strength I needed. Looking back, almost two years later, I'm so grateful for everything; I'm even grateful for how hard it was because I'm a much stronger person now. I can see how God was even more present than I felt at the time. My daughter's an amazing young woman, and I am so proud of her." —Linda, mother of three

Center Yourself with an Active, Flexible Spiritual Life

"I get up early every morning to be alone and read *A Course in Miracles*. I write down everything that I'm grateful for and set my intentions for the day and the rest of the month. I've been doing this since my children were babies. i might not get the breakfast dishes done but my morning wouldn't begin without this ritual." —**Wynn, mother of three**

Some parents of teens maintain a spiritual routine that remains the same for years. However, between the demands of work and home, partnering and parenting, it can be hard to find the time to engage in what connects you with the Higher Power. This holds true regardless of how old your children are, but rising early to meditate is even less appealing after waiting up until the wee hours for a teen driver to pull into the garage.

My daily ritual once included walking meditation, journaling, yoga, and affirmative prayer. That morning round seems like light years ago. With two teens in the house and a career that's more than full time, I connect with God in shorter moments throughout the day, rather than an extended early morning period of peace.

I grab *Daily Word*—a little magazine with sacred messages for each day of the month—and close my eyes as I take a moment to center my spirit. I open my eyes and read the thoughts and meditations, reflecting on their relevance in my life. Sometimes, I flip to a random page of a favorite spiritual book such as Catherine Ponder's *The Dynamic Laws of Prayer* and let my index finger rest wherever it may, trusting that the message my finger found is exactly what I need to focus on. I check my breath pattern throughout the day, remembering to inhale deeply, *inspiring* in the truest sense of the word as I fill my heart with Spirit and let my shoulders relax.

I remember to tell the people I love that I do. The very act of recollecting how important they are to me brings me home to myself. I find opportunities to practice gratitude and appreciation for ordinary experiences—for waking up earlier than usual and enjoying the peace of a quiet house, for a phone call from a friend at the right time, for the warm smell of the furnace turning on, or the delicious taste of a chocolate I discover in the pantry.

My spiritual practice has recently expanded to include listening to inspirational music. Whitney, my sixteen-year-old, created a few CDs for me to use while I work. These songs of worship and praise lift me up and allow me to be a part of Whitney's unfolding faith. I might not be completely comfortable with some of the heavy-handed lyrics or the bass level in a few tunes, but my spirit opens song by song.

Some parents catch spiritual nourishment on the fly—literally. My friend Amy says, "Running is prayer and meditation for me; sometimes, I actually chant a prayer in time to my feet hitting the pavement. Other times, I just let my mind go blank. No matter what, I always come home calmer and more clear."

Prayer doesn't have to be an incantation of well-known words, such as "*Our Father.*" Prayer is simply talking to God.

"Sometimes, when I'm driving, I imagine that God is sitting in the passenger seat. I just say what's really bothering me; I can be completely honest, without having to worry about saying it the right way or offending someone."

—**Marcia, mother of four**

Finding touchstones throughout the day is one way to help us remember to connect with God. Use an action that you repeat at different times— pouring a cup of coffee, taking a bathroom break, fastening your seat belt—as a reminder to breathe. Check in with yourself, or offer a silent word of gratitude for blessings you've received and those that are still on the way.

Faith Moran, senior minister at the Spiritual Life Center in Sacramento, California, talks about the value of being "prayed up." By establishing and maintaining an active relationship with God during the times when life is calm, we can get right down to business when the going gets tougher. It's easy to understand the concept when we think about lapsed friendships of the human variety. If we've lost touch, even with someone very dear to us, it takes a little time to reconnect. Spending some time maintaining the relationship every day makes it easier to lean on the bond you've built when you need it.

Sometimes, daily spiritual practice routines can grow boring or burdensome. We cling to them out of habit, and inspiration turns into obligation. At these times, when meditation or prayer feels like a "must" instead of a "can't wait," we're far better off trying something new: reading a few passages from a sacred text, walking under vibrant autumn leaves, taking a quick nap. The purpose, not the form, of spiritual practice is what's important, and we can gauge how effective it is by the peace we feel as a result.

To nurture your spiritual connection as you parent your teen, try any of these ideas:

- Cultivate an attitude of gratitude. I recently heard someone describe gratitude as "the mother of all prayers." Nothing opens your heart like actively appreciating life. If you're stumped for something to be grateful for, start small—a warm house, a good cup of tea, the vibrant rosebush you pass on the way to work. One friend of mine keeps her gratitude list in her checkbook. She finds it helps when money panic sets in. Many parents of teens tell me that once they shift to being grateful for their son or daughter's positive qualities they move away from nagging and judging to acceptance.

- Incorporate nurturing practices for all your senses. Beautiful music on the ride to work, soothing lotion on your cracked elbows before bed, soulfully prepared food rather than frantically fixed leftovers, a crystal pitcher of lemon ice water, and lavender oil sprinkled inside running sneakers are actions that may rekindle your connection to Spirit.

- Acknowledge and accept *dis*connection. Spiritual practice isn't about always being connected with Spirit; it's about continually reconnecting. We all have moments when our nerves jangle, impatience surges, or we feel low and alone. Pretending otherwise perpetuates these feelings; acknowledging them diminishes their hold on us.

- By adding more nourishing people, food, and activities to your life, you are strengthening your connection with God. When you replace that nightly glass of wine or heaping bowl of ice cream with sparkling water and a soak in the tub, you experience the same relaxation without dullness the following morning. When you speak kindly of others rather than looking for their flaws, you open your heart rather than clouding it with negativity. Allow Spirit to seep into your life and replace any behavior that numbs and barricades you from experiencing deep spiritual satisfaction.

• Develop an evening ritual of closing the day by turning your thoughts and worries over to God.

Create a Circle to Nourish Your Spirit

I once heard that individuals united in focused prayer create a powerful force for healing—the "power of the group squared." I love that idea and encourage you to find a group of like-minded parents to meet with during your children's teenage years. A magic synergy happens when parents come together, willing to bring a spiritual perspective to bear on daily life with teens. We can acknowledge struggles, keep an eye on the high road, and provide honest, compassionate feedback for each other.

For some parents, a spiritual circle is found in a church, temple, or mosque. For others, a select group of friends, who may live hundreds of miles from each other and might rarely meet, constitutes the same thing, as experienced by this mother of two: "I have five friends who I know will always tell me the truth. They are my lifesavers. We're scattered around the country but keep connected with phone calls, e-mails, and a girls' gathering every year or two."

There's nothing like the wisdom, conversation, and support of other parents to sustain and guide us in the most important job we'll ever have. For that purpose, parents have formed Spiritual Parenting Groups in locations around the world and meet monthly. Visit www.SpiritualParenting.com to find a Spiritual Parenting Group near you or begin one of your own. There are many tips and ideas there to help you get started.

It's a special boon if your circle includes parents whose teens are a few years older than yours. The teen years have a rhythm of their own, and someone else can help us discern the pattern in what seems like cacophony.

"Being a part of a Spiritual Parenting Group has been a lifeline for me as I parent my three kids. There's none of the competitive edge I find when I'm with other parents who make comments like, 'Oh my son is a varsity swimmer, what sport does your son do?' Or 'Joe is being recruited by three colleges because of his brilliance in science.' My parenting group is about building each other up and sharing ways to be the best parents we can be. I am totally honest about what's going on with my kids without any shame or embarrassment. Another mom with older kids gave me a great head's up on the dip her kids felt sophomore year. I'm so grateful!"   **—Susan, mother of three**

When our children are struggling, and that may mean a very different thing from one family to another, it seems to reflect on our strengths and foibles as parents. Sometimes, we can be tempted to cover up these challenges. The truth, though, sets us free. As we share our struggles with each other, willing to lend an ear and shoulder to support someone else, we, too, will have a lighter load.

And when it's time to celebrate a graduation, concert, report card, or first job, this same circle brings full joy to the table, appreciating the smooth stretches because they've been along for the bumpier parts.

To create a nurturing spiritual circle, try these suggestions:

• Start small. Ask one good friend with whom you share some spiritual beliefs if he or she would be interested in exploring the idea of spiritual parenting with you. If so, create a weekly phone check-in time and make it part of your appointments.

• If you would like to meet with a larger group, begin putting the word out through your teen's school, your religious community, or your neighborhood. You can also place an announcement in the local newspapers, school newsletters, parent organization's newsletters, pediatrician's offices, or on busy bulletin boards around town.

• To keep your group running smoothly, try the following:

• Accommodate and respect each member's pace.

- Allow the group to evolve naturally with the most organic format, pace, flavor, and focus.
- Remain open to feedback.
- Keep the group open to everyone's religious beliefs.
- Don't bend to everyone's whims, but do acknowledge and take in all opinions and suggestions.
- Keep it light and fun so you might learn from one another.
- Use one Principle per month, from the ten in this book, as your discussion topics to help you stay focused.
- Create an e-mail list or call-chain system where changes in schedule, location, or messages can be sent.
- Celebrate often!

Embrace the Mystery

From one moment to the next, we may not know who we're living with when we have a teen in the house. Opinions, reactions, hairstyles, career plans, clothing, and dietary preferences can change overnight. The vast majority of these choices don't stick, and they can provide a great source of entertainment. Someone once said that God has a terrific sense of humor. Many parents of teens will confirm the truth of this perspective.

> "My son went through a phase of wearing black eye makeup to school. He thought he looked very cool. I hated it and had to bite my tongue every morning. One day, he came downstairs wearing bright red eye shadow. It was so incredibly ugly that I started to laugh. I turned away so he couldn't see me, then choked out, 'Nice makeup.' He said, 'Thanks!' and went out the door a happy guy." —**Tim, father of one**

It can be difficult to draw a straight line between the way a teen of fifteen talks and behaves and the young adult who emerges over the next few years. If we took seriously each of the myriad ways that our teens experiment with being in the world, we'd lose sight of the complete quilt that is being woven and see only each jagged stitch.

The mystery of living with teens is that underneath all the posing and experimenting, an adult is gestating. It's as though the things we can see, what our teens say and do, are an eggshell. Protected within is a thoughtful adult developing, with God's ever-present guidance. At times the shell thins in places and we catch glimpses of the person who will one day emerge. Eventually, the shell falls away, leaving a radiant young adult.

Each experience our kids undergo, their successes, challenges, heartbreaks, and jubilations, are part of this gestation process. Sometimes the impact of a particular event in a teen's life seems clear. More often it's a part of the great mystery, as in the following story.

Kara, seventeen, was driving herself and three friends down a two-lane country road on a warm, sunny day. Her father was driving the vehicle in front of her. They were returning home from her rural boarding school campus after packing up her dorm room at the end of her junior year.

A truck turned onto the road in front of her, between their two cars, and Kara swerved to avoid it. Her right front wheel left the asphalt road and went into the gravel shoulder. She lost control of her car. It slid at fifty miles per hour across both lanes of the road, hit the far side of a culvert, flipped into the air from the force of the impact, and landed on its roof. Her father watched, horrified and powerless to stop the scene unfolding in his rearview mirror.

He turned his car around. The seconds it took him to cover several hundred yards seemed to take an eternity. The accessories of a teenager's life littered the field surrounding the silent, mangled car. Centrifugal force had scattered a stereo, bedding, schoolbooks, backpacks, makeup, and clothing.

Kara's dad later said, "Intellectually, I knew from the look of things that someone could have died. The entire rear of her car was gone. In my heart, though, I just *knew* that everything was going to be okay."

As he pulled to a stop, all four girls were crawling out of missing car windows. Emergency vehicles soon appeared, and supportive school personnel, having heard of the accident, also rushed to the scene.

Kara was the only one who didn't need medical care. The other girls went by ambulance to the hospital, where two were later admitted. They eventually recovered fully from their injuries and the story might have ended there. However, two years later, Kara reflected on her experience. "At the time, I knew there was a reason for my accident. I didn't know what it was, but I just knew there had to be a reason."

In fact, as time passed, she became aware of a number of ways her life had changed irrevocably as a result of her accident.

Her friends and their families embraced her as she made the rounds of hospital rooms that night, apologizing for her role in causing her friends' pain. Other friends called her to make sure she, too, was okay.

"I felt so guilty but no one blamed me. Everyone else forgave me, so I had to focus on forgiving myself. That was the hardest thing of all," said Kara.

She eventually bought another car, saving money from her part-time job and scouring newspaper ads for the right one.

"I loved the car my dad gave me, but I'm prouder of the one I bought myself. I learned how good it feels to take care of myself," she says.

Most fundamentally, she learned something that many of us never do. She recounts the story of the accident itself.

"In my memory, I'm inside the car until the moment it hits the ditch. Then I can see the whole thing from fifteen feet or so above the car. I watch it flip, and, at the same time, I can see the girls inside the car. I see *myself* inside the car, and I feel so sorry for these girls and for their families. I feel how scared they are, and how much their families will suffer if they die, and my heart aches for all of them. Then the car stops moving, and I'm back inside, crawling out of the window.

"I know now that I am not my body. I am so much bigger and more lasting than my body is."

What Kara learned as a result of her accident shapes her daily life. "Every day is a gift. I know how thin the line is between being here and not. It's easy to die.

"Also, I am so grateful for everyone in my family. I know how important I am to them, and how important they are to me. I know, without a doubt, that God loves me and that God is with me every moment, even when I will eventually leave my body for good."

These lessons were unclear in the immediate aftermath of her accident.

Yet they emerged over time as she and her friends healed from the physical and emotional trauma of what could have been a fatal accident. The cumulative impact has been enormous. Although she lives a few hundred miles away from her family now, she stays connected, frequently expressing her love for them.

As she puts it, "I always tell my mom and dad that I love them when I say good-bye. I know there's no guarantee that I'll see them again."

When our teens experience traumatic events that seem to make no sense, we can acknowledge their pain and gently ask them to consider the possibility that meaning will emerge over time. By embracing the mystery of life, we, parent and child alike, open ourselves to all that it has to offer. Albert Einstein sums up this idea succinctly, "The most beautiful thing we can experience is the mystery."

Try these suggestions to magnify the beautiful mystery that comes from raising teens:

• Develop your capacity for response-ability, the potential to choose how to respond, rather than react automatically. Build in a pause between your emotional reactions and your verbal responses. The space of time needed for a few breaths is sufficient. Often, a pause lets you see other response options.

• Reflect on the times that you've been wrong in your assessment of a situation. If you're like me, there have been plenty! Rather than shrinking from these memories, use them to explore how hidden aspects of situations reveal themselves over time.

• Cultivate your imagination. Create alternative explanations, even ludicrous ones, for events and situations in your teen's life. Thinking outside your usual box will help you sense the broad palette from which God paints. This strategy can have the added benefit of increasing the humor quotient of your parenting life.

• Remember that you don't need to take on the role of God in your son's or daughter's life. It's your job to trust in God, turn to God within, then let go and love your teenager.

• So many of us get caught up in thinking of God as a giant vending machine who distributes what we've ordered if we just ask in the right way. God is not limited by form. Don't put so many restrictions on God's outlets for pouring blessings into your family's life. "Dear God, please let Joan get into Harvard with a full scholarship and then go to Stanford Law School and then . . ." Try, "I let go and trust that God is working for the highest and the best in Joan's life and career. I trust that she will be accepted into the perfect school at the perfect time with the perfect funding available." You don't have to figure out all the details, just simply live moment by moment in the mystery of this creative presence and give thanks for the good when it appears daily.

Welcome God as Others into Your Life

In a recent public opinion study released by Public Agenda, 66 percent of the teenagers polled said, "Faith in God is an important part of my life." Yet, 49 percent also felt that most kids their age need more guidance and attention from adults.

Parental guidance and attention is one way God's light flows to teens. We may think that when our kids were younger we had more opportunities to be a beacon of light or God in action. If our teenagers stop turning to us, we can still make sure that they're not spiritually alone. Teachers, coaches, aunts, uncles, youth ministers, neighbors, older friends, employers, and mentors can all be extensions of God's love in a teen's life.

As our children mature, they increasingly look to others for support and guidance. The headmaster of a small Mennonite school in Salem, Oregon, says, "Teens desperately need guidance, and they're often not willing to accept it from their parents. We believe in surrounding teens with loving, caring adults, and we're fortunate that we have the organizational support to do so." At this school, as at many others across the country whether religiously affiliated or not, teachers and advisors leave their doors open for teens who need to talk. They may provide rides for those who need them, a few dollars for a sandwich, or a few words of adult wisdom that come at just the right time. A small kindness can engender the confidence a young person needs in order to cope with the many challenges strewn on the road from adolescence to adulthood.

Others who bring soulfullness into our teens' lives sometimes do so with explicitly spiritual messages. In some communities, organized religious activities such as Young Life, Focus, or youth groups affiliated with specific congregations are very active. However, we can also look behind the content to discern where our teens are hearing the voice for God. One father says: "My son's guitar teacher would probably never say the G-word, but he teaches him more about living spiritually than anyone else right now. From him, Kevin learns about integrity and self-expression, about being true to his heart and caring for other people, too."

We can welcome God working through other people in our teen's lives by supporting those relationships that we would like to see flourish. As we do, our kids have vivid examples of various ways that they too can allow God to work through them.

A fifteen-year-old describes her youth group leader: "I watch Kate talk to kids and she doesn't even have to use the word 'God.' She just accepts them as they are and it's inspiring. By watching her I see that the best way to spread God's light is to live it and to be kind, loving, and nonjudgmental. I'm starting to use my life like Kate does. There's a very weird kid in my World Cultures class. Lately, I've just been saying 'hi' to him in class and in the halls. I saw him smile for the first time the other day when we passed by one another. I want to use my life to get closer to God and this is as a result of watching Kate live hers."

The idea that God speaks to us through other people can become an intriguing idea for our teens to embrace. Once they begin to become aware of how God is using other people to reach them, they may become more receptive to those who cross their paths.

Mary, a high school junior, was beginning to feel suffocating stress around the college admission process. Her parents couldn't mention the word "college" without Mary retreating to her room, shifting to an ugly mood, and diving deeper into her fears. At swim team practice early one spring morning, a member of the prior year's team, Kyle, returned to greet his old teammates. Kyle was a freshman at the college of his choice and was eager to share his experience with Mary. He explained how the admissions process worked, told how he had trusted in fate, but did the footwork, and encouraged Mary to keep working on her swimming. He went on to suggest she even come for an interview at his school where he felt sure the swim coach would love to meet her. Kyle humanized the big, scary college choice issue for Mary, becoming a human voice for God in her landscape of college fears.

We can become more verbal with teens who are open to our support and opinions. Teens aren't closed down to their parent's ideas as much as our culture would tell us otherwise. A mother talks about one voice of God in her daughter's life: "The wife of her high school soccer coach, Janet, is a great asset in my daughter Natalie's life. I suggested that she use the long bus rides to games as opportunities to talk to Janet about certain issues. While I don't always agree with Janet's religious beliefs, I know that she has my daughter's best interests at heart. I am so grateful for her presence on the team bus. Natalie looks forward to this time to bounce ideas off of Janet."

Our teens shine Divine light just as brightly as anyone else. Their presence in our lives calls us to be bigger, better, *more* as parents and people than many of us ever thought we could. We become who we're really meant to be when we allow ourselves to expand past what we believe our limitations are. And there's nothing like a teen for helping us accomplish just that!

To welcome the presence of God in your adolescent's life, try to:

- Listen with your heart as your teen talks. God shows up in our kids as grounded enthusiasm and self-confidence. Notice the people your teen mentions when he or she seems most comfortable and at peace.

- Support these relationships by making it easy for your teenager to be with the people who bring out the best in them. If another adult is important in your son or daughter's life, try to see it as a blessing, not a personal affront.

• Suggest these individuals as resources when your teen is trying to make a choice or wondering about an issue. "Maybe you could ask Mrs. J.," you might say.

• Don't be surprised when another adult comes up with the same ideas that you first suggested. It's the idea, not the originator, that is important. Acknowledge how smart, insightful, or cool that individual is, and be grateful that the ideas hit home.

• Remember that teenagers are often social animals. Many begin their personal exploration of God through community. Allow God's light to shine into your child's heart through positive groups of other people.

• Don't discount other teens as vehicles for Spirit. My daughter Elizabeth looks up to Liza, who is a grade above her in school. She comments on Liza's kindness and willingness to go the extra mile for someone else: "Mom, Liza is the nicest girl I know. All her choices seem to be positive and sincere."

• Talk about how Spirit shows up in your life using examples of how others have helped you solve a problem or offered you loving kindness.

• Facilitate opportunities for your teen to be around other interesting adults. Include your kids in dinner parties or arrange a ski weekend with a few other families whom you admire. Perhaps your church, mosque, or temple has a need on the vestry or leadership board for a teen representative.

• Encourage your son or daughter to express their spirituality through their humanity. They, too, can be God in action. Remind them that their age, frailties, or perceived limitations are no obstacles to God. If God is using them to carry out the plan of good in this world, then how might they operate in their daily lives? The writer Mary Daly said, "Why indeed must 'God' be a noun? Why not a verb—the most active and dynamic of all."

Questioning Religion

"I think church has done the most to turn kids off from God. You are made to sit there and listen to stuff like 'God caused a plague to kill thousands of people' or 'The mighty voice of God says we are sinners.' Yea, like that's going to make kids comfortable with Spirit."   —**Brian, fifteen**

Kids want and need to define their own sense of spirituality so that they might create an intimate relationship with God that takes them from childhood to an adult spiritual life. "The movie *Lord of the Rings* was a cool way for me to talk to my friends about religion and the Bible. Frodo is like powerless, but is trusted to destroy the ring," says thirteen-year-old Max.

It can seem paradoxical that the process of developing a personal relationship with God is often also a social one. Teens depend upon information from others, especially peers, to expand their thinking. They need others to serve as mirrors as they discover who they are becoming. Teens consistently tell me that their friends are their touchstones for behaviors they want to avoid and attitudes they may want to try on. A teen's relationship with God can be intensely personal and fiercely expressed, as well as private and heavily social.

Teens search for a sense of belonging. Ideally, they find their roots of connection within their families, but they often look elsewhere. It's a natural part of their movement into the world. And this search elicits mixed reactions from parents. As one mother of an eighteen-year-old says, "My son became very involved in Young Life, carrying a Bible in his backpack. He started hanging around a group of Christian kids and going to a very conservative church with them. I wasn't comfortable with that. But the group gave him a way to avoid things like drinking, drugs, and sex. Their values worked for him."

One might assume that parents would be thrilled their kids are interested in spiritual issues. While many parents are pleased, others feel threatened and fear that their value system is being rejected when their son or daughter questions the family's religion or pursues a spiritual tradition about which they know little. Parents may wonder "How can you do this to me?"

Some teens embrace Buddhism or Islam while others become born-again Christians or devout Catholics. While some come from religious homes and are now exploring a religion other than that of their parents, others were raised with little or no religion and are finding one on their own.

Yet the life of the Spirit is much more than just decisions about faith. We have a choice to be a part of our child's exploration process, joining them in their quest for knowledge and individual sense of spirituality, or viewing their journey as a personal threat. One mother of four was crushed when her teenage son abandoned the religion of his youth. "Matt was an altar boy and we sent him to religious schools. He is now sixteen and tells me he isn't sure he wants any of this dogma."

When encouraged to point out Matt's positive qualities, his mother's entire demeanor changed. "He is so kind. This is the kid who shovels sidewalks in the middle of the worst storms for unsuspecting elderly neighbors. He is quick with a smile and a great student. Matt is tender with his little sister and sings in all the school musicals. He's a great kid."

When she stepped back from her own fear about Matt's spiritual questioning and examined his life, Matt's mom was finally able to acknowledge a spiritual young man who was right where he should be in terms of his development of faith. Matt, like many teens, was in the midst of questioning beliefs from his childhood and exploring his religious convictions by weighing dogma versus rules of the heart.

If your child is exploring a faith other than your own, here are a few suggestions:

- Define what you believe as a parent. Your beliefs are usually broader and more personal than labels like Reformed Jew or Methodist or Buddhist. Parents should be able to state what their beliefs and values are so that their children really understand them. Some parents have drafted a spiritual mission statement for their personal clarification of their credo. If your children choose to explore other beliefs, at least they will understand what values are held at home.

- Attend a religious service at the house of worship to which your child has been drawn. Seeing and hearing this faith firsthand will allow you to have conversations about it with your child and to better understand why they are attracted to a particular belief system. For example, if your teen expresses interest in Zen, find a monastery in your area that you both could visit to learn more, check out books from the library, or go online and get more facts.

• Look for commonalities between your belief systems. There are many paths to God. What's most important is that your teen finds one that works for her, not that she follow in your footsteps. Know, too, that temporary wanderings don't necessarily reflect life choices.

• Sign up with your teen for a class on world religions at a local university.

• Think of spirituality as a way to connect with your teens throughout your days together. All too often, I speak to parents who have been raising their kids without a spiritual awareness and when a disaster strikes, God is where they turn. The always available Divine Source answers a very primal need.

• Ghandi taught that God does not belong to any one religion. Catch yourself when you begin to equate spirituality solely with religion.

When Your Teen's Faith May Be Detrimental

How do you know when your teen's exploration or embracing of another faith has gone too far? Much depends on his spiritual temperament. While every teen is unique, you have to determine what is "too far" for your son or daughter. It's important to separate your issues from your child's. For example, just because you don't embrace Islam or the born-again belief doesn't mean that these spiritual avenues are inherently bad.

However, a young person's exploration does have the potential to become dangerous. The warning lights should go off when:

• The particular faith or group that your child is examining identifies itself as the *only* one to follow or the only way to God/Allah/The Divine.

- People promise things to your adolescent if they join the group such as material or emotional inducements to become "one of us."

- Your son or daughter pulls apart from the family to follow the faith. Some separation is normal, but when the group seems to be driving a wedge into your relationship, concern is appropriate.

- Your teenager spends an inordinate amount of time with the faith group to the exclusion of other activities and other friends.

If you think that a situation is getting out of hand, first have a frank and open discussion with your teen and express your concerns. Second, approach the adults who are the leaders of the faith group with which your child has become involved. Most likely they are not villains. In fact, your child may be taking things much further than the leaders would recommend. If it still seems as if the situation is out of control, seek outside help from a therapist or counselor.

The key to helping our teens deepen their connection with a loving God is to help them understand that there is no great religious or sacred attainment that is a prerequisite for a relationship with the Almighty. There is no person they must go through to reach God. Anyone who wants to feel God's loving presence will indeed feel God's loving presence. How our sons and daughters develop their awareness of God is as dimensional as their personalities. Some might meditate or chant while others use traditional prayer. Some might resonate with gospel music while others feel God's light through building a house with Habitat for Humanity. Some might simply look into their hearts each day and ask "God, what is it I should do today?" Other teens might find God through religious community.

As you begin to tune more and more into God's never-ending presence and help your teen rely on this power, remember the sage words of Mother Teresa: "God doesn't require us to succeed; He only requires that we try."

Parents' Insight-Building Exercise

We can get so caught up in the drama of daily life with a teen that we forget about the quiet, calm thread of God running through every day. Our children's sometimes frantically active lives and schedules can distract us from our central need to "be" as parents.

Take a moment now to acknowledge the tremendous challenges and joys of parenting an adolescent. Feel the common tie you share with parents all over the world as you create an environment into which a young adult can safely and successfully emerge. Let the warm light of God caress your strong parenting shoulders, relaxing them and cascading into your heart.

You are filled with God's light and love, protected and safe. Kahlil Gibran speaks of parents as the stable bow from which our children's lives take flight like arrows. Let the solid strength of Spirit fill you. Feel yourself sink into the chair as the light of God warms your back and legs. Place your feet on the floor and feel them rest there, firm and solid.

See yourself as encircled by a radiant light, restoring and nurturing your spirit. Release any concerns about parenting into God's care.

Linger in the experience of feeling fully surrounded and protected by God's light and love for as long as you wish. As you return to the room, breathe in deeply and release your breath fully. You are parenting in the light of God.

Parents' Check-In Questions

* How have I experienced God's presence in my life?

* Where do I see evidence of God in my teen's life?

* What have I done to nurture my spirit this week? What worked best for me?

• What am I grateful for right now? What is my deepest gratitude?

• When did I feel most disconnected from Spirit? Is there a different choice I could have made at that time?

• What could I do this week to more fully embody the presence of God in my own life as well as my teen's?

• Do I consider the religion of my youth as my primary source of spiritual enrichment? How does my early faith experience relate to my sacred path today?

• Is there another adult who might provide my teen with spiritual understanding? How can I encourage that relationship?

Conversation Starters

Many parents find that car time is a good time for initiating conversations. There is something about the hum of wheels, the slap of windshield wipers, and the close physical proximity that makes even the most taciturn teen more likely to talk. As always, the more we listen attentively, the more teens feel encouraged to continue. The next time you're in a car with your son or daughter, try starting a conversation with one of the following questions:

• Do you believe in God?

• Now that you're older, how have your ideas about God changed?

• Are there times when you feel as if God is really present in your life?

• If you could ask God for one thing and know that it would happen, what would that be?

• What's your favorite way of praying?

• Are there songs that make you feel close to God?

- Do you and your friends ever talk about God?

- Is there anyone in your life that you think demonstrates God in action? How so?

- Do you believe you are part of something more than just the "stuff" of everyday life? In what way?

Understand That All Life Is Connected and Has Meaning

"Being out in nature got me through the awkward teenage years. I chose to be close to trees and plants rather than the always-shifting social realm. I did sports and excelled in academics but, finding myself, my true self, was always in nature." **—Matt, thirty-three**

"When I read *Tuck Everlasting* I finally got the 'circle of life' thing. One of the characters says 'You can't have living if you don't have dying.'" **—Ellen, thirteen**

* * *

If our teenage sons and daughters are going to survive and thrive, they must know that their lives have deep meaning and great worth. Teens hunger to feel they are a part of something. Their need for acceptance runs deep and is often assuaged by peer groups—affiliation with a certain school, team, style of music, or club. Many teens, however, still feel a lingering sense of longing. I believe this is a spiritual yearning to feel connected to their Creator and to all of creation.

Adolescents need opportunities to recognize that they are never alone, no matter how different they may feel. They, like us, crave experiences of plugging into the ultimate *oneness* that includes every living thing on earth. We can help them—and ourselves—find and strengthen this connectedness in relationships with people—and with nature itself.

Nature

"The deeper we look into nature the more we recognize that it is full of life, and the more profoundly we know that all life is a secret, and we are all united to all this life." **—Albert Schweitzer**

We are intimately connected to everything we can see—and all that is beyond our immediate vision, too. We are bundles of atoms and molecules, made of the same elements that our world is made of. In the beautiful book *Songs of the Spirit, Blessings of the Flesh,* Matthew Fox says, "Over 60 percent of the atoms in our material bodies were once inside the flaming inferno of the cosmic fireball. Every single hydrogen atom in our bodies was once part of the Big Bang itself. Forty percent of the atoms in our material bodies came from older stars. This cosmic connectedness is shared by all life forms on this planet, be they horses, flowers, fish, or insects. It is also shared by rocks and stones and water and air—all the nonliving matter."

Many teens, however, don't see the intrinsic value of nature. To them, shopping malls are more valuable than open space. Intimacy with the natural world has often been replaced by intimacy with the electronic world in the lives of our sons and daughters.

Researchers have shown that exposure to wild lands brings a host of developmental benefits, including instilling navigational skills and improving cognitive ability. Contact with the natural world also opens our hearts to the spark of life in all living things.

I believe that linking with the power of nature can quite literally save kids' lives. Teenagers are social creatures. If they feel socially isolated, and studies reveal that millions do, the results can be devastating. Nature, however, never rejects them. Nature's predictable cycle centers teens when their world seems rocked by daily ups and downs.

My brother Mark Walch is a wilderness therapist who has worked with kids for over twenty years. In wilderness therapy, teens experience group living, individual and group therapy, physical challenges, and skill mastery, like fire-making and backcountry travel. Mark believes strongly that the benefits of teens connecting with nature fall into a number of categories. For one, the alternative lifestyle associated with caring about nature appeals to teens. Being "outdoorsy" can help them work out the developmentally appropriate urge to be different.

The earth and natural systems also give teens something to feel part of. Nature unconditionally accepts people, but it also imposes rules from a larger system than teens can fight, which gives them reassurance about boundaries and personal limits. Nature allows them to belong to something without having to conform.

Mark says, "Teens want to feel that they can take responsibility for themselves. When it's cold, it's up to them whether they wear a coat or not. Conforming will make them feel warmer, but they get to choose. Realizing that they can't out-bravado nature can give them a sense of humility, too."

He also believes that the physical world gives teens a chance to demonstrate physical mastery through hiking and climbing, and that the sense of accomplishment is real and lasting. Climbing a pike doesn't depend on being part of the in crowd and the memory of it can't be taken away by unkind words.

Whatever aspect of life appeals to teens, says Mark, they find it reflected in nature. Poets can appreciate it, and jocks can experience it.

The degree and way in which our teens reap these benefits when they connect with the natural world is shaped, in part, by their spirituality. Experience with particular religious traditions impacts them in certain ways. Some environmentalists suggest that the Judeo-Christian tradition, for instance, believes in a world created solely for the benefit of man. And yet, might we humans have twisted sacred teachings for our own benefit? In the *HarperCollins Study Bible,* Ecclesiastes 3:19 states: "For the fate of humans and the fate of animals is the same; as one dies, so dies the other. They all have the same breath, and humans have no advantage over the animals; for all is vanity."

In Judaism, the Torah outlines a series of ethical environmental obligations. The Torah, in Ecclesiastes, Rabbah 7, says: "When God created Adam, he showed him all the trees of the Garden of Eden and said to him: 'See my works, how lovely they are, how fine they are. All I have created, I created for you. Take care not to corrupt and destroy my universe, for if you destroy it, no one will come after you to put it right.'"

In other religious traditions, humans are seen as part of, rather than ruling, nature. Followers of Hinduism, for example, believe that certain rivers and mountains are sacred, as they give and sustain life, and that all plants and animals have souls.

Religions are evolving to embrace an understanding of human's spiritual link with nature in today's world. I found it encouraging that the Sierra Club and the National Council of Churches cosponsored a television advertisement opposing drilling for oil in Alaska's National Wildlife Refuge. The narrator intoned a Jewish prayer interperted from the Torah quote above in which God says: "This is a beautiful world I have given you. Take care of it, do not ruin it."

New alliances are being forged to link religion and nature, spirituality and environmental consciousness. Teens by the thousands are drawn to this union. They resonate with the principles of Deep Ecology, the concept that there are no superior or inferior things. They are passionate about caring for the environment and the future of the planet. It gives *meaning* to their lives. They are also attuned to the idea of good and evil, and the ethics of Deep Ecology call them to identify how this fragile planet is being damaged, who the culprits are, as well as how to be accountable in their own lives.

Religious beliefs and traditions influence a teen's attitude toward the natural environment; so do family values. The decisions we make about such seemingly innocuous matters as lawn care send messages to our children. In many parts of the United States, where water is often at a premium during the summer months, for example, do we insist on maintaining a broad expanse of dark green grass during hot, dry weather or allow our lawns to go dormant? Few teens grouse about the greatly reduced mowing needs of a brown backyard, by the way!

Talk with your teen about topics such as local land use and environmental issues. In many areas, preserving native species means restricting human activities. Trusting that all life has meaning requires that, as a family, we must ask ourselves other tough questions, such as:

* Do humans have any ethical obligations with respect to the natural world?

* Have we the right to take all the Earth's resources for our own use?

* Do other species have an intrinsic right to exist?

* What does our religion have to say about humanity's relationship to the rest of the living world? What do other religions have to say?

* How can we as a family honor our Earth?

Trusting that all life is connected forces us to ask difficult questions; it also brings simple joys—when we pay attention. Many of us are so caught up in our daily routines that we've lost contact with these daily glimmers of Spirit. Our teens, in particular, are brainwashed to honor perfect pectoral muscles and expensive cars rather than the gentle hum of a bee or the brilliant colors of a setting sun. How often do we stop to smell the special scent of fallen leaves in autumn or feel the warmth of the soil in spring? Helping our teens feel at one with their everyday surroundings, the Earth, and the Universe, allows them to experience a deeper sense of connection.

Feeling a part of nature is different than passively observing it. Passive observation is thin nourishment for the soul—and poor stewardship of the Earth. Only a few generations have brought our planet to the brink of total destruction by lacking an understanding of our unified link.

Traditional Native American perspectives suggest that a harmonious relationship to the world requires us to move beyond the role of observer into active participation. Shamans talk with the plants, animals, rocks, wind, and all creation with whom we share the Earth.

Chief Seattle spoke of the Suquamish people in 1854 when he said, "Teach your children what we have taught our children—that the Earth is our mother. Whatever befalls the Earth befalls the children of the Earth. . . . The Earth is precious to God, and to harm the Earth is to heap contempt on its Creator."

I recently had the honor of hearing conservationist and primatologist Jane Goodall speak at Harvard University's Gutman Library. My daughter and I were thrilled to be in her presence. She talked about her Roots and Shoots Program and how kids truly can save the world—a powerful charge for my sixteen-year-old to hear. Goodall said, "Roots creep underground everywhere and make a firm foundation. Shoots seem very weak, but to reach the light, they can break open brick walls. Imagine that the brick walls are all the problems we have inflicted on our planet. Hundreds of thousands of roots and shoots, hundreds of thousands of young people around the world, can break through these walls. We *can* change the world."

To support your teen in developing a deeper connection with the natural world, you could:

• Support and join environmental and nature preservation groups.

• Draft a family letter to the editor of your local newspaper about local environmental issues that matter to you.

• Write to politicians and business leaders about how to create a greener planet. Brainstorm these ideas as a family.

• Expand family recycling activities. If your community doesn't offer curbside recycling, a teen with a driver's license can deliver paper, cans, glass, and other items to the nearest recycle center.

• Give your teen a tree on his birthday. Plant it near his bedroom window or near his school or a place that has special meaning for him. It will help remove greenhouse gases from the atmosphere as well as be a reminder for how he valued nature at this particular age. The scrawny weeping willow tree planted for my brother Tim's tenth birthday is now a towering

graceful guardian of the land on which it sits. Tim is forty-one and s
calls with fondness the day his tree was planted.

- Many communities have Earth Day celebrations or Bike to \
days. Bring them to your teen's awareness, even if he or she choose
to participate.

- If you have a teenager who is a fanatic about car-washing, make
he understands the damage that detergents or solvents can do to the l
watershed. Offer biodegradable alternatives to harsh chemical cleaner

- Consider a family camping trip, even if it's been a while since you
all slept in a tent. Adolescents can gain a deeper clarity when they e
perience a clearer, simpler life. They focus on the inner rather than t
outer, on a qualitative rather than a quantitative life. When I was th
teen, I was invited to a friend's cabin in the woods. We spent evenin
sitting in front of a fire, no distractions. I remember being hypnotized b
the flames, and captivated by sitting in silence with only the light of th
fire. It was a revelation for me. I heard my inner voice. I began to writ
poetry—terrible poetry, but the muse was unleashed in the stillness.

- The National Wildlife Federation has a Web page devoted to specific
events and situations to which teens can become involved. Send your
teenagers a link to the site, www.nwf.org, and encourage them to decide
how they can become involved—whether it is by making their high school
campus greener or simply writing to Congress about cleaner water.

- When you and your teen are out enjoying nature, whether walking
the beach, hiking a rugged trail, or simply heading outside to pick up
the mail, make sure to talk about and point out the sacredness of the
land, water, air, and sky. Share the beautiful words of Emerson: "The
doors of the temple stand open, night and day, before everyone."

- There is a lot of information available for the teen who is moved to
explore the deep connection between the environment and religion. A
good, albeit dense, beginning is the Forum on Religion and Ecology.

ill re-   on this interreligious, multicultural, interdisciplinary ini-
              ilable via the Internet at www.environment.harvard.edu/
              n.html. The Forum Web site is a major research-oriented
York   iling various aspects of religion and ecology and how these
not   teract with other disciplines such as science, ethics, econom-
              ion, public policy, and gender in the larger global context.

ure   teens are walking billboards for rock groups, clothing de-
cal   or retail stores. Many kids choose organic and their clothing
.   nat choice. If your teen is not yet a convert to all things "green,"
ve   ght purchase an all-cotton organic tee shirt for your son or a
x-   "no sweat" sneakers made in socially responsible factories for
e   aughter. Check the Resources section in the back of this book for
-             online sources.
s
              e is growing awareness of the ways in which our spiritual well-
              directly linked to the health of ecosystems, bioregions, and Earth
              dvocating an integrated human-Earth relationship gives our teenagers
              work from which they might live their lives in harmony with all liv-
              ngs.

Animals

"The greatness of a nation and its moral progress can be judged by the way its animals are treated."   **—Mahatma Gandhi**

Kids are used to speed and quick results; nature teaches patience. Car-
ig for and being aware of animals also teach our teens responsibility and
perseverance, compassion and generosity.

I grew up in a home where nature and animals got top billing. My
mother tied herself to an ancient live oak tree in Mississippi in the 1960s so
it wouldn't be taken down to expand the highway. She rescued neglected
animals from a petting zoo and they moved in with us for a time: monkeys,
deer, antelope, and even an armadillo we named Archie. We had horses,

cats, dogs, and various other living creatures move in and out of our family. We appropriately named the huge spider outside our front door Charlotte, and adopted her into our menagerie. Living this way, the lesson was to respect, honor, and love all living things.

Respect for all living things begins at home and extends naturally out into the world. Many children love animals and, as they grow up, begin to recognize the deep kinship and sense of responsibility they feel toward them.

One fifteen-year-old girl who looks pretty tough with a lip ring and spiked hair says: "After the crazy day at school it calms me to just spend a few minutes with my cat. She's always there for me—through thick or thin."

Indeed, pets can teach our teens volumes about unconditional love. In the trusting, adoring eyes of a dog, for instance, our teen can perceive the reflection of a God who loves them deeply and constantly, no matter what team they play on or what grade they got on the math test.

As adolescents connect with animals close to home, some begin to take a natural interest in how animals are treated in other settings. People for the Ethical Treatment of Animals (PETA), for instance, has eight thousand members between the ages of thirteen and twenty-four. While PETA's radical techniques have garnered much disapproval, its mission and methods resonate for many teens. Quoted in *The New Yorker*, a PETA representative commented, "Teens want the truth. We walk the talk. You cannot call us hypocrites."

For some teens, part of walking the talk of caring about all life is adopting a vegetarian diet. Adults can be tempted to tease a teen about this choice, grumble about the inconvenience it brings, or simply refuse to accommodate it. If we see, however, vegetarianism as a spiritual practice—one that brings our teen into greater connection with the world as a whole and the creatures we share it with—it's easier to honor and accept this choice. Last Thanksgiving, I served a tofurkey (turkey made of tofu) alongside the more familiar main dish to honor my daughter's choice to become a vegetarian.

Kindness and compassion are fundamentally spiritual qualities, whether they're directed at humans or animals. Every living creature is worthy of our respect. Just as our teen son or daughter is not alone in this great big cosmos, what he or she does matters. What he does or doesn't do to the animals in his life matters. Teaching teens compassion for other animals and respect for nature will cause a ripple effect and contribute to the creation of a safer, more tolerant world.

To help your teenager find a deeper connection with nature and animals you might:

• Validate and value your adolescents' relationships with their pets. Studies prove it—time spent with our pets can reduce our stress. Our cocker spaniel, Comet, is truly a stress reducer for Elizabeth. He curls up next to her as she lies on the floor doing homework, and her breathing slows down. I can see the tension from the day at school begin to melt away. Her rhythm shifts when she greets her dog at day's end. Whitney has the same "de-stress" relationship with her beloved cat. Don't discount your teen's time spent with their pets; in fact, encourage more of it. Rather than always focusing on the tasks and chores that come along with pet ownership, encourage some special bonding time.

• If your teen has become too busy for the golden retriever in his or her life, bring the family pet to attention in a lighthearted way. Point out the canine hallmark characteristics of endless love and eternal optimism: "You know, she only gets that excited when you come in the door." At our house, we sometimes put words in our dog's mouth by speculating about what he'd say if he could talk: "Maybe *tonight's* the night I get to have a nice long walk." No guilt trips necessary.

• Support your teen in starting an animal rights group at school. They can visit www.worldanimalnet.com for a list of local animal rights groups that can help them in their launch.

• Your son or daughter might want to hold a garage sale to finally get rid of all those Beanie Babies or stuffed animals and give the proceeds to an organization that champions the well-being of living animals.

Join your adolescent in looking under the surface of what appears to be healthy treatment of animals. Nature films, for instance, seem to give us brilliant glimpses into the natural world and thus foster our appreciation. I recently heard an interview on National Public Radio's *Talk of the Nation* that shook me. Gregg Mitman, Professor of Science Studies at the University of Wisconsin and author of *Reel Nature: America's Romance with Wildlife on Film,* revealed that directors of nature documentaries often stage action that is intended to appear natural to viewers in order to create a show that is dramatic. This program also pointed out that there are game farms that rent out animals for films and photo shoots. Producers then set up situations to capture on film. Often, these forced encounters result in harm to animals. Many times the animals are not taken care of properly on the farms, where inexperienced staff and incorrect food lead to illness. And what becomes of aging animals that are no longer needed to perform? Most nature films, however, are wonderful glimpses into the animal world and raise awareness and resources to save wildlife.

Focus on your day-to-day actions that might affect animals. Before choosing a shampoo or cosmetic, my daughter Elizabeth calls the manufacturer to find out if they test on animals. I am in awe of her ability at age thirteen to ask questions and push harder for the truth. She is amazed at the hedging response from most companies, "No animal products are used in the shampoo" goes a typical response. She counters with, "Well, do you test on animals?" The reply, "Not sure, you'll have to talk to our corporate offices, or our New York office, or call another time." She doesn't give up even when left on hold for long periods. "Okay, what's that number?" and on and on until she discovers if she will or will not buy the product she is researching.

Taking Positive Action

"History, although sometimes made up of the few acts of the great, is more often shaped by the many acts of the small." **—Mark Twain**

If we know we are part of all creation, then it must also be true that we can change the world by changing our lives. Our individual actions do make a difference—to the environment, to the animals we share our planet with, and to our fellow human beings.

Adolescents need opportunities to recognize that they are not alone—

no matter how different they may feel. They need to know they're not alone in their wishes for a better world and their desire to believe in the goodness of people, as well as in the pain they feel over life's injustices. Social activism and reaching out to make a difference give them that assurance.

Respecting others and embracing the multiplicity of humankind engenders racial harmony and enables our teens to appreciate each other's unique qualities. It even allows punk rockers and pop music aficionados, Gothic devotees and *Sound of Music* fans to peacefully coexist. When our teens think of their spirits as a part of the universal Spirit, they realize that their thoughts matter and their actions reverberate.

In Gregg Braden's book *The Isaiah Effect,* he says, "For centuries, prophets and sages have suggested that one-tenth of one percent of humanity, working together in a unified effort, may shift the consciousness of the entire world."

Quantum physics tell us that it is not clear where one thing starts and another ends in the endless field of energy that permeates our universe; we're all connected now. Chaos theory demonstrates that small differences can yield huge consequences; what we do echoes into our world.

Not all kids are going to become social activists. Their personalities and temperaments may be less bold and public in the world. But the truth is that we are all challenged to make ethical choices day by day.

In an environment where thousands of teenagers suffer from emotional violence in the form of bullying, harassment, intimidation, humiliation, and fear, it is clear that this message about acting ethically towards one another is not on the tips of most parents' tongues and has not seeped into most teen's souls.

Tony, age sixteen, attends a suburban high school of approximately one thousand students, "Everyone in high school gets teased. You just have to learn to deal. Yeah, sometimes the teasing turns to threats and stuff. Teachers don't do anything and parents don't hear about it because kids would get it worse if their parents showed up. It makes me feel bad to see it but I don't really do anything."

Accept the fact that there is some degree of bullying and emotional violence in your teenager's school. Talk to your kids about it. Are they ever afraid? Have they been involved in intimidating other kids? If they are an upperclassman, how are they helping the younger kids? How might they counteract the negative energy kids are putting out? Can they stop gossiping, excluding others, hazing for clubs and teams, or taking part in put-downs? Teens can be good at hiding the unsavory parts of their lives. Naming these alienating behaviors brings them into the light.

"We must not, in trying to think about how we can make a big difference, ignore the small daily differences we can make which, over time, add up to big differences that we often cannot foresee."   —Marian Wright Edelman

I attended a wonderful family holiday party this year where the hosts had hired a group of their daughter's teenage friends to serve and clean up. The party ended, the kids finished their obligations, and one of the boys offered to drive everyone home. About two miles from the party, they spotted an elderly woman on the front lawn of her house wearing a light nightgown and holding a flashlight. The young man driving immediately stopped the car and jumped out to ask if the woman needed any help. The woman, acting confused, said she thought her house was on fire and couldn't understand where the fire trucks were. The kids sprang into action. One called 911 on her cell phone, one grabbed the garden hose and headed for the garage where he saw smoke, and two kids held the woman's arms as she struggled to go back in the house, even after answering their questions that she did live alone and no one was inside. The teens waited for the fire truck to arrive and still they continued to take action. They made sure the woman was escorted to a neighbor's home where she could wait inside in the warmth. The next morning, a few of the kids returned to the house to inquire about the women's well-being and to ask if there was anything they might do to help her.

None of these teenagers were social activists. They're ordinary kids who were able to respond immediately in a way that helped to make a huge difference in the life of one woman.

Many people wonder why teens today are so different from their protest-marching parents of the 60s and 70s. I believe that they aren't out there marching because they are online, working, studying for college entrance exams, involved in multiple extracurricular activities, and racing to the rhythm of a frantic culture. I also am meeting many teens who have a sense of hopelessness about changing the world. They have a "Why bother? Everything's so screwed up," attitude.

I'd like to see more teens get out into their neighborhoods and communities and make their corner of the world a better place to live. I'd like to see teens act more kindly to the kid in front of them in English class or speak up when someone's reputation is being trashed. I'd like to see them stop shunning the Goth kid in the lunchroom or the kid who collects stamps and instead take the time and have the courage to open their hearts without judgment.

Many teens suffer from feelings of loneliness and isolation. In fact, one of the things that puts teens at risk for suicide is loneliness. If kids began to move into their communities in a more hands-on way, perhaps that loneliness would be replaced by the inclusion that comes from giving. If they were kinder to one another, the toxic sense of rejection would be replaced by the tonic teens must have: acceptance.

Social activism is perfect for teens who desperately want truth and righteousness. The thrill of standing up for what they believe in also resonates for this risk-taking period of life. Remaining silent when a teen sees wrongdoing eats away at her spirit.

Author and civil rights activist Derrick Bell says, "An ethical endeavor at which you can work with passion and integrity is a key component in a satisfying life."

Some ways you might help your kids take action to make their world a better place include:

* Help teens recognize instances of stereotyping, prejudice, and discrimination. Talk with them about how they might respond to such attitudes and behaviors when they see them in action. Television news and entertainment shows, movies and newspapers often provide opportunities for discussion. "What would you do if you saw someone being harassed on the street?" Remember, it's also vital that your kids

see you taking action when you can and standing up for what you believe in.

• Give your child a chance to stand up for her beliefs in the safety of your own home. Have debates at dinner, listen to her views on an issue you might not agree with, give her a forum for self-expression. We must first voice our opinion in order to solidify our beliefs. Then comes action.

• Help kids recognize wrongs both in their daily environment and the world at large. Support them as they try to make them right. This might mean writing a letter, speaking up to a friend, holding a poster, spearheading a group at school, or simply saying a prayer.

• When you or your teen need to give a gift, consider giving from one of the many socially responsible organizations. There are both religious and secular groups who offer the opportunity to give needy families everything from a milk cow to a year's supply of rice. There are also catalogs that sell crafts made by disadvantaged artisans. Check out the Gift listing in the Resources section.

• Support your teen in coming up with creative ways to donate resources to a cause they believe in. A high school senior in my town asked kids to forgo renting limousines for the prom and instead give the money to an organization that recycles prom dresses for girls who can't afford to buy new ones. Another young woman I know loves horses. She chose to take riding lessons every other week rather than weekly and uses the money she saves to donate hay to a farm that shelters old, abused, and abandoned horses. Your teen might want to skip going out for dinner this month and give the money she saves to a local food bank.

• To change the conditions of our outer world, we can actually change ourselves. When we do, the conditions of peace or joy are mirrored in the world around us. To bring peace to the world, for instance, we must first become more peaceful. What a powerful concept for our teens to embrace. Their feelings can change the world in which they live.

• Praise your teenager for kind deeds, empathetic actions, and community service excellence—rather than for losing a few pounds or getting a date for the prom.

• Community service has become another form of moving up the college acceptance ladder. I see kids racking up the hours without really caring how. I see parents forging signatures and fudging hours so their children can look good on paper. If your teen's school requires community service hours, help him figure out what he cares about and how he might give of his talents to make a *real* difference.

• A friend of mine shared a great suggestion for kids who aren't into volunteering. She says, "My stepson needed to borrow a substantial sum of money from us to repair his car. We gave him a choice of paying interest on the loan or working off his interest through a community service activity. He chose the latter and made arrangements to play music at a retirement center. It didn't change his life, but it got him out into the community—which was what we wanted."

• Kids can take action by using the power of their pocketbooks. Teens account for about $150 billion a year in revenues in the U.S. alone. Many teens I know are involved in boycotting certain companies whose policies or work environments they oppose. Erin, a seventeen-year-old high school junior, wrote me recently: "I'm boycotting all the teen magazines for girls that feature anorexic models and articles about how to get a guy. That seems to be all the mags out there. It doesn't seem that my little efforts will matter, but they matter to me. I'm against sexualizing teen girls."

• If we are all connected and all life is one, what about cloning? How does your teen feel about the concept of genetic manipulation and engineering? Kids can and must join in political conversations to explore the connections between science, policy, spirituality, ethics and the law. This is the world they will be running in a very short time.

- The Sufi poet, Hafiz, wrote a poem called "You're It." Share these words with your teen, and demonstrate with your own life that the game begins right now.

You're It

God

Disguised

As a myriad things and

Playing a game

Of tag

Has kissed you and said,

"You're it—

I mean, you're really IT!"

Giving from the Heart

It's not easy for our teens to focus on goodness and sharing when the world around them is applauding power and possessions. We can counteract this group thinking by helping our kids tune in to the gratifying internal reward that comes when they give.

Recently, my daughter's friend lost her father in an accident. I was amazed at the compassionate response from her school community: Students were given a full day to grieve, to talk, and to float through the school with caring adults. The middle-schoolers then launched into action. They created a bulletin board for their classmate, posting up photos of her with her dad and words of support. They also put together a box of caring notes for her and organized people to prepare meals for her family.

When tragedy strikes nearby, parents are often consumed with shielding their children from pain rather than supporting them in reaching out to the real victims. Through reaching out, as this class of kids illustrated, we begin to heal our grief.

Being of service can be seen as a spiritual act when we accept and recognize the presence of God's energy in all living things. Sure, most teens are focused on self-satisfaction, and it's developmentally appropriate. But they also waver in and out of feeling lonely and isolated. By opening their hearts to give, they think beyond themselves and experience a unity with Spirit. Charles Dickens said, "No one is useless in this world who lightens the burden of another."

My friend Elyssa, age sixteen, recently returned from a one-week trip to Kentucky with her church's youth group. She says, "It totally changed my life. I'm still there in my mind. The feeling of actually building a house, of seeing walls go up and being a part of that was astounding. I felt like I mattered and that all of us kids together could do something good and solid. I became so close to the other kids on the trip because we were united by doing this positive thing, not just complaining about school or goofing off."

When we help kids ask "What might I give?" rather than "What might I get?," we help them open themselves to amazing blessings. By volunteering, our teens not only help make the world a better place, but also enrich their own lives. They might discover a passion they never knew existed, learn new skills, make new friends, deepen their sense of connection to something important, and develop a new perspective.

Often, and this can be a tough one, we parents assume they don't have time, are unable to share, or that volunteering isn't a worthy endeavor. We don't give them opportunities in their lives to share themselves. Kids get the message that they shouldn't feel so deeply for strangers or be quite so charitable with their things.

Our kids can be our teachers, and my thirteen-year-old was recently mine on this topic. She was heading off to school one morning with all of her white shirts, including a brand new one, stuffed into her backpack. When I asked her what was up, she said, "It's dress rehearsal for our play at school today and we're all supposed to have a white shirt for our costume. I'm bringing some extra ones in case someone forgets." My first reaction was, "Oh, not your new crisp white shirt . . ." but, feeling very humble, I bit my tongue. Elizabeth is no Mother Teresa but she has experienced the positive energy that comes from thinking of others and sharing in her everyday life.

Teens can make a difference each day. They can touch other people's lives through sharing simple efforts: a smile, a nod, a shared laugh, a kind word, a whispered prayer for someone else. All it takes is opening our hearts to what we have to offer, moment by moment, to make someone else's life better.

Acts of kindness move teens out of their self-imposed self-centeredness. They realize that it's an illusion to suppose that they are alone floating round in the great cosmos. The root of kindness is identifying with others. When we bring joy to people other than ourselves we feel joy. A pretty simple system. We can help our teens close the gap between themselves and others.

Encourage and model generosity, not just financially. In giving, our teen breaks down the walls around him. Any teen can do it. He doesn't need to be an A student, an athlete, or in the popular crowd. When teens are generous they discover themselves. Giving opens the path to spiritual wonder.

Giving begins at home. Encourage family caring by becoming a more caring parent. Come up with ways to foster kindness among siblings—emphasizing the teamwork of family rather than competition among one another. Encourage your teens to show love to their extended family and to be thoughtful friends. Parents are the mirrors on how to do this well! Don't be afraid to admit when you've been moving too fast to take a chance and show kindness. In fact, recall it and let your teen join you in thinking of options you might have taken.

Sharing is sparked by empathy. Just because your kids are older, don't miss an opportunity to focus on what it's like to be inside the skin of someone else. "I feel so badly for Karen. She was all set to go to the dance and her date changed his mind. What a terrible thing for him to do. She must be very disappointed and a little embarrassed." It becomes a habit to reach up and out of ourselves when we empathize.

In this competitive world, kids are told, as they get older, to win rather than to help someone else make it to the finish line. Make your home one that applauds caring, sharing, and empathy—the true winning qualities.

Friends

"Normal means being accepted. I want to be normal." —**Beth, thirteen**

Kids long to fit in and be part of a group of friends. They hunger to feel connected and to know their lives have meaning. Friends frequently supply both.

A shift in friendships is often part of the teenage package. Friendships begin to be formed based on interests and how kids see themselves. The result of this shift, however, is some kids are left on the fringe, feeling a deep lack of connectedness.

As children grow into adolescence, the social realm demands more and more of their attention and energy. Friends become the secure passage between family and the world. At least, we hope that's the role of friends in our children's lives.

Cliques seem to be inevitable, and exclusion, power, worthiness, and social rules become the minefields kids must navigate. Our teenagers crave a sense of belonging at the same time that they come face-to-face with the shaky rules of cliques. They lose their social innocence and we, their parents, ache for the hurt they often face.

Many schools have initiated bully-proofing curricula that focus on strategies to diffuse the bully who threatens physical harm. But far more common is the emotional cruelty that permeates the shining halls of our schools.

A strong spiritual connection can help kids weather the storm of fitting in. Friends stamp an indelible mark on children's psyches. Many adults I have worked with still smart from a middle school caste system that ranked them as misfits.

More than anything we would like to deliver a sense of belonging to our kids along with their clean laundry and warm dinner. The truth is, children need to develop their own survival skills—with us always at the ready should they need advice, a sincere hug, and assurance that they are loved and are part of this team called "our family."

When I asked Whitney, my sixteen-year-old, what she would say to younger kids about navigating the social jungle, she said:

There are four ways for kids to survive cliques:

1. Make friends outside of school who are involved in something you have an interest in such as a sport or club.

2. Develop a good relationship with your guidance counselor.

3. Come up with some tried and true "comebacks" to those hurtful comments sure to be slung your way. NOTE: There is a fine line and a clear distinction between maintaining self-esteem and sinking to the level of those who speak hurtfully.

4. Develop a self-confidence that keeps you from stooping to the levels of others who are less secure.

Some ideas you might try to help your teen handle the issue of friends include:

* Talk to your child about the cliques in her school. What are they called? Where does she think she fits in? Is she happy with that? Opening up conversation can be just the permission she needs to unload her feelings.

* Continue to reinforce that finding self-acceptance is the ultimate peace. Discuss your teen's standards for accepting himself. Is it always related to how he stacks up in his social chain? Share your own struggles claiming this peace.

* Show kids examples of how our thoughts ultimately govern how we feel. If we allow our fears—and most adolescents fear not being liked—to play repeatedly in our minds, they strongly affect our feelings.

* Take a stand on rumors, backstabbing, and belittling. When you hear kids talking about others unkindly, put a stop to it.

* Speak up. Talk to the school administrator about what you see if there is a problem.

* Encourage your teenager to try kickboxing, karate, yoga, or other self-empowering activities that help build assertiveness and control.

• Be clear with all kids who come into your home about your expectations and rules. There are different values and different rules from house to house. Kids appreciate knowing what your family believes in, what your rules and rituals are, and they usually adhere to them. In our house, for instance, we take our shoes off, we light candles, we say a prayer before meals. Most of my daughter's friends fall right into our rhythm when here. They pause and pray with us, they put on a pot of tea and know right where the "stress buster" tea bags are; they curl up on the faded yellow couch. Give your children's friends the gift of clearly articulating your family's way of doing things if you want them to feel comfortable.

Golden Rules for All

The term "Golden Rule" sounds so very clichéd that I tend to dismiss things written with those words in the title. Yet the premise of the Golden Rule is at the core of understanding that all life is connected and has a purpose; expressed in many ways across cultures, it's a universal spiritual teaching. When we discover that most religions articulate the same Divine concepts, it reaffirms how connected we all really are. As one wise fifteen-year-old told me, "God is bigger than any one religion."

The Golden Rule is also at the core of becoming a more spiritual parent. You might share this list with your kids, or simply post it on the fridge for all to consider.

• Christianity:
"All things whatsoever ye would that men should do to you, do ye even so to them."

• Judaism:
"What is hurtful to yourself, do not do to your fellow man."

• Islam:
"No one of you is a believer until he loves for his brother what he loves for himself."

- Confucianism:

"Do not unto others what you would not they should do unto you."

- Buddhism:

"In five ways should a clansman minister to his friends and familiars—by generosity, courtesy, and benevolence, by treating them as he treats himself, and by being as good as his word."

- Hinduism:

"Do not do to others, which if done to thee, would cause thee pain."

- Sikhism:

"As thou deemst thyself, so deem others. Then shalt thou become a partner in heaven."

- Jainism:

"In happiness and suffering, in joy and grief, we should regard all creatures as we regard our own self."

- Zoroastrianism:

"That nature only is good when it shall not do unto another whatever is not good for its own self."

- Taoism:

"Regard your neighbor's gain as your own gain, and regard your neighbor's loss as your own loss."

And finally, let's not forget how connected we are to our child. It may seem that we are in and out of sync during the teenager years, so it takes reminding ourselves that this is our precious baby—with longer legs. Extend a big dose of empathy to your teenagers and treat them with the respect and appreciation you wish to receive. They are moving through a period of life that isn't always serene or straightforward. Your actions reverberate into their hearts and souls now perhaps more than ever before.

David, nineteen, says, "My greatest sense of belonging is within my own family. They are the only other humans who care about me unconditionally. As I get older, I realize the value of the relationships I have with my family, and how they have strengthened me as a person, especially when I didn't think much of myself."

Parents' Insight-Building Exercise

Set aside fifteen minutes. Turn off the ringer on your telephone, let the dog out, turn off your computer, and put a sign on your door that says "Deep Thinking Going On—Please Come Back Later." You may want to put some soothing music on if that helps to block out the household or office noises that can so easily pull you back into the fray.

Now, close your eyes and inhale deeply. Drop your shoulders, drop your jaw, and relax your hands. As you continue to breathe deeply feel your body settling into the chair or bed. Relax even more deeply and let go. Imagine yourself moving upward, floating out of your body, and above your physical surroundings. You are moving even higher and feel no limitations. You are now looking down at your home, your family, your town, your state, your country, and now the Earth itself. You are filled with love and compassion for all that you see and you watch with a detached wonder as the Earth comes into clearer focus. A web of light begins to wrap itself around the Earth and its features as if an illuminated spider's web. Observe this glistening glimmering sheath of brilliant light as it gently embraces the land, the water, and all the countries. You see that this web of light is really pure love. Your heart is overflowing with love as you begin to understand that all living things are connected by this web and this love is available to us all. Now your vision begins to focus on smaller and smaller parts of the earth. You see your state, your town, your family, and your teenager. You watch as little strands of this web of light that so easily surrounded the earth begins to float toward your teen. He reaches for the strand and is instantly filled with light as he makes the connection. Your child is now hooked into the web and his being is vibrating with love coming to him from this union with all living things. He smiles and opens his arms, still holding onto the web of light. You sense that your child is a part of all life, that he is not lonely or afraid but bolstered by this joining with a loving, sharing universe.

Stay in this meditation as long as you like. Then gently come back to your body, your room, and your breath. Take another deep breath in, then out. Take out your notebook and write down any thoughts you might have had or images you want to remember from this meditation.

Parents' Check-In Questions

- Do I live in harmony with nature? How so?

- Does being in nature sustain my spirituality?

- How do I feel about the animals in my life?

- What cause pulls at my heart strings? How might I take action for this cause?

- Do I know how my teen is labeled in school? Does she fit this label? Does she like being labeled in this way?

- Who are my child's closest friends?

- How might I make our home more friend-friendly?

- How might I make our home more earth-friendly?

Conversation Starters

Talking to our teens about how all life is connected and how they are part of that life can be tricky turf. We don't want to set up any more to do's in their busy lives or sound like a preachy nag. We may worry about causing them to feel guilty if they don't want to volunteer, or that we might be fostering a harsh "giving is better than getting"–type mentality. Use opportunities that come up naturally to talk about what *you* believe in and why.

Earth Day is celebrated in many communities both large and small and is a great touchstone for involvement or at least discussion with your teen. My small town of Concord, Massachusetts, has a charming parade complete with nature floats that are launched at twilight down the Concord River. This is the perfect time to talk to my teens about our beautiful Mother Earth and our opportunities to nurture Her.

Some specific conversations starters might include:

• What do you think of community service hours mandated by schools? Does this take some of the good out of your service contributions? How?

• How might you take action to create change for the better in your school? Here at home? In our neighborhood? In the world?

• What do you find easy to give?

• What do you experience when you give?

• What have you given in the past year in terms of time, service, love, money?

• When did you feel as if you really belonged?

• Have you ever felt that sense of belonging and connection in nature?

• How can we bring more nature into our home?

Words Can Profoundly Change Lives

"The things I really regret are the words I've said to my kids in angry moments that just aren't true about them. I generally realize this within the hour and we talk about it." —**Molly, mother of two**

"My parents spend more time correcting the words I use than listening to the words I say." —**Katie, sixteen**

* * *

I t's easy to coo and goo words of love to our precious infant. It's fun to sing silly poems about how much we adore our toddlers. It's even pretty common to tuck our ten-year-old daughter's hair behind her ears, peck her on the cheek, and tell her how we adore every freckle on her precious nose. As our children grow, however, the busyness of our lives can intrude upon these simple words of love, as can our kid's physical size and the size of their attitudes.

We need to remember that our teens may be struggling with low self-images and their need for love and acceptance is at an all time high. Now is not the time to hold back positive words. Tell your teenagers how they delight you, how much you respect their choices, your amazement at their abilities, or your appreciation of the way they solved a problem. Loving words from a parent fuels a child, no matter their age. Your positive, authentic words can be the grace that salves their fragile spirits.

Many spiritual texts and sacred people who have gone before us affirm the power of words. The Bible talks about the strength of the spoken word quite often. God said, "Let there be light," and there was light. At Jesus' command, the seas were calmed, the sick were healed, the blind could see, the deaf could hear, and the dead came back to life. Jesus also used his word to inspire and change hearts. When he spoke to a group of fishermen, they dropped their nets and followed him.

Buddhism uses chanting mantras as a means of practice, and the recitation of verses as a way of cultivating an awareness of the qualities of the Buddha.

Words have the power not only to manifest things in the world but also to change them. Confucius, when asked what his first deed would be if he were to become Emperor of China, replied, "I would reestablish the precise meaning of words." All religions, cultures, and civilizations have taught that *your word is your power*. Early Buddhist texts provided incantations to heal illness and bring prosperity to the land. Spoken words infuse the intention of thought with the power of breath. Naming ceremonies in traditional societies continue to celebrate this sacred activity, attaching language to life.

There is a saying that we should use our words for only three purposes, to "heal, bless, or prosper." Imagine if we set out each day knowing that our words had the dynamic power to cure or destroy, to build up or tear down.

Words crystallize our thoughts. As parents of teens, the power of our thoughts as words goes far beyond what we imagine, deep into the hearts and souls of our children and out into the world around us.

Ralph Waldo Emerson reminded us that "Words are also actions, and actions are a kind of words."

Prayer

When we think of words in the context of spirituality, we often think first of prayer. Certainly, in prayer, our heartfelt words take flight with the angels, unifying us with the implicit power of Spirit.

Praying is one of the most natural human experiences, and can also be one of the most empowering and transformational. We can't, however, push our teens into it. There is a certain amount of honing that will happen as they explore prayer before finding a personalized rhythm and style that suits them. Our notions about prayer change as our relationship with God evolves. There are many different forms of prayer, and our teen's spiritual temperament can lead them to that which resonates most fully.

A high school senior who takes part in her school plays says, "I don't get down on my knees or anything but before I go out onto that stage I'm in the wings praying away. I may not look like I'm praying but I'm completely focused on my connection with God. It helps me to know I'm not alone and I can go out there after I pray."

Another high school student, a freshman, wrote me about his experience with prayer: "It's not about Hebrew words I learned from my bar mitzvah but about my feelings of being a part of a deep religious tradition. I can just feel the power of my Jewish tradition and that is a form of prayer."

And nineteen-year-old David, a college freshman, says, "Sometimes grades stress me out. I have a scholarship, and sometimes I feel like my life is over if my GPA sinks too low. Other times, lack of romantic companionship bothers me because that was something I always had back in high school. I hold positions in some organizations, and when things go wrong I get stressed. Overall, I remain fairly calm. When I do get nervous or anxious, I can usually pray and it all gets easier. Or I find it helpful to get away from people and just go to a quiet place and sit down a while. I play guitar, and that allows me a lot of opportunity to worship in my private time. Usually when I think about it, the things I'm worrying about never matter enough to stress out over anyway."

For many teens, prayer is another example of being let down. Sara, sixteen, said, "I've been praying for peace but it hasn't happened yet." When we pray but don't see answers, we might begin to feel that there must be something wrong with us, our prayer methods, or our spiritual connection. Let's assure our teenagers that we aren't always able to recognize an answer to our prayers. We may receive exactly what is needed, but not have the wisdom to see it quite yet.

I do believe that the practice of prayer is a willingness to relax into the sacred and to honor the vast power and love always there for us in this bountiful universe. When we see our prayerful words in that context, rather than as a magic spell for wish-granting, then we will begin to experience the results that prayer and placing ourselves in the presence of the Divine bring.

We can expose our teens to the many ways various cultures use prayer. We can also demonstrate a menu of prayer options by exploring prayer ourselves and sharing our journey. Then, when we say, "Let's pray about it," we have choices for how to begin.

Some additional thoughts on how you and your teen can tap into the power of prayerful words:

- Metta meditation is an ancient practice that is meant to help us reach across to others when conflict arises. "Metta" means loving-kindness so "Metta meditation" means the meditation of loving-kindness. Buddhists use this meditation to cultivate openheartedness and centeredness in all relationships. You don't have to be a Buddhist, however, to practice Metta meditation. Say the following words when you wish to transmit love and send light to your teen, or anyone else. The effects are remarkable.

May **I** be filled with loving kindness

May **I** be happy

May **I** be peaceful and at ease

May **I** be well

May (child's **name**) be filled with loving kindness

May (child's **name**) be happy

May (child's **name**) be peaceful and at ease

May (child's **name**) be well

May **we** be filled with loving kindness

May **we** be happy

May **we** be peaceful and at ease

May **we** be well

• Thich Nhat Hanh, in his beautiful book *Present Moment Wonderful Moment*, says, "Words can travel thousands of miles. May my words create mutual understanding and love. May they be as beautiful as gems, as lovely as flowers." Use Thich Nhat Hanh's thoughts to create a prayer for your family. "Today, may my words create mutual understanding and love. May they be as beautiful as gems, as lovely as flowers. May I have confidence and courage with these words. Amen."

• Write your own parenting prayer. As our children become teens our prayers often shift slightly. My prayer recently has been, "May I reach my highest and best divine potential as a parent. May I remain compassionate and mindful without losing my self. May I craft a life of loving and supporting my children without pressuring or controlling them. May I overcome my limitations and fears, and envelop and support wonder and magic in our life together as a family. May I empower my children with love always." Begin your prayer with: "May I . . ." and see what words flow.

• When your teen is faced with an obstacle, encourage him to pick one word that might address this situation, for instance "peace," "understanding," "resolution," or "calm," and bring it to mind throughout the day. Often focusing on one affirmative word can switch us out of our circumstances into a higher place of resolution. My daughter has been feeling stressed with some big tests coming up. Her word of the day has been "steady." She begins to panic about her workload and whispers to herself "steady!" It seems to help.

• Words aren't always necessary for prayer. Simply feel appreciation and gratitude in your heart, as if your prayer has already been answered, even if circumstances tell you otherwise. Rather than praying with our heads, this prayer is from our feeling modality. Rather than pleading for something or attempting to make something happen, wordless prayer allows us to experience the gratitude for what we wish to come to pass. This can be the most powerful of prayers.

• Asking for prayer from others and offering it in return can be an enormous gift of Spirit. Many times, close friends have held my prayers as their own during times I found challenging. As we include others in our personal prayer life, our teens see us choosing to amplify our own connection. And we can certainly invite our children into the process, asking them to remember others who need prayer or offering to hold them in silent, close connection with a loving God. Author Celia Straus left a prayer on her teenage daughter's pillow each evening. Those prayers have been collected in Celia's book for teenage girls, *Prayers on My Pillow.*

• Write a letter to the Source that fuels and guides you. It may feel awkward and a bit strange to put pen to paper or fingers to keyboard for this purpose. Think of it as a way to focus your thoughts, clearly express your thanks, release your worries, or ask for guidance. Writing to God can be like talking to a close and trusted friend. It may also be similar to a good journaling session. There is something very soothing and freeing when we reveal our innermost thoughts and desires in a context that is safe and free from judgment.

When we pray, we wrap our words with conscious spiritual intent. All of our words, not just those used in prayer, have powerful effects that we can use as we spiritually parent.

Loving Words

We love our teens, but often our words don't demonstrate that love. At the same time, as much as our culture would tell us otherwise, teenagers still want to hear how we feel about them. "Do you love me as much as my brother?" "Do you care as much now that I'm almost an adult?" "Would you love me even if I dyed my hair blue, broke your favorite vase, or drank beer?" Mother Teresa so wisely pointed out that, "There is more hunger for love and appreciation in this world than for bread." She could have been speaking about our teenagers who need to hear: "My love is always with you," and "It is okay to make mistakes."

As spiritual parents, our charge is to love all the time, not just when our adolescent's room is neat, the report card is stellar, or her attitude is positive. It's not easy. We often don't feel very loving towards our growing sons and daughters. Our emotions may be triggered by a teen who complains about her wardrobe just as we're writing a check to pay off the Gap credit card. "I sure don't like this teenage person I'm living with these days, but I do love him very much," said one frustrated father.

We must continue to turn to our inner Source of guidance so we can love through our anger, our frustration, our disappointment, and our fear. When we dig deep in our souls for patience, we have the strength to be more understanding with our teens and to work a little harder at putting ourselves into their place rather than finding our place as their parents uncomfortable. With patience, we become better able to demonstrate our caring with our words.

Remind your children how much you love them, even when it might be a struggle. They need to regularly hear words of encouragement from their parents. Brianne, sixteen, who recently broke her wrist, received some much-needed affirmation at just the right time. "I know that my parents love me because they keep encouraging me through this tough time. It's so hard to get my work done at school but they never force me to do homework when I'm not feeling well. They tell me to do it later or to rest when I feel like resting. The other night my Dad said how proud he was that I was trying so hard."

It's often difficult for kids to say something to a parent about their pain or pleasure. So when they have the courage to share something intimate, in my experience, they are looking for initial acceptance and affirmation rather than judgment or solutions. Do you want your teen to confide in you? Remain accepting and affirming when your son or daughter goes out on a limb to share, and save the lectures for later.

Words have the power to transform. Celebrate your love by practicing the following ideas:

• Be thoughtful with your word choice, tone, and timing. Author Christopher Morley wisely stated that, "If we all discovered that we only had five minutes left to say all that we wanted to say, every telephone booth would be occupied by people calling other people to tell them that they loved them." September 11, 2001, proved Morley's point. Tell those you love how much you love them—often. Look into your teen's eyes and speak from the depths of your heart. Bless her with your words of love. "I give thanks today for the gift of you in my life. I love you today and always. I will hold you in my heart forever. I love you, _____."

• Remain attentive to the words you use as you part in the mornings and last thing in the evenings.

• Ask your teen what helps him to feel really loved. If he's a typical teenager, he will probably be embarrassed by the question, but the simple effort of asking reminds him you care. Our teens are multidimensional, fascinating human beings and, by knowing their likes and dislikes, we learn more about their unfolding personalities. Maggie, fifteen, says, "My dad asked me the name of my favorite ice cream. I was pretty surprised he didn't know but he's a busy guy. It made me feel so special when he came home the other night with Mississippi Mud. He nailed it." And Rich, seventeen, feels his parents have missed the boat: "My parents haven't a clue what I like and dislike. All they seem to care about is my sneakers left on the stairs, and how much gas I use in the car."

• Written words can be very powerful. Send your teenager an e-mail with positive words affirming his importance in your life. If your teen uses a cell phone, text message a sappy missive. Post-it notes can help prompt your child to remember so you don't have to fall into nagging. Sometimes I'll leave a giant yellow Post-it note on the bathroom door with the simple words "litter box." And, although it has become lunchtime sport amongst my daughter's friends to read them, I often include notes with their lunches or tucked in their backpacks. Now, however,

I'll add a line or two for their friends: "Hi, Kristen!" or "Good luck at fencing tonight, Eva!"

• Don't forget recorded words. Leave your teen a message on the answering machine, "Hi, it's Monday and even though you are right down the hall, I wanted you to know, I LOVE YOU and thanks again for making a great breakfast on Sunday. You're the best."

• I recently heard about a group of women in Nantucket, Massachusetts, who are knitting shawls to pass along to those who are sad, sick, or in any kind of trouble. They gather together to knit these shawls, praying aloud for the people who will use them. Imagine wrapping your teen in a shawl of prayer and love just as you swaddled him in that first receiving blanket. You might create some sort of visual representation of your love for your son or daughter. If you knit, create a bright funky scarf. Affirm positive words about your child as you knit. "Each stitch holds a bit of my love for you." Or, if you are hopeless with handcrafts as I am, you might weave together a special poem or decorate a box or picture frame with positive words that describe your teen. Cut the words from magazines or print them using different colors and fonts on your computer. They may think it's corny but deep down your kids will be touched that you care so much.

• Take a moment to pause and recall the times in your life when someone said something to make you feel loved. What is the first scenario that comes to mind? What was said to you? What might you say to help your teen feel that same sensation of being loved?

• Offer lots of words of praise when appropriate. The appreciated teen is far less likely to have an attitude problem.

Words of love can seem like such a small thing, easily overlooked in the daily hustle. Over a lifetime, they make all the difference in the universe. I was blessed to be with my father when death was drawing near. Not a day goes by that I don't think of his description of moving towards the light. He said, "I see now that all that truly matters in life is love. We just need to love each other."

As we strive to move ahead in life, get it all done and raise successful kids, think of the parting words of my dad. Love each other. Love your teenage son or daughter, and you will deeply nurture their spirits while enriching your own soul.

The Power of Stories

Stories have the potential to enchant, touch, and transform us. Why is it, I wonder, that we here in the Western world often pack stories away in the attic with the picture books as our children grow?

Stories show us what is possible, what has come before us, and what is happening at this very moment. The art of storytelling carries a wave of continuity and meaning that teenagers instinctively respond to. Stories can convey ideas, beliefs, traditions, knowledge, and moral standards in powerful ways.

Teenagers are bombarded with stories through the movies, television, magazines, newspapers, Internet, and video games they take in, as well as the urban legends and myths passed down to them from their peers. They have stories about most everything—themselves, others, events, and circumstances. In fact, who they are and how they perceive themselves is always a story—a linguistic construction. "I'm a good field hockey player but have terrible skin and will never get a boyfriend." "I'm all about my parents' divorce." "I'm the kid no one misses if I don't show up at a party." "I'm a skateboarder with attitude."

Writer and political scientist Hannah Arendt says, "The story reveals the meaning of what otherwise would remain an unbearable sequence of sheer happenings." As teens search for meaning, it would be unbearable for them to think of the events of their lives as "sheer happenings."

We can use the powerful words of stories to spiritually nurture our kids and weave a new thread into the tapestry of stories making up the texture of their lives. Consider the following ideas:

• Teens are vulnerable to taking on the stories of others in ways that leave them out of touch with their authentic selves and, as a result, are not the authors of their own stories. Encourage your teen to write (or think about) the story of how she'd like her life to unfold. This is a private endeavor, not for you to read (or hear) but for her to play with the power of words so as to craft a vision of her future. Explain to her the power of her own narrative rather than reacting to a story that happens *to* her.

• Teenagers are faced with tough decisions. They are eager to know how others have coped in similar situations. Tell your kids stories from your teen years; challenges, overcoming obstacles, esoteric explorations, humorous realizations, and finding your passion. Hearing our stories helps our kids to realize that we are human too and that their feelings are normal. If your teens are like mine, you'll probably hear "Not that story *again*," but press on. Encourage family members and friends to also tell their stories to your teenagers. These tales can broaden your teen's perspective on life.

• Cognitive scientist William Calvin, in an article in *Scientific American,* described how from stories, a child learns to "imagine a course of action, imagine its effects on others, and decides whether or not to do it." In a very fundamental way, storytelling and decision making are related. Find stories from other teens and use these words as a segue into discussions about making decisions. These stories help open conversation around sensitive topics. To get you started, the following teens share their stories about sex.

"I thought that having sex would make our relationship stronger, but really all it did was destroy it." **—Meline, sixteen**

"I never thought I'd be saying this, but I wish I'd waited to have sex. You know, when you're a guy you're supposed to just want it all the time. Sometimes it seems like sex is all the guys I know ever talk about. So I was thinking that I should do it. I didn't want to be the only one who was a virgin. So I went out with this girl twice, and we had sex. We used a condom and everything. And the sex was okay, but I didn't really know what I was doing and it felt awkward. Afterwards, I wished that I had known her better and could have talked with her about it. Then she missed her period, and we both really freaked out! We weren't even together—the sex was just a one-time thing. She wasn't pregnant. But I realized how quickly I could mess up my life—and hers. So I decided to wait until I'm in a long-term relationship before having sex again."   **—Andrew, seventeen**

"I've made the decision to abstain from sex until I'm married. It seems like a long way away and lots of my friends are making different choices. I'm clear with what I believe and I just hope I can find a boyfriend who feels the same way. That would make life a lot easier."   **—Melody, sixteen**

• The world of literature offers a plethora of coming of age stories that have accompanied and nourished generations of adolescents through the passage to adulthood. Expose your teen to books such as *Anne Frank: The Diary of a Young Girl, The Catcher in the Rye, A Separate Peace, The Adventures of Tom Sawyer, To Kill a Mockingbird,* and *A Tree Grows in Brooklyn.* Some recent coming-of-age stories include *Peace like a River, The Secret Life of Bees, Speak,* and almost anything by Toni Morrison.

• One mother of a sixteen-year-old daughter finds that reading aloud to her daughter is a warm, nourishing, bonding experience, "Kate just recently asked me to read *Tom Sawyer,* her favorite book, to her. It was a delightful adventure. Every couple of nights, I'd snuggle in next to her in bed and read a chapter. Had I suggested such an activity I'm sure she would have balked, but coming from her it was a lovely opportunity to get close again."

• Kerry Kennedy Cuomo, in her powerful book *Speak Truth to Power,* has gathered stories of individuals facing oppression from around the world. She says, "I believe their stories must be told because when people hear these tales, they too will take up a cause whether to stop child la-bor and sexual slavery, to assure free expression and the right to practice one's faith, or the right to credit for the poor and to a decent, healthy environment all causes which will make for a more just and decent world." Reach deeply into the world in which you live to read and discuss true stories so your teen might be ignited to take action in his life and make a difference.

• Create a list of the books that have had an influence on your life in some way. Share that list with your teenage reader. Ask her to create her own list of transformational titles. Swap lists with other families.

• Start a mother/daughter or father/son, or father/daughter, mother/son book club. Your busy teen may resist a formal arrangement, but if you invite a few others over to discuss a favorite book, they may open up. Literature can often open the door to discussion about some of the tough topics your teen is facing.

• Stories play an important role in how kids learn. Researchers found that high school students recalled up to three times more when history textbooks were translated into the story-based style of *Time* and *Newsweek*. Encourage your teen to transform dry details he must memorize into vivid stories that come to life.

• Stories can shape, expand, and begin to answer the questions our teens are grappling with, such as "Does my life have meaning?" "Who am I?," "Am I part of something bigger?" Your children are not too old to hear the story of how you address these questions. "I believe that you belong to the universe. A magnificent power greater than you or me has put you here. This power, I call God, wants you and needs you. Your spirit, which is vaster than your body, is a unique, creative, unlimited entity and it will always be connected to God. No matter what you've done or will do you are God's beloved one. This might sound corny but it is the truth as I have come to know it. If this is all true about you, it's also true about me, your sister, your math teacher, everyone. So trust this universe. Trust that you are enough as a grand spirit in human form and trust that other people are trying to answer these very same questions."

Negative Talk

"Whatever you are saying about someone, they could be saying about you."
—Katie, sixteen

Teens' words are often extreme, dynamic, and all or nothing. "Life sucks!" "I hate that teacher." "I'll never step foot in that house again." They aren't usually very discerning with their words and speak in the flurry of passing emotion. The sixteen-year-old home on a Saturday night for the first time in months cries out, "I have NO friends."

In addition to complaining, the way we're all tempted to, teens can—just like us—use words in caustic and cutting ways. In my experience, most teens use negative speech to test out their standing in the world. "She is such a loser!" would empower the speaker of these words to define herself as a "winner."

Jean, the mother of three teenagers, uses two words to halt negative talk in her family. She says, "My son at sixteen, was often quite judgmental to the degree of degrading other people or things. So I started talking with him about how his words have impact and asking him what impact did he really want to have. Did he want to be negative? So we developed a little fun thing we do together that helps us to be positive rather than negative. It is called 'Cancel that.'

"If we catch each other saying a negative phrase, we say, 'Cancel that' and we envision the red circle and the strike-through mark just as if you were looking at a No Parking sign. It has become pretty exciting. For instance, in the morning, if someone is mentioning something negative, another will say, 'You need to cancel that.' Or, if I say something negative and I don't really want to continue I'll say, 'Cancel that.'

"My son turned some kids that he didn't like before into friends with this perspective and it really surprised him. He came home one day and explained that by canceling the negative things he thought about a person and thinking about them in a different way, he found out they had a lot in common and he really didn't know the person before."

It is important for teens to realize that their words have meaning. If nobody ever tells them that they are continually negative, for instance, they won't know. Kids need the feedback.

At certain ages between twelve and twenty, kids are tempted to cop an attitude. If we tolerate a certain way of talking from our teens that we find unacceptable, our own spirits suffer. We need to help our kids reframe their self-involvement by refusing to respond when attitude presents itself—even through their tone of voice. For instance, your son may need a ride to the game, but he isn't going to get one from you if the request comes in that tone. (Often, the presence of friends escalates this tendency. Take your teen aside for a private conversation, rather than embarrass him in front of friends, or put it off until later.)

We all need to be reminded of the power of negative speech. Small talk can have large consequences. The following tips are to help you and your kids refrain from gossip and hurtful words.

- It's easy to let our emotions get the best of us, especially when we are teenagers and it often feels as if these vast emotions are controlling our every move. Encourage your child not to believe everything he hears. One simple comment can travel fast and furiously, destroying a person's reputation. Just think of the childhood game of telephone. One person starts off and by the time the statement has reached the end of the circle it has completely changed. Take responsibility and check out a rumor before believing it to be true. A good piece of advice comes from the following saying: "Do not repeat anything you will not sign your name to."

- Establish a family "gossip jar." When anyone is caught gossiping by another family member, they add a quarter (or a dime or a dollar) to the jar and a tally mark under their name. At the end of a month (or a week or two), the person with the least number of tally marks gets the contents of the jar.

- One mother of two teens used the above strategy to eliminate widespread complaining. She noted that an unanticipated—and fun—part of the process came from family members trying to trick each other into forfeiting some cash. "'Man, your back must be sore,' my son would say to me. I'd respond, 'Nope, nothing I can't handle!' in a perky tone even when I did feel certain twinges."

• Help your child understand that a friendship built on gossip has no future. Mark Twain once said, "It takes your enemy and your friend, working together, to hurt you to the heart; the one to slander you and the other to get the news to you." Encourage your kids to surround themselves with friends they can trust rather than basing someone's value on their ranking in the social strata.

• Choosing silence rather than speaking negative words is always a good choice. In our Western culture, we are uncomfortable when there is a lull in the conversation, so we feel we need to fill it up with words. Often, the words we grab onto aren't the highest possible choices. There's a wonderful old saying, "Talking comes by nature: silence by wisdom." A friend of mine who grew up in India once remarked, "When I attend a party with others from India there will be long moments of silence. Our words are carefully chosen rather than banal small talk."

• Misery loves company, but it's unrequited. Nobody likes a whiner, or a complainer, a kvetcher. Don't dwell on problems; concentrate on solutions. Resolve how you can handle an issue, rather than lament why you can't. This is advice for us as parents but also for our teens. They can become locked into each problem they face, and we can help them shift the habit.

• Could your use of clichés be limiting your experiences? Take a look at the negative habitual phrases that might have crept into your speech such as, "You can't fight city hall," "Life sucks and then you die," "It's better than nothing."

Even in Jest, Words Can Hurt

Hurtful words at home are common because home is a safe place where teens can verbalize their frustration. Words have power, as we know, so flinging them around in anger can land a nasty sting. If this is happening with your teen, let him know that he has a right to express his opinions and that you want to understand how he is feeling but his choice of words isn't working. Ask him to try again to tell you respectfully what is troubling him so that you might understand.

Of course, teens are much more likely to express themselves respectfully when that's what they learn at home. We need to examine our own speech. Are we rude to one another? Do we speak to our teens in a tone and manner we would never use on someone outside the family? How readily do we apologize to our teens when we've done injury? Are we overly critical, finding fault with things we'd overlook in anyone else?

Criticism from a parent, however judicious and well-intentioned, can be crushing. A good formula for correction is to first offer a compliment; mention what it is your teen could work on, than end with another compliment. For instance, the following might be a way to help your new driver to become even more conscientious: "Fantastic job remembering to hang the keys on the key hook. I was so happy this morning that I didn't have to spend five minutes hunting for car keys. Please remember to fill up the gas when the gauge reads empty. By the way, I was amazed that you took the time to back the car into the garage. I never think to do that and it makes exiting a whole lot easier. You're really coming along in the driving department!"

Try some of the following to shift away from negative words in your family:

- Swearing does no good. It brings our energy down, illustrates our limited vocabulary, and often disrespects sacred figures, Jesus Christ for instance. We don't wash our children's mouths out with soap anymore; in fact, many parents accept lazy language as, "just the way teens are." After all, we hear these words on television, or include them in our own conversations. Make an effort to eliminate swearing from your own vocabulary and point out when your teen casually curses. Remind her that by not swearing she will appear smarter.

• Teens may appear grown up and easily able to handle joking words from a parent, but that's not always the case. Be sensitive with teasing words during these years. Harmless teasing between teens isn't always harmless either. Harassment has crept into our teen's speech and become more and more rampant amongst our high school halls. Harassing words are hurtful, damaging, and yes, illegal, when they cross the line and threaten personal safety. Teach your teens to treat one another with consideration.

• Be aware when you respond to your teens with absolutes. Rather than, "You are hopeless at doing your chores!" you might say "Let's come up with ways you can remind yourself to clean the bathroom in the future."

• When you constantly describe parenting a teen as strife-ridden you set yourself up to be frightened, stressed, and annoyed. Decide to stop talking about your situation this way. Instead of saying, "Yup, life is never dull with a teen in the house. You know terrible twos, now tumultuous teens," try "My son is on the brink of big things, he's working through the details and it's my privilege to be there to help when I can." Can you feel the difference?

• Disagreeing isn't always a bad thing. Help your sons and daughters learn the fine art of articulating their viewpoints and disagreeing respectfully. Perhaps dinnertime is a forum for discussion in your family when every opinion is respected. This is great preparation for adult life and builds a teen's sense of self-worth.

Bring your teenager's attention to the inner dialogue constantly running through their minds. Our negative inner script is that little voice that tells us we are too fat, too thin, not pretty or popular enough. It belittles us with statements such as, "You're such a loser, what were you thinking?"

"You are out of your league here so just shut up." "You can't possibly measure up." Often this critical voice is the voice of a society that wants the perfect teen, that person who couldn't exist. This limiting voice prevents our sons and daughters from discovering their true selves. Help them become aware of the negative script and understand the power it has as it grows over time. Liken their negative inner script to a paper cut. Ask them to think about getting a paper cut every time they get dressed, have something to eat, go to school, talk on the phone, play sports, study, or just hang out. That's a lot of paper cuts. Unless you want to bleed to death, you'd better make a conscious decision to change the script! Shift the word commentaries running through your head to more positive expressions. "I look great in this outfit." "I'll give it a try." "No harm done." "I'm completely cool here." We must help our teens to turn up their present-tense positive self-talk to overcome cynicism, negativism, and defeatism. Every picture and thought that we send to our brain is taken as total truth.

A teacher of seventh grade girls recently told me, "Each year I'm hearing more and more girls put themselves down more and more of the time with the 'Oh, I'm so bad at that' kind of comments. Some of this rises, of course, out of that 'please stroke me, stroke me' need they have but, then again, some of it seems to come from something else I can't put my finger on."

The self-defeating limiting phrases these girls use, when said often enough, will begin to map out their reality. Repeat "I'm terrible at geometry" enough and watch your grades go down. I suggested this teacher bring the girls' attention to their words and help them do a correction on the spot.

The derogatory word habits of these twelve- and thirteen-year-olds, as well as the examples above of negative inner scripts, are word habits that can become toxic. Our own spoken-word habits with our teens are just as hard to break. "How many times do I have to tell you?" "You don't have to be a Rhodes Scholar to get an A in that class." "You drive me nuts!" "What were you thinking?!"

Saying No

"I wish parents understood that it stinks when we can't do something we really wanted to. Let us voice our anger." **—Meg, sixteen**

Teens, like the above sixteen-year-old, should voice their anger respectfully to their moms and dads. Many parents, however, hesitate to say no to their teens for fear of that anger. They may also hesitate to say no because they worry about damaging their teen's self-esteem or alienating themselves from her. A teen's security, however, ultimately comes from knowing you are lovingly in control and call the ultimate shots. You love her, you respect her, you care for how she feels but, in this situation, the answer is "NO."

Be careful not to change your mind based on your teen's reaction after you have issued a well-thought-out "no." Remaining consistent and true to your word alleviates negotiating, complaining, and pleading, even though it's tough to accept that your child might be unhappy, and even tougher to have her demonstrate that unhappiness with drama and bravado.

It's always a good habit to take some time to think before responding. "Can I go to the concert on Saturday night with Mary then spend the night at her house?" Your immediate response might be "no," but if you say instead, "Give me some time to think about it, check my calendar, and talk to Mary's mom," you will make a clearer, better informed choice.

Be thoughtful, too, about the tone behind "no." It can make all the difference in the world. A firm "no" in a calm and confident tone of voice conveys a very different message than a quavering "noooo" that invites argument or a blustery "NO" that breeds resentment. In my experience, the more comfortable we are with saying "no," the more calmly we can deliver the news.

It is one thing to stick with "no" once you've said it, but could you give your teen more "yes" messages?

Many of us rattle off a quick "no" without giving it much thought. Consider the following when your teen wants to do something and you are about to deliver a habitual "NO!":

- Could this be harmful to my teen?

- Does it violate our family's rules?

- Will my teen be in a safe environment with friends I approve of?

- Do I trust my child with whatever situation may arise during this activity?

- Is saying "no" about me? Might I be afraid of what others think of me because of my child's choices? Be honest. Does the spiked hair or tattered jeans cause you embarrassment?

Support your teen's individuality by saying "yes" to their choices (as long as they aren't permanent, dangerous, or go against your spiritual beliefs).

You Just Don't Understand

Many teens don't talk to their parents because they don't think their parents will understand. When teens only hear reprimands or instructions, they may feel that a parent doesn't care how they feel. Silence, then becomes a teen's weapon. It's their way of saying, "You can't control me anymore."

Don't pump a recalcitrant teenager for information, rather allow conversation to develop slowly and naturally. A sullen sixteen-year-old who slams the bedroom door on a concerned parent but instant messages for an hour with his best friend doesn't need to hear, "It seems you always find time to talk to your friends but never to me." He may need time to work through a problem on his own or to assess whether his friends' perceptions are the same as his. It's normal for teens to shift their interest away from family and toward their friends. Rather than nagging or complaining that they aren't talking, create opportunities to be alone together so natural conversation arises.

I recently received the following question from a mother. "I have a fourteen-year-old daughter who I feel spends too much time on the phone and computer with her friends. I know the importance of peers at this age— but when it seems friends know your child better than you, what can be done? She is aware that we feel shut out but does not seem to care. She can talk to peers for hours but can not speak to her family for one minute. I've yelled, I've cried, I've even told her that she doesn't appreciate all I've done for her. Should I limit her access to peers even though she will probably be mad? Help, I want my daughter back!"

This mother's feelings are hurt. She wishes the relationship she had with her dear daughter wasn't changing. But by laying on a guilt trip, crying, and limiting the child's access to peers, she will only drive a further divide. Instead, she might create opportunities to talk to her daughter by arranging a dinner out or offering to pick her up at school. She might move the computer to a central place in the house, limit her daughter's phone and computer time, and work on her grief over losing the companionship of her little girl.

Teens usually become secretive, aloof, and pull away from their parents because they think we couldn't possibly understand their lives or they don't want to disappoint us by revealing their less-than-perfect selves. They may also believe that they can handle things on their own. And then there are the times when adolescents don't engage in conversation or answer questions because they quite simply are awash in confusion. They may not have the words to explain, even to themselves, so they certainly aren't going to appear so vulnerable in front of their parents.

Sometimes there is nothing you can do to help your teen open up and you simply have to wait for him to come around on his own time. I'm an impatient person and this is the toughest letting go I've had to do as a parent. But, by turning to God, I am comforted. "Help me be fully present and supply my daughter with whatever it is she might need today and stop trying to control in what way or when she shares with me. I know she has a close relationship with Spirit and trust that she is guided each and every moment by that Source."

Many parents of teens feel that their charge is to give advice. Before their children leave home, they seek to fill them up with all that has been left unsaid. In truth, most of your work is done, so you can relax. Now is the time to listen and, rather than advise, clearly articulate limits, expectations, and support your kids as they explore the ramifications of their decisions.

Tell the Truth—the Whole Truth

"I discovered that our fifteen-year-old daughter was lying because she didn't want to hear "no." But also that her fear of telling us the truth was based on misunderstood statements that we'd made. So, now we're going to write down some basic ideas and make sure that the communication lines are open and nongarbled. Hopefully, things will shape up." —Jay, father of one

Lies, deception, and dishonesty are unattractive Spirit-squashing traits to be sure. The very words sound sordid and dark and way beyond anything that would touch our orderly lives. Yet, teens lie. And teens hear their parents lie. Often, kids are nurtured in an uneven emotional environment where lies, evasions, and double messages are the rule. We don't mean to be models of dishonesty, but habits are hard to break.

When we lie, we create distance between ourselves and the person to whom we've lied. We shift into a dishonest relationship where true authentic connection becomes hampered. It's difficult for soulful growth of any kind to occur when we create an atmosphere of distrust. An African proverb says, "One falsehood spoils a thousand truths."

The CHARACTER COUNTS Coalition recently released their national survey of high school students. The quantified falsehoods were staggering. In the past twelve months, 92 percent of the high school students surveyed lied to their parents, and 79 percent said they did so two or more times. In the same time period, 78 percent lied to a teacher, 58 percent two or more times. More than one in four, 27 percent, said they would lie to get a job.

I did an informal study of my own over the past few weeks. I spent time talking to teenagers about lying. Here's the essence I gleaned of why many of our sons and daughters aren't telling the truth:

• Kids don't want to let their parents down. They feel an enormous pressure to live up to the high expectations their family has for them. Lying is often easier than disappointing Mom and Dad.

- Fear of punishment is a big incentive for kids to lie.

- Lying doesn't really matter, they think. What difference does it make, in the scheme of things, if I tell a lie?

- They use lying as a way to seek revenge against "the system."

- Some kids lie because that's what they hear at home. They use lying to get out of jams because it's what they've seen their parents do.

- Many kids have admitted that telling a small lie is a way to test the waters, to gain independence. It's an aspect of rebelling, of pushing boundaries.

- There is a fine line between exaggerating and lying and many kids continue to ignore it.

- For some teens, lying is a way to finally get their parent's attention. The statement, "I hate school, my math teacher has it out for me," may peak a parent's interest.

When our kids lie, an emotional minefield is ignited for many of us. We may recall shame-filled and punishment-ridden religious teachings of our youth. We aren't terribly concerned when our toddler lies about sneaking a cookie but we somehow never pictured our almost full grown young adult lying to us about where she spent the evening. After all, we have taught her it's wrong. Haven't we?

Try some of the following ideas to foster a sense of truthfulness in your teenagers:

- Begin by making sure home is a safe place. Kids usually lie when they are afraid to tell the truth. Do your teens feel comfortable talking to you or are they fearful of the repercussions of their truthful words?

- We can do the courageous and difficult work of getting honest in our own lives. We need to be honest with our children and especially with ourselves. Stop telling small white lies to get yourself out of uncomfortable situations or sidestepping the truth in order to get what you want. "You didn't receive that paperwork? Gee that's odd because I sent it last week." Be truthful and your teen will see how you take responsibility. "I'm sorry I should have sent the papers but I just haven't gotten to it. I will send them by overnight mail at my expense."

* Again, examine your interactions with your kids as reflections for how they behave with you. We lose our credibility with teens if we are less than honest. What they want is parents who are "real" and tell it like it is. When we do the tough work of getting honest with our kids, they will have more courage to do the same with us.

* Being loved and feeling a connectedness with others, especially their parents, is absolutely vital to kids. So when that closeness is at stake, the practical implications don't much matter. A lie is minor next to losing the love of your parent. Make sure you are loving and honoring your teens—not just managing their lives by delivering rules, consequences, or voicing your expectations.

* Lies become habitual. Stop them when they start by deep and honest communication. Consider sharing the Character Counts statistics (at the start of this chapter) with your son or daughter and use the study to spark conversation about how lies show up in their world. What do they observe about dishonesty around them?

* Come up with ways to let your teens have more control over their lives and rebel without resorting to lying. Give them alternatives. Gayle, mother of thirteen-year-old Sam, says, "I asked my daughter if she had fed the pets this morning. She announced that she had. I looked closer and responded, "Sam, you did not take care of the animals, did you?" She giggled as if she had done something cute. I said, "Look you can be angry, you can stamp your feet, but you can't lie to me. It's not fair for us to be untruthful to each other but, more importantly, there are consequences to the animals you love."

* Often a teen will lie rather than risk losing the closeness of a friendship. There is a Hopi saying that helps us understand, however, that

lying impacts our own spirits. "Lose your temper and you lose a friend; lie and you lose yourself."

* When your teen does tell a lie, hard as it is, make sure she takes responsibility for it. Jane, mother of fourteen-year-old Mark, was horrified when his teacher phoned to say Mark had called another child a racist name. Mark denied it to his mother, so she went to bat for him. After getting the principal involved and much back and forth, Mark eventually told the truth. He had indeed called the child by this name. His parents were mortified. They insisted that Mark write a letter apologizing for wasting everyone's time with this incident to the child, the child's parents, the teacher who had stood by Mark, and the school principal. It can be humiliating when our teen lies so publicly, but we need to get over our own egos and make sure he faces his mistakes. A mother of two teens writes, "My son told me a lie over a year ago when he was twelve. The most painful thing about the experience still is that I knew instantly the reason he was lying was because he was afraid of what I would do if he told the truth. As gently as I could, I walked him through the process of getting through the fear to telling the truth. When we finished talking he understood that there would be consequences for the original action that inspired the lying, but that I would not be angry if he told the truth—quite the opposite: I would applaud the difficult task of truth telling. He hasn't—knock on wood—told a lie since."

* It's not easy to rebuild trust after our teen has lied. It's important, however, to take action to regain trust in order to heal the relationship with your son or daughter. Begin by noticing when you're tempted to withdraw in anger or mistrust. Take a small step in the other direction, instead, moving a pace toward your teen emotionally. Focus on the things that your teen does right—there are bound to be many.

Communication Is Key

Have you talked with your teenager lately to spell out those things you assume she knows? Statements such as, "Even if you screw up, tell me the truth and I will respect you for that." "You can always come to me with problems." Or "There's nothing you could do that would make me stop loving you." Communicate the all-important "I believe in you" in words your teen understands. "Teen speak" is an altogether different language, and by the time you finally master it, it changes. The essence of what you want your teenager to know, however, will translate if you are authentic and honest.

I want my girls to know they can count on me no matter what. When they worry about disappointing me, however, miscommunication can set in.

Whitney began fencing this winter. She's doing a great job, made the varsity team, and has committed herself to working hard. I love learning about my children's interests and being a part of their activities. With this one, however, Whitney was clear that she didn't want her dad or me to attend the fencing matches. Of course, my feelings were hurt. I imagined that she was embarrassed to have her parents in attendance. I assured her I wouldn't yell her name and would discreetly watch from the corner of the gym; I really wanted to see her fence. During family dinners Whitney described in detail the events of that day's match but no invitations for a viewing were offered. Finally, one cold Thursday afternoon as I was driving her to lift her saber in competition, Whitney said, "Mom, I would just get too nervous at this point if you were watching me." She's a girl of few words, but by saying those, I understood.

How often do we misunderstand our teen's actions, take them personally, and allow a wedge to drive its way into our relationship? A simple sentence might open the door to understanding or illuminate that we are completely on the wrong page. It's easy to fall into the stereotypical assumptions; in my case, I assumed Whitney was embarrassed to have her often outspoken, very excitable, and proud mother draw any sort of attention to her. By patiently waiting, however (which is not easy for me), I was able to hear the words that helped me to understand.

When is the last time you talked with your teen about topics that might make you both uncomfortable, but need to be addressed such as drugs, grades, alcohol, future plans, speeding, or sex?

When talking with your teen about sex, be clear about your own sexual values and attitudes. Yes, you need to have these discussions, as awkward as they might be. The National Teen Pregnancy Prevention Research Center recently released a report that found 20 percent of kids fourteen years old and younger, have had sex and the voices of their parents are stunningly absent in their lives.

Communicating about sex, love, and relationships is successful when you are certain in your own mind about these issues. To help clarify your attitudes and values, take time to ask yourself the following kinds of questions:

* What do I think about abstinence until marriage, given that the average age at marriage these days is twenty-five?

* Was I sexually active as a teenager and did I regret it?

* Was I sexually active before marriage? Will I share my own story with my teen?

* What do I feel about teens using contraceptives?

* How can I help my teen make discerning choices about becoming sexually involved?

Most parents think that the number-one reason teens have sex is raging hormones. But they are wrong. In one large survey, only 4 percent gave pleasure as the reason and only 10 percent said they were in love. Peer pressure—everyone else is doing it—and curiosity were the main reasons. Knowing this, communicate to your kids how they can remain true to their own beliefs and postpone curiosity until they are deeply in love and old enough to handle the consequences.

Never be reluctant to share your thoughts and beliefs about sex with your teens. For instance you might say, "I think kids in high school are too young to have sex, especially given the risks." "Our family religion says that sex should be an expression of love within marriage." "You will find yourself in a sexually charged situation so you need to think about how

you'll handle it in advance. Have a plan. Will you say no? How will you negotiate all this?" "It's okay to think about sex and to feel desire, everybody
does! But it's not okay to be unprepared, to get pregnant or get somebody
pregnant or to contact a sexually transmitted disease." "One of the reasons
I don't want you to drink or use drugs is that it can blur your reasoning and
plans when it comes to sex." "Your body houses your beautiful spirit. Think
carefully about what you do to this sacred vessel."

Miscommunication can be one of the biggest roadblocks to a strong relationship with our teens. Some other ways we can use our words to communicate more clearly are:

• When you speak to your teen, make your intentions understandable
with up front statements rather than sarcastic questions. When we are
direct with our words there is less possibility of miscommunication.
Rather than, "What were you thinking? Did you assume your laundry
would get done all by itself?" try, "If you want clean jeans for the
dance tonight, do a load of laundry." A mom who wants her daughter
to stop playing the stereo so loudly asks, "Do you want to go deaf?"
The daughter cranks it up even louder. Mom, now frustrated, yells,
"What did I just say?" Still no response. Rather than these open questions, she could simply, directly, and respectfully ask her daughter to
"Please turn down the music because I can't concentrate on what I'm
doing with music blasting and I'm worried about damage to both of
our hearing."

• We don't want to argue with our teens or experience their sour moods.
So, rather than experience a dose of their attitude, we cushion our words,
beat around the bush and ease into what we mean. We end our requests
with, "okay?" or "all right?" We say, "Don't talk back to me, okay?" The
question implies we are looking for our teen's agreement on the matter.
We handle uncomfortable topics by easing into them or talking around
them, saying "It was a terrible day" instead of "You were obnoxious to
everyone at church this morning." We set up statements with words such

as, "Now, don't get mad but . . ." Instead, let's do our kids the favor of being clear and direct without worrying about their responses.

• With teens in the house, many parents find the majority of their words to be complaints. Be careful, however, of how you phrase your "complaints." Using terms such as, "You always" or "You never" sets up confrontation and a wall between us and our teens. It is better to be straightforward with the particular issue at hand. "Please hang up the towels after you shower. I get cranky when I have to step over them to brush my teeth."

• Create your own parenting rules—your teen doesn't need to know what they are. These can become your fallback guidance when interacting with your kids. Perhaps your rules could begin with one of the following:

"Don't jump to conclusions."
"Let go and let God."
"Stay real with my teen."
"Don't worry about what other people think."

• Sometimes the easiest way to communicate with your teenager is through a letter. God will direct your words and the timing of when to share it with your son or daughter. The key is not to give up, but to continue opening to Spirit for guidance on the best form of communication to use. I received the following note from a mother recently: "Lately my thirteen-year-old does not want me to touch her or give her *any* advice. The narrow windows that she opens for any physical affection are very rare and I've learned to put off whatever I am doing to take advantage of these moments. A few months ago my daughter asked me, 'What do you believe?' My answer was short and sweet . . . '*love*.' Although concise, I didn't feel it was enough. I thought about your advice in a workshop I attended and decided to put my thoughts into words. I wrote her a four-page letter to communicate exactly what I meant. Now, even though she doesn't want to 'hear' me, I have noticed that the letter is open and next to her bed quite often."

The wonderful author Florence Scovel Shinn wrote in the 1920s about the power words have to shape our experiences. She said, "We cannot always control our thoughts, but we can control our words, and repetition impresses the subconscious, and we are then master of the situation."

Whether you are writing letters, praying, speaking loving words, or apologizing for ones you'd like to take back, your words have a tremendous impact on your life and the lives of those around you. As you pay more attention to what you say and how you say it, you will notice the impact on what you experience. You speak—and so it is. Help your teens master their lives by using the simple technique of conscious word choice. What they say is what they get.

Parents' Insight-Building Exercise

A wonderful technique for communicating to your teen, when it seems she is not interested in talking, is to practice the following simple visualization. Picture yourself hugging your receptive child, telling her how much you love her. Say the words you haven't been able to say recently. Speak from the heart and visualize your teen listening with uncrossed arms and direct eye contact. Imagine that you understand and accept one another fully in this interaction. See yourself communicating openly and honestly saying what you need to say and listening to her words. What does she want you to know? Enjoy the image of the two of you spending relaxed time together. Feel what it is like to be in harmony. When you feel as if you have said what you need your teenager to know and you have heard her authentic response, then slowly come back to the room and go about your day.

Parents' Check-In Questions

• Do I have old associations with the words of formalized prayer? If so, what are they?

- Is there a prayer from my childhood that is still of comfort to me today?

- When is the last time I told my teenager I love her? How did I say it? What was the response?

- How might I sprinkle more encouraging words into the lives of my kids? Leave notes in their backpacks, on the car dashboard, or send encouraging e-mails.

- What can I do to handle my own feelings and stress so that my words are thoughtful rather than reactionary?

- How do I react when my teenager's words are "in my face?"

- Do I have some negative word habits I'd like to break? What are they? (complaining, gossiping, muttering put-downs, sarcasm)

Conversation Starters

- What's your favorite word? Why?

- Can you remember a time when I've misunderstood something you've said to me?

- Are you ever afraid to tell me the truth?

- How do you think we can communicate more clearly with one another?

- Is honesty a quality that you find of importance in your relationships? Why?

- Are you embarrassed to compliment other kids? Is it easier to tease them or just have idle banter?

- Do any of your friends lie to get themselves out of jams? You don't have to tell me their names, but how do you think the lying affects their lives?

• I was reading a book that said "what we say is what we get in life." So if you say, "I stink at math," then you aren't helping your chances at a good math score on the test. Do you believe that?

Listen Fully, Acknowledge Deeply

"Listening to my kids without jumping in with my fears is hard. It takes a lot of faith for me to remember that I've already taught them what they need to know to make their decisions. I role play a lot with questions like, "So if you do go to the party and there are drugs, what are some options you have?" It's training mixed with trust and a confidence that my teens will make good choices." **—Anne, mother of three teens**

"I can't talk to my parents, they never listen. They always jump to conclusions before they let me explain. They say they are listening, but they are definitely not." **—Anonymous, fifteen**

* * *

In an online survey I asked teens "What do you wish your parents did differently?" The overwhelming response was not what I expected. I expected them to want more freedom, a later curfew, or another gadget. Instead, what teens said they wished their parents did differently was listen to them more often. I received responses like these: "I wish my parents really listened to me instead of just acting like super mom and super dad." "I would love it if my mom was around more often to hear what was going on in my life. We rarely catch up." These teens didn't mean they wished their parents gave them solutions, advice, or solved their problems. They simply wanted to be heard and respected.

There is a common misconception that our teens don't need us. They do. The Global Strategy Group polled teens and parents regarding their concerns about communicating with each other. The top worry among parents was drugs. However, 21 percent of the teens reported, "Not having enough time together with their parents" as their top concern. So, if teens got what they wanted, more time with an attentive parent, then maybe parents could worry less about drug use.

There is no shortage of polls and surveys when it comes to parenting teens. The YMCA recently released a study that showed family household conversations have decreased by 100 percent in the last twelve years. It's hard for our teens to be heard when we aren't having conversations. They desperately want our attention and love and one way we give that is by listening to them. We miss an awful lot when our teens, exasperated at unreceptive parents, choose to go elsewhere with their thoughts and ideas.

It's hard to listen to our teenagers when what we really want is to get our opinions across or to be right. It can be difficult to listen if we don't take our kids seriously; granted, that's sometimes tough when the package our teen presents has pink hair, or odd looking attire. To make it easier, practice listening to the real meaning of what your teen is telling you rather than the dramatic impact, the bravado, the surly tone, or the super-sweet delivery.

Bring yourself to the moment rather than allowing your fidgety mind to scan and notice your preexisting views, fears, or beliefs about what you are hearing. Doing so is easier when you have a predictable time to be with your teen or a ritual you share, such as Saturday morning breakfast, or even the routine drives to the orthodontist or cello class.

My daughter Whitney and I began a walking routine together. Whitney found a walking workout in a health magazine and posted it on our bulletin board, subtly suggesting we might follow along. I can't quite understand the mathematical calculations that go into figuring out our heart rate, but I do understand the importance of this morning rhythm we have developed. As we walk briskly along our neighborhood streets, all sorts of conversations are spun, giving me glimmers of who this young women is becoming and what she holds dear. Whitney is quiet and introspective, so the Zen-like movement somehow frees up her sharing mechanism. I, in turn, have tried my best to become more comfortable with the silences that fall between the talk and hold myself back from aimless chatter.

I'm grateful for this time with Whitney. I'm glad I told her that walking with headphones—her first instinct—wouldn't be quite as much fun for me. I'm glad that my assumptions about who she is are being replaced with conversations that allow me to be the lucky recipient of her wisdom. A new strand is being woven into our relationship, and I'm gaining a deeper understanding of this fine person, all under the guise of getting in shape.

We all want our teens to feel cared for and loved. We want them to know how important they are to us and to feel comfortable speaking openly about their lives, their worries, and their dreams. By listening to our sons and daughters during their teenage years, we tether them more firmly to their spirits even in the face of the world's opposition, and help them feel safe with the people who truly matter the most, their parents. While there are no guarantees in parenting, I've seen that the most spiritually grounded teenagers have parents who truly enjoy listening to them.

Plan some time to listen to your teen in ways you might not have tried.

• As you listen to your teen, practice letting go of any assumptions you have about who he is and remain open to his truth in this moment. We often have to override our lazy thoughts and create a new mental habit to keep this listening technique going. Next time you are in conversation with your teenager, pretend you're meeting him for the first time. How might you listen to this person if you knew nothing about his background?

• Designate an afternoon, an hour, or an entire weekend when you can shed your agenda and focus entirely on your teenager. Allow her to call the shots about what you do and where you go. My husband, although he isn't keen on popular music, fondly recalls the time he spent five hours at an outdoor rock concert with our daughter. It wasn't until the guy behind them threw up that he called it quits.

• Stop what you're doing and look into your teenager's eyes. Really hear her. Listen to her tone of voice as well as her words. Watch her body language. These are the details of truly listening with an attentive spirit.

• If it's appropriate, reflect back to your teen the emotions he is feeling when he shares something meaningful with you. It's remarkable how often a simple reflection of feelings, when done with no judgment or criticism, can create a sense of relief. "Oh, my Mom understands how completely nervous and humiliated I was. . . ."

• Remain flexible so you're available to listen when your teen is ready to talk. This is tough for me, as I'm not a night owl and my older daughter comes alive after nine p.m. One mother of three said, "I look forward to the evenings after the younger kids have gone to bed because that seems to be when Carolyn, my thirteen-year-old, and I have some nice warm talks. We both have come to quietly count on these evening hours."

• Ask questions with the intention of listening to the answers rather than making your child defensive. Ask questions to get information— not to prove a point.

• Remember, listening doesn't mean you necessarily agree with everything being said. Therein lies the challenge of finding the patience and willingness to suspend judgment and demonstrate your openness to hear your child's views. The idea is to think before you react. One sixteen-year-old shares a bit of illumination on this. "Sometimes kids don't mean to have an attitude. They just act that way around their friends, and then they bring it home. They are joking around and trying to see if their parents are uptight. If parents don't react, then kids might be more likely to share things with them because they feel like their parents are open."

- Keep your child's confidence. He won't come back and share if you can't be trusted to keep the information between the two of you. This seems obvious, but it can be very difficult to keep quiet when what our teen tells us makes great conversation on the playing field sidelines or at the next cocktail party.

- Neutral ground can often be the best place to talk: a restaurant, shopping mall, tennis court, or coffee shop. When your teen hints about wanting a latte or a scoop of ice cream, hop in the car and join him in a special drink or treat. It's truly about more than just the java or chocolate sauce.

- Be willing to play chauffeur. As one mother of a fourteen-year-old puts it, "I see driving my son and his friends to and from activities as a great chance to be visible. I get to meet the kids, see where they live, hear what they talk about, as well as have the security of knowing where they are and what they're doing. Plus, they love that I'm willing to listen to their music on the radio while we're driving!" Whether you're taking them to the mall, to the movies, or to play practice, time in the car with your child and his friends gives you a great opportunity to be visible without interfering.

- Listening isn't the same thing as snooping. I am frequently asked if it is okay for a parent to read their child's journals, letters, or e-mails. I believe that if a parent suspects that their son or daughter is in any kind of danger, if he or she has started to act differently, or if there is evidence of trouble, then first talk to him or her. Only if it is a situation that could harm your child physically, mentally, or spiritually—you suspect he's using drugs, for example—may you invade personal space. Ask yourself why you need to snoop. Often, it's because we want a closer relationship with our sons and daughters. Come up with ways to have that closeness without invading their privacy.

- Reward your teen's honesty. If your seventeen-year-old admits he dinged the car door when filling up the gas tank, let him know you appreciate the guts it took to tell you the truth rather than pretending nothing happened.

• Listen to your child without judgment. Judging sounds like this, "That wasn't a very good choice you made," rather than "How did it feel when you made that choice?" which deepens the conversation. Expressing how she feels, without editing for your benefit, allows her to look deeper within to her rich, always available Source, for insight and sustenance. You won't always be there for her, but this inner wisdom will. Articulating her beliefs and trying them out on you is safe ground. She can look within for guidance then practice voicing her opinion in the secure framework of a loving parent. Your judging words may put a halt to this.

• We listen, we affirm, we acknowledge, and we provide a safe haven for feelings to come out. But how do we know when we need to take action for our teen's safety? When our kids sound as if they feel helpless, isolated, angry, or afraid, we have a warning sign. Listening to our adolescent's words to us, their conversations with friends, as well as what they don't say, can sound an alarm.

• Many of the most important conversations I've had as a parent have come unexpectedly. Recognize the importance of casual conversations. Spontaneous conversations show our children that we always care deeply for them and can be trusted to listen to what matters in their lives. That trust lays the foundation for their ability to trust God with similar conversations.

• Create a family tradition in which everyone shares one or two anecdotes from their day. Teens will balk at this new "sharing" concept but when you make it nonnegotiable they will come to accept this day's end routine. During our evening meal I often ask, "What was the best thing that happened to you today?" The answers give me wonderful glimpses into my daughter's lives.

• Listen to what other adults in your teen's life have to say about your son or daughter. We are often hesitant to "bother" a teacher or youth leader and yet a quick call or e-mail to "check in" on our son or daughter is perfectly acceptable.

• Respect your teen's boundaries knowing that some teenagers say "I don't want to talk about it" or "It's not a big deal" because they're not sure their parents are really interested. Be persistent without being pushy. Assure your teen that you are genuinely interested in and concerned about her life and that you're always available to listen. Then, just stay close for a while and see if she doesn't open up.

• Listen without trying to fix things. Fixing things sounds like this: "I'll just call your teacher and see if we can't schedule a retake of that test." A better choice might be, "What would you have done differently?"

• Listen without criticizing. Criticizing sounds like this: "You did it again. You're never able to get anywhere on time," rather than "How do you feel when you are late for an event?"

• Listen without discrediting. Discrediting your teen sounds like this: "It couldn't have been that bad" or "You shouldn't be disappointed because you didn't really try very hard." To deepen conversation and be a receptive listener you might say, "I can tell you feel badly about what happened."

• Listen without interrupting. Interrupting might sound like this: "Wait a minute, before you go on let me ask you something . . ."

• Listen, listen, listen . . . and it's also critical that you express your own ideas. I've learned a couple of questions that I've used over and over to find the right time to do so. "Is there anything else?" allows me to make sure I'm not interrupting an important flow of ideas or emotions. "Would you like to know what I think?" frames my input as opinions, not commands. I ask this when "No" or "Not right now" is an answer I can accept and I'm willing to zip it accordingly. "I have some strong feelings I need to share with you. When would be a good time?" is useful for making it clear that I have something to say without stepping on my daughters' conversational toes.

It's Not Always Comfortable

There are many emotional triggers that can stop us from listening to our kids. Talking about drugs, sex, your recent painful divorce, her latest diet, his questioning of God, might be difficult. So instead of listening, you might fall into the trap of warning, nagging, or simply tuning out. Chances are your teen isn't looking for another lecture. What she wants is information and advice about something that is important to her. Some teens, too, think best out loud. "How can I know what I think until I see what I say?"

When you begin to feel anxious about a topic your teen brings up, make a conscious effort to control your feelings and listen. Discern if she wants more specific information or simply your loving presence.

When we're in touch with our best selves as parents, we don't stifle our children's honest questions. Doubting spirituality, wanting more information about sex, and questioning family changes is part of being human. Spiritual and emotional growth can only come when kids are given permission to wrestle with the tough questions.

The Centers for Disease Control and Prevention recently released a study that proved how important talking about sex and drugs is. In the study, the behavior of adolescents who didn't discuss sex or condoms with their mothers showed a higher participation in sexual activity, compared with adolescents who did discuss sex or condoms with their mothers.

We might not listen to our teen because we assume we already know the information. "I know you think you thought you knew what you thought I said, but I'm not sure you understood what you thought I meant" can be true for both parents and teens. As we make the effort to avoid jumping to conclusions, we can listen more fully to our teen's response to questions ranging from the mundane "Is there anything special you'd like for dinner tonight?" to the logistic "Let's discuss the use of the car this week. Where do you have to be when?" and, ultimately, to the critical "I think I'm pretty clear on your beliefs about drinking but, now that you're sixteen, what's been happening when you walk your talk?"

Many parents have developed the habit of discounting what their teenager says because it sounds silly, pompous, or irrelevant. Teens may present poorly, but once you get past their first attempts at communicating, which may be full of words such as "like, stupid, whatever, dude," you'll find the depth of feeling and thought lurking beneath the fluff.

Some things to try when you're tempted to tune your teen out include:

- If you're backing off an uncomfortable topic, be as honest as you can with yourself—and your teen—about why you're avoiding the discussion. Are you afraid that you'll find out information you'd rather not know? Are you anticipating a protracted argument? Do you fear judgment or criticism from your teen? The more authentic you allow yourself to be with your son or daughter, the more permission you give for him or her to be the same way with you.

- If you're feeling overwhelmed or distracted when your teen brings up a topic that will require your close attention, take a moment to shift priorities if you can. How can you rearrange the next hour so that your adolescent knows how important his need to talk is to you? If it's impossible to make space for soulful connection in the moment, make a date to do so in the immediate future: after dinner, before bedtime, over a cup of coffee in the morning.

- What if you live with a teen who never brings up the subjects you most want to discuss? A tactic I've used successfully with my most reticent teen is to introduce the topics of sex, say, or substance abuse more generally. "I read an interesting article today that said that 20 percent of all teens have sex by the time they're fifteen. Wow, that shocked me." Treat these topics the same as you would any other subject of general interest and you might find that words start to flow.

- Remember the virtues of passing phases. To date, every teenager I've known has been right about *everything* at one time or another. The need to be right, I believe, is an awkward and passing attempt to garner adult power. When I remember this, I remember that I can afford to be wrong on certain subjects.

The Power of Sound

"We need to find God, and he cannot be found in noise and restlessness. God is the friend of silence. See how nature—trees, flowers, grass—grows in silence; see the stars, the moon and the sun, how they move in silence. . . . We need silence to be able to touch souls." —**Mother Teresa**

Noise, unwanted sound, is derived from the Latin word "nausea," meaning seasickness. Can you recall a time you felt dizzy and knocked off balance by the swirl of sound? Now think about your teenager's soundscape and how he might be affected by this sound environment.

Noise is among the most pervasive and frustrating sources of everyday annoyance. Noise pollution is so prevalent because most of us have become accustomed to the constant sounds with which we are bombarded. Many who are creating the noise don't care enough or aren't bothered enough to correct it for others. The teen practicing drums is focused on his music and may forget that his neighbors' bedroom is only a few inches from his thundering instrument. An enthusiastic jet skier may be aware of, but dismiss as inconsequential, the interruption her loud machine inflicts on the beachgoers longing for the sound of healing waves. The family dining in the booth next to yours is apparently unaware that they aren't in their own kitchen and carry on with voices that blast into your sphere, ruining your visions of a quiet evening of much-needed conversation with *your* family.

I had the pleasure recently of speaking with Joshua Leeds, a pioneer in the psychoacoustics field and the author of *Power of Sound*. Joshua explained the enormous impact sound has on our neurological system. He sees "conscious sound awareness" as the next step in responsible health and wellness practice.

Leeds has witnessed sound offer healing results in kids with autism, learning disabilities, balance issues, and some levels of sensory delay.

The following are some ways you can take action to control the impact sound has on you and your teens:

• Work consciously to design your family's soundscape just as you would design your landscape or home interior. Remain attentive to the sounds coming from your television, computer, and CD player. Delay noisy lawn mowing in the morning to respect your neighbors—and let your teens know about their potential impact on the soundscapes of neighboring residences. Use your car horn discriminatingly. Scan your family's everyday environment and do what you can to minimize chronic sound interruptions. Remember that arguing, talking angrily, and shouting are harsh sounds that disrupt the peace of any home.

• Respect silence in houses of worship. One frustrated sixteen-year-old said of her church experience: "I sure don't feel God here. All these people are talking and chatting. I can do that at parties. I can't hear God's voice in this space."

• If you determine there is nothing you can do about the chronic noise where you live, consider toning down the sounds with white noise devices, soundproofing panels, ear plugs, water fountains, or nature sound recordings. Ask your teen if he would like to shift the sound quality of his bedroom. The purchase of a sound machine, with lots of audio options, might tempt him to give up rap before bedtime.

• Point out the subtle sounds in your environment and help your kids notice and honor them—a purring cat, distant church bells, the sound of rain on your roof, a crackling fire, or the crunch of fall leaves underfoot. They might roll their eyes and call you "very weird" but they *will* notice next time.

• In the early 1900s, "quiet zones" were established around many of the nation's schools. These protective areas were intended to increase educational efficiency by reducing the various levels of noise that were believed to interfere with children's learning and hamper their thinking ability. Researchers looking into the consequences of bringing up children in this less-than-quiet world have discovered that learning difficulties are likely byproducts of the noisy schools, play areas, and homes in which our children grow up. Have you stepped into a classroom in your child's school lately? The noise levels are alarmingly high. Be bold, suggest classical music be played over the school's intercom rather than the annoying bells signaling class changes.

• Designate a quiet space for your teen to do her homework—no television, no blasting music, no telephone calls with friends. Noise negatively affects our ability to learn and concentrate. A new study was recently released showing that, regardless of what they tell you, teens don't tune out sound when in a chronically noisy environment.

• Turn down the sounds in your home as bedtime approaches. Dr. Edward F. Crippen, former Deputy Health Commissioner of Detroit says, "The din of the modern city [includes] noises far above levels for optimum sleeping. Result: insomnia and instability."

• Loud sounds do affect hearing loss. Joshua Leeds says "If your teen is listening to music with earphones and you can hear the music, it's too loud." I was astounded to read a study that showed a mere thirty minutes of continuous sound in a video arcade can cause permanent hearing loss.

• Leeds also believes that rap music is "sonic valium," dulling kids' nervous systems. Many teens I have worked with have become desensitized to sound and as a result, like with any drug, need to increase their exposure to be touched by its effects. Notice if the volume is increasing when your son or daughter listens to music.

• Noise renders us less tolerant of frustration and numb to the needs of other people. It can cause your teens to feel more aggressive and you to lose patience quickly. I'm fascinated with the studies I've found on this topic and the following one in particular left me stunned. Results indicated that while a lawnmower was running nearby, people were less willing to help a person with a broken arm pick up a dropped armload of books. Another study of two groups of people playing a game found that the subjects playing under noisier conditions perceived their fellow players as more disagreeable, disorganized, and threatening. Noise can heighten conflicts and increase tensions—no doubt about it.

• Teens spend an average of 10,500 hours during their four years of high school listening to music. Their choice of lyrics says a lot about what they feel. Listen to what your kids are saying by what music they are listening to.

• Help your teen become conscious of her use of sound and offer some alternative suggestions as a test. Form your own little study with the help of your adolescent. "How do you feel after listening to this?" "Were you able to fall asleep easier with this music?" "Just play this CD when you study for a week and see if your grades change or you feel less stressed."

The right sound environment affects our bodies, minds, and spirits. Be a conscious creator of the sounds your teenagers take in when you have control of the environment and use sound as an audio vitamin to nourish their very beings.

Exercise Your Inner Guidance Every Day

"I call intuition 'cosmic fishing.' You feel a nibble, then you've got to hook the fish." —Buckminster Fuller

Our teens can take us to the edges of what we know—and beyond. Unsure if we're up to the task, we often find ourselves in territory we never thought we'd explore. Rick, father to a seventeen-year-old son, describes the challenge he feels: "When Justin was younger, I looked forward to his teen years. I thought parenting would be so much easier when he didn't need all the daily care of feeding, bathing, homework, lessons. It's much harder than I ever expected; I wonder if I'm doing the right things for him."

We'd go crazy if we needed to come up with all the answers. Fortunately, we don't. Jane, with two teenaged daughters, talks about an inner tool she relies on: "I learned that one of the ways God speaks to me is through my gut. If I feel like a little buzz of electricity is dancing through my belly, it's a clear message to put my foot down or ask more questions."

The still, small voice of inner guidance expresses differently for all of us. Some feel nudgings, some of us hear words, and still others see pictures. You don't need to be a psychic, a yogi, or a Zen monk to discern your sixth sense. All it takes is a willingness to try and trust that what we sense is indeed valid. No matter how or when we experience our inner guidance, this voice of God within is always available to us.

However, it's difficult to distinguish between guidance and gut reactions if we only try to tune in when the stakes are high. The still, small voice gets drowned out by emotions and stress. It's like trying to remember our long-ago CPR lessons when placing our hands on the chest of a victim.

By listening to our inner guidance on a daily basis when the stakes are low, we learn what it feels like. A mom of two teens puts it this way: "If I get a feeling while driving that I ought to make a particular turn or take one road rather than another, I always honor it. Sometimes, the reason is obvious; I see something or someone that I wouldn't have otherwise. More often, though, I do it without knowing why or caring."

Guidance is like a muscle; it grows stronger with exercise. I have learned that if I depend on my guidance to lead me through my days in the smallest of ways—whether a second cup of coffee would work for or against me, what music would be most healing, whether I should pick up the phone and make a call—then I can more easily hear or feel that same voice when I'm upset.

Inner guidance allows us to discriminate between fleeting desires—chocolate, revenge, self-aggrandizement—and what we *really* want. God speaks to us through our most heartfelt desires, as well as small nudges; and as we act on them, everyone benefits.

Dropping down to our intuitive knowing can help us make decisions. If you find you are often second-guessing and questioning yourself when it comes to decisions having to do with your teen then you might be disconnected from your intuition.

To explore and strengthen your inner guidance:

* Pay more attention to your gut feelings. If you have a hunch, follow it—and notice what happens as a result.

* Use your inner guidance to make seemingly inconsequential decisions throughout the day. We get to know God through little things.

* Avoid mental arguments with yourself about what the voice of God leads you to do. Intuition and reason are two very different processes and our brains often want to override our intuitive leadings. Thank your brain very much for sharing its perspective and follow your guidance.

* Listen to the signals your body sends you—nervous stomach, headache, feeling off-center. I heard author and creative expert Julia Cameron interviewed recently and her wise advise included the following "Your body is the first line of defense signaling danger. Creative people really need to learn to listen to their bodies, because often their heads are slower to catch on to something suddenly wrong. We tend to want to lead with our heads. We tend to say, 'That's not rational.' And actually our intuition is our early warning system."

* If you have time to include walking in your schedule I find this is often the easiest way to access my intuition. My body is moving through space, I don't have to channel my mind, and thoughts filter up to the light of awareness.

* If we think of our intuition as "the voice of Spirit within guiding us" then we are Spirit's means to reveal action. So, if we listen to our intuition, then move into action based on that knowing, we will experience right results. Pretty simple, yet pretty profound—stop, look within, listen, then take action.

* To distinguish your gut feeling from a "should," use the following: A "should" may feel heavy and unexciting. Intuitive wisdom will feel freeing and energizing.

* The best way to determine if your teen may be in or heading towards turmoil is to use your own feelings as a guide. Start by asking yourself

what worries you the most about your teen and/or your family dynamics. Trust your gut! You really do know your teen better than anyone.

- At the core of your being lies Eternal Spirit. Try the following affirmative words to help remind you to tap into this powerful spiritual tool that is always at the ready:

"I connect easily and often to my inner wisdom to receive all the answers I need. I live in a world of infinite possibilities and am guided by this always available Sacred wisdom. Today, and everyday, I listen to the voice within and have the courage to follow through with action."

We can encourage our teens often to rely upon their inner sense of knowing. When they invite us to listen as they struggle with a decision, we can gently remind them that their hearts already hold the answers. Figuring out how to go within for these answers is truly the golden compass that will guide our sons and daughters throughout their lives.

One mother recently told me, "What I really want for my daughter is a way for her to find a centering point within. I know it's there and she knows it's there but in this crazy culture it's hard for her to find it." Figuring out how to listen to her intuitive voice is one way for this daughter to find her "centering point."

Honing their intuition helps kids solve problems, make good decisions, resist peer pressure, forge a deeper more loving connection with themselves, stay safe, trust their own instincts, and lead happier lives. Exploring their intuition also helps kids identify their deepest desires. One of the gifts we can give our teens is the opportunity to freely explore their desires in search of their most deeply held urgings. Indeed, this is their brilliant purpose; their gut feelings are prompts to get closer to this desire.

Zoning out to music, video games, or even electronic solitaire can be distractions teenagers use for not thinking, not listening, blocking out thoughts and certainly their intuitive voices. A fifteen-year-old girl says: "I usually don't quite know what to do. So much gets in the way like my friends and their ideas, what will people think of me, and what my parents will do or say. I can't take it all in so I slap some earphones on and listen to music so the world will go away. I'd rather do that than deal." Escaping with music can offer a much-needed respite from the world but shouldn't become a habit that blocks our spiritual connection.

When our teens give importance to their inner awareness, they can begin to find a deeper sense of being pleased with themselves. They won't have to look outside themselves so much of the time for answers. Divine wisdom within tells them what they need to know, rather than relying on *People* magazine, MTV, or peers for the way.

In *The Art of Living,* Epictetus said, "In trying to please other people, we find ourselves misdirected toward what lies outside our sphere of influence. In doing so, we lose our hold on our life's purpose." When we listen to the voice of Spirit within, we can grow closer to the truth about every aspect of our lives. When we listen to the people we love, we come to know their truth.

Parents' Insight-Building Exercise

Close your eyes and see yourself standing tall and confident, secure in knowing that you have access to the wisdom of the universe. Feel this empowering truth. See your inner power growing more and more each day as you listen to the wisdom from within more often. Picture yourself pausing throughout a typical day easily receiving this Divine guidance. You are receiving the information you need to solve a problem, move forward toward a goal, or parent more lovingly. In your mind's eye, imagine your day going easily and smoothly as you begin to apply this inner wisdom to your life. Feel the joy of having this constant and immediate access to wisdom. Take a moment, right now, to listen to what your guidance is whispering. What is the first thing that comes to mind? Simply acknowledge it without dwelling on the message and breathe deeply. Now let these images go and move out into your day, knowing that by taking the time to listen to your inner guidance you will create all the good you can imagine.

Parents' Check-In Questions

• When I know something is going on with my teenager, how do I initiate conversation and what is my listening style?

• Is it difficult for me to listen without jumping in to fix things? If so, how might I listen without always wanting to solve my child's problems?

• When do I listen to my teen? (driving to school, eating dinner, etc.)

• How might I increase that listening time in the next week?

• Are there some topics I avoid talking about? If so, what are they and how might I open my heart and my listening apparatus to hear what's going on in that department?

• Is there some way I can create a home with fewer constant sounds? How?

• Have I ever gone against my intuition and allowed someone else to convince me what was right for my child? How can I better tune into my gut feelings when it comes to decisions about my teenager?

Conversation Starters

• I've read recently about the power of sound in our lives. Are there sounds in our house that bother or distract you?

• Describe the soundscape that works best for you when you are studying.

• Has there been a time you recall feeling as if you've been really listened to?

• Is there something you want to talk about that you haven't been comfortable coming to me with?

• Do you think you use your intuition? How so?

• Have you ever done something your gut feelings warned you against? What happened?

Supported Dreams Manifest Miracles

"If I did it, so can you. Don't let naysayers discourage you. When I first started, folks said, 'You're too young, you have to have hundreds of thousands of dollars.' But I've read about Madame C. J. Walker who built a multimillion dollar business by starting with what she had and going door to door. I know about the work of Imhotep, the world's first doctor and multi genius. I can look at Venus and Serena Williams on television and know that we can beat the odds. We've done it before. But it takes discipline, a strong sense of yourself, and support from the 'village.' I know this to be true because that's how I did it."

—Kenya Jordana James, thirteen, founder of *Blackgirl Magazine*

• • •

My friend's son Ethan has dreamed, at least since he was old enough to talk, of being a firefighter. He's never entertained any other idea. Now seventeen, Ethan volunteers at his hometown fire department, has passed advanced first aid and CPR exams, and can't wait to graduate from high school and take firefighter entrance tests.

For many years, Ethan's parents have known exactly how to support his dream. I paid a family visit last week, and Ethan showed me the book his mom gave him for Christmas. It was a firsthand account of the World Trade Center apocalypse, written by a New York City firefighter.

In my experience, Ethan is the exception. He's been very clear about his dream from an early age. Many teens take far longer to understand and articulate their dreams.

However, a dream lies inside the heart of every child. When my daughter Elizabeth was quite young, she shared some wisdom with me that sums up this chapter's principle. She said, "God has a lot of wishes for this world. I think that each time a baby is born, God puts one of those wishes into that baby's heart." Similarly, author and speaker Jean Houston says, "We all have the extraordinary coded within us, waiting to be released." What could be more extraordinary than the divine spark of our deepest desire?

As spiritual parents, our job is to help our children nurture their dreams and uncover that sacred desire. Each individual—child, teen, or adult—is a unique unit of human potential, a drop in the human ocean that is Spirit expressing in this world. Fred Buechner, called the finest religious writer in America by *The New York Times,* says, "The place God calls you to is the place where your deep gladness and the world's deep hunger meet." As we encourage our children to embrace the deepest desires of their hearts, we get out of the way as they develop into exactly who they're meant to be—with God's help.

The desires God plants in our hearts have a life all their own. If you're like me, you know people now in their thirties, forties, or beyond who are remaking their lives to follow long-dormant dreams. As spiritual parents, we want to help make the road between having a dream and living it as short and straight as possible for our teens.

We want them to avoid the experience of a man my friend Rose, a counselor, told me about. A successful surgeon, he struggled with deep depression despite being affluent, highly regarded by his professional colleagues, and well-respected in his community. Over time, he realized that he'd abandoned his true calling—a love of language—at a very early age. Born into a family of doctors, he'd followed the path they assumed he would. However, his deep affinity for the world of words didn't fade; he even chose to go to medical school in Paris, learning about the intricacies of the human body in French.

He would, he realized, have loved a career as a university professor: teaching the language and literature of another culture and sharing his love with students. After coming to this awareness in his late forties, he faced the choice of continuing in a familiar and lucrative career that felt like going through the motions, or reinventing himself.

This fellow had a career and lifestyle that many people would envy. However, it was a complete mismatch with his heart's calling.

By helping our teens nurture their visions of who they are, we may be able to spare them years spent pursuing goals that are off the mark of their personal dreams. And with that we help them find something beyond value—an authentic sense of purpose in the world.

A sense of purpose isn't something we can give to our kids. They must find it for themselves through an inner process that unfolds during the teen years and, ideally, blossoms as they become young adults. A sense of purpose comes from connecting the deep currents in our hearts with the abilities of our hands and minds, bringing meaning to our daily activities. It's the answer to the fundamental spiritual question, "Why am I here?"

Dreams and Accomplishments

An important step on the road to helping our teens realize their dreams is to distinguish between heartfelt visions and accomplishments.

In our culture, we are what we do. From the moment our children are born, we measure their accomplishments: from APGAR scores in the delivery room through marking the age at which they walk and talk to the standardized testing that begins in elementary school. By the time teens start sending out college applications, they're largely defined by a GPA/SAT combination.

Reducing the magical complexity of young lives to a series of numbers zaps teens' souls. Those whose performance is solidly average—or less—are acutely aware of a sense of failure. Those who excel are in danger of succumbing to the 90th percentile spell: a sense of self-worth that depends on continuing stellar scores. In either case, the temptation exists to define one-self by performance on external measures.

To help our teens live their dreams, we must help them understand the distinction between accomplishments and the dreams in their hearts. One results from studying and certain innate strengths; the other arises from Spirit and self-awareness. One is in plain view; the other speaks with a still, small voice. One pleases the world; the other resonates with a sense of purpose. Ultimately, when we're doing what we love, external measures of success both come more easily and diminish in comparison to the personal satisfaction we feel.

I recently heard Armand Nicholi speak; he's the author of *The Question of God: C.S. Lewis and Sigmund Freud Debate God, Love, Sex, and the Meaning of Life.* He said that in his psychiatric practice he works with many "successful" people—those who have won MacArthur Genius Awards and Pulitzer Prizes. Often, he said, they express emptiness even after achieving such remarkable successes. "Is that all there is?" they ask. "I'm still empty inside."

The link between dreams and the kind of achievements that make the world sit up and take notice can be slender. Of course, a teen whose deepest desire is to get a degree from an Ivy League school will need some impressive accomplishments to gain admission. And academic scholarships make the difference between community college and a private university for many graduating high school seniors.

On the other hand, dreams don't depend on racking up a series of impressive numbers. Many, many adults live rich, rewarding, dream-driven lives—far more than the 10 percent who fit into the top percentiles on standardized tests. A teen who's called to work for social justice or pursue spiritual training may not need stellar SATs to manifest his or her dream. Teens whose callings run toward artistic endeavors find paths to achieving their dreams that don't depend on admission to the Pratt School of Art. Even teens whose hearts quicken at the thought of owning or running a business, writing The Great American Novel, or solving complicated theoretical math problems don't necessarily need to attend Harvard or MIT to make their dreams come true.

Dreams are sinews running down the core of our lives, gaining strength and working their way into expression as we understand, honor, and nurture them. Accomplishments are often like sensations dancing across the surface; delightful or uncomfortable, they can distract us from deeper spiritual callings.

To further explore the difference between accomplishments and dreams, consider trying some of the following ideas:

• How do you spell success? Envision twenty years into your teen's future. What qualities do you hope to see foremost in his or her life? Love, recognition, financial success, spirituality, community involvement, peace, prestige, good relationships with friends and family? All of these—and more—are positive attributes, but which are most important to you? Ask your teen to join you in the same exercise. What qualities would define your teen's ideal life as an adult? As your teen matures, his or her vision may shift, so this is a conversation worth having several times. Be careful not to judge what you hear, rather just listen. A vast gap in your response and your child's may point to a subtle cause of friction that may be a static undercurrent in your relationship.

• Talk to adults who have followed their dreams to create lives filled with a sense of God-given purpose. What were their paths like? How large a part did worldly accomplishments play in their lives? Did these achievements distract them from their dreams or facilitate their realization? Share what you find out with your teen.

• As your teenager enters the phase of life where SATs, college admissions, and scholarships loom large, take the long view to help him keep a sense of perspective. Great SAT scores, admission to the college of his choice, and a National Merit scholarship are all noble accomplishments—but they may have little to do with what happens down the road. Similarly, starting classes at a two-year college for academic or financial reasons doesn't mean dreams can't come true.

Exploring Possibilities

To connect with the extraordinary within, teens need to explore, test, and try out various behaviors. As parents, our job is to encourage this exploration.

Easy enough to say. However, all too often, we're tempted to put a twist on their exploration by turning it into something more or by shutting it down, inadvertently or intentionally.

It's easy and natural to latch onto our teen's assets and want to prune and nurture them for the world to see. However, this might send the wrong message, that they are their talents. "Jim is a runner." "Mary is an equestrian." "Meet Sam, he's our musician."

Overabundant praise can sound like pressure to the sensitive ears of an adolescent. Certainly, we want to let our teenagers know when they've done something we admire, but it's more important that they appreciate their own endeavors. "That seems like something to be proud of. Are you?" might be a more appropriate response than "I'm so proud of you!" Making too big a fuss over a talent might also send the message that your child needs to know what she is going to do with the rest of her life. Many teens—as young as thirteen, fourteen, and fifteen years old—have told me that their biggest source of stress is deciding their career path.

When we, as parents, see our teen's talents and abilities, we naturally want to encourage their development. We can do so by following the wisdom of author Martha Grimes, who said, "We don't know who we are until we see what we can do."

However, we also have to pay close attention to what their inclinations are. For instance, my daughter Whitney is a wonderful photographer. Her black and white photos are truly stunning displays crafted from an often-surprising perspective. Whitney quietly accepts my enthusiastic responses to her photos, content to pick up the camera when she feels moved. My mind whirls with ways she might share her visions with others and opportunities for her to extend what is, to me, an obvious talent. "You could offer 'alternative senior photos' so kids could choose your cool portraits rather than the stiff air-brushed versions they've used for twenty years," I say. "Oh, Whit, check out this photo contest. Your shot of the American flag hung on the side of a barn at sunset would surely take first prize."

On and on I go with my personality's way of being in the world. My vision of Whitney's capabilities and her vision are often different. Whitney, rightly so, sees herself learning, exploring, and beginning photography; end results would be premature. Balancing my perspective with what is going on inside her is an important touchstone.

Other times, our response to our son's or daughter's talents, abilities, and interests is mixed—or even negative. Their fear of our criticism may prevent them from exploring the very avenue that will lead them to their heart's desire. Our teens are exquisitely attuned to our opinion of their efforts, finding innuendo even in our casual comments and questions.

Allowing our teen to explore a dream we can't relate to can bring us to the edge of what we hold dear in our own lives. Julie, the mother of three, talks about her oldest daughter's passion. "Emily wants to be a fashion designer. I'm a little ashamed to say that out loud because it seems so superficial. It's not something I would ever, ever do myself. However, I can't deny the truth of it for her. Last year, she started college at an excellent liberal arts school and did fine. But this year, transferring to an art school to study fashion design, she's on fire. A year ago, I don't think she felt strong enough to stand up to her dad and me and say, 'This is what I really want.' I can't relate. But I can see how excited she is, and that has to be good enough."

Sometimes, a long-standing family tradition can make exploring another path seem like a teen is getting ready to move to another country altogether. At these times, we have to carefully gauge our responses, keeping in mind that God knows our child better than we do. My friend Carol is a highly intelligent, dynamic business coach with scores of client success stories to share. However, her father is a nuclear physicist. Her brother is a systems analyst, and her younger sister is a tenured professor of electrical engineering. Carol simply keeps quiet about her business when her family gets together because repeated put-downs and questions ("Now what is it that you do again?") have hurt her. A seventeen-year-old voices similar feelings when she says, "I feel stranded in a family of high achievers." How alone they each perceive themselves to be!

Peers, too, can limit a teen's willingness to explore options. A teen who chooses to pursue a dream that departs from the course his or her friends pursue can face ridicule or criticism. And teens who care about anything with the passion that fuels dreams may swim against the cynical current that seems to run through our culture.

Another soul-bruising situation arises when we compare kids to adults. Forgetting what we were doing as a teen, we somehow expect our children to perform at a level beyond their reach. Imagine how this could cut away at their self-esteem.

I'm not suggesting that we need to treat our teens as fragile butterflies while they explore their dreams. This does them a disservice in the long run. As adults, we know that negative responses are an inevitable part of life. As the saying goes, "You can please some of the people all of the time and you can please all of the people some of the time, but you can't please all of the people all of the time." We're responsible for offering constructive criticism and for balancing its impact with appreciation and acknowledgment. In this way, we help our teens develop the perspective and self-confidence to explore and pursue their dreams, despite criticism from teachers, peers—and even us.

To expand your thinking about exploring dreams, consider one or more of the following suggestions:

* As is the case with every aspect of spiritual parenting, affirmative prayer is a great way to set intention and align yourself with Spirit. Try words like these or find those that feel more comfortable to you:

Dear God, thank you for the opportunity to witness this life taking shape. May my child feel free to explore the depths of his heart, safe to try out all possibilities for his future, secure in his acceptance in this family. May I see with Your eyes, hear with Your ears, and speak with Your words as I witness and respond to my child. Help me to be a loving component of his life's mosaic by saying and doing the highest and the best. May my child grow to be fully in harmony with your perfect plan for his life.

• Make a short list of your teen's talents, abilities, and interests with which you feel a kinship. Allow your guidance to tell you what to include. Focus on each one in turn, bringing it clearly into mind. Acknowledge the divine gift it represents and appreciate the ways in which your life is enriched by its presence in your child's personality. Release the development and expression of each talent back into Spirit's domain.

• Make a second list—this time of your teen's talents, abilities, and interests that seem foreign or incomprehensible to you. Focus on each one and bring a clear picture of it into your mind. Consider how you feel about it: embarrassed, anxious, uninformed, left out? Now consider the possibility that it, too, is a divine gift, the meaning of which you cannot understand from your current perspective. Release its development and expression into Spirit's hands.

• Ask your teen if there's a particular skill he or she would like to develop, and then listen carefully to the response. Write it down. Tuck the paper in your calendar and over the next few weeks bring to mind any resource—a person, book, movie, class, supplies—that might help your teen deepen this skill or talent. Whisper the following affirmation, *I draw to me and accept divine insight and serendipitous coincidences that help* _____ *deepen her talent for* _____.

Whose Dream Is It, Anyway?

"What's important to me hasn't changed because my daughter's heart takes her in other directions. I feel a sense of loss about what I hoped we would share. All the time, though, I learn a little more about how to live gracefully with it, how to see beyond my feelings to the joy in her life." —Jen, mother of two

It is immensely flattering and affirming when a teen shows interests that are similar to our own. In some cases, similar dreams do run through families. In my experience, though, it is more often the case that a teen's dream departs from what his or her parent would have chosen at that age—or would choose today.

In order to partner with our teens in nurturing their dreams, we must be able to distinguish between their heartfelt callings and our own. Our children have their own divine purpose in life, and we act in alignment with Spirit when we help them to uncover it.

Keeping in mind that teens crave our approval and affirmation, it's easy to see how our responses could steer our children in directions toward which we feel familiar or comfortable. Even without intending to do so, we might evidence more interest in art, say, as opposed to environmentalism. A teen will readily distinguish between interests that spark enthusiasm and interest on our part and those we find challenging to converse about.

Other times, our attempts to mold our children in certain directions are overt. A successful biochemist I know recently announced that his older daughter, age ten, would be the family doctor and the younger girl, age six, would become a lawyer. He was completely serious. Already, his older daughter takes advanced math classes in summer school, and her younger sister is encouraged to state her opinions and argue them at the dinner table. Whether or not either of them has natural leanings in other directions is immaterial in this family.

If we feel that our own lives contain missed opportunities, we sometimes reflexively work to provide those for our children—whether or not they're particularly interested. My friend Sam, a highly successful leader in health care, has a career that he finds deeply rewarding. However, one of Sam's regrets is that it wasn't financially possible for his family to send him to an Ivy League college. He went to a private university in the Midwest: a good school, but not one that leaps off the pages of his resume.

Sam has worked very hard and made many sacrifices to enable his children to attend excellent colleges—still not Ivy League, but a notch above his own alma mater. Of the three who have entered or graduated from college, one has chosen to be unemployed rather than finding a job that would make use of the expensive degree Sam funded, and one transferred to a community college. Only one child graduated with the kind of honors Sam envisioned for all three.

To the extent that we address our own dreams, we more easily separate personal desires and drives from those that run through our children's hearts and souls. When we nurture our teen's highly personal heart visions and partner with Spirit in helping a uniquely wonderful human realize his or her full potential, we free them from the weighty obligation of living *our* lives, as well as their own.

Supporting our teen's God-given dreams can take us to the very edges of what we hold dear and tax our reserves of understanding and compassion. And yet, if we aspire to be truly spiritual parents, we can choose to embrace the process as key to our own spiritual growth.

To explore more about distinguishing between your dreams and those of your teen, try one of these ideas:

- Set your intention with affirmative prayer, using words like these:

"Spirit, thank you for the experience of being a parent. I am so grateful to witness and support my child as she uncovers her dream and brings it into experience. As I attune to Your wisdom, I easily see the difference between the dreams in my heart and those that fill my child with joy and excitement. Infuse me with energy and inspiration to make my dreams come true while supporting my child to follow her own."

- Grab a pen and a piece of paper, and find a few moments to spend in a quiet place. Write a paragraph or two in answer to each of the following questions:

  1. If you could do anything in the entire world, money and time being no object, what would you do? How would you have answered this question when you were your son or daughter's age?
  2. When you look back at your teen and early adult years, what regrets do you have? What opportunities would you have enjoyed that weren't available to you?

- Now take a moment and read what you've written. Are your answers similar to the dreams you believe your teen has? If so, consider the possibility that your teen has unconsciously taken on the responsibility for living your unfulfilled dreams.

• If you suspect that your teen's dreams and your own are confused, begin by acknowledging that to your son or daughter, then give him or her permission to revamp the vision taking shape in his or her heart.

Dreaming Big

"My mom always told me that I could do anything I wanted to. If I wanted it badly enough, there'd be a way to make it come true. She's been right so far."

—Heather, twenty-four

"If your dreams don't come true, either you don't believe they can or you're not working to make them happen."   **—Rich, nineteen**

Victor Frankl was one of the great authors and speakers of the twentieth century. He survived a Nazi concentration camp, and he tells us why. "Others gave up hope. I dreamed. I dreamed that someday I would be here, telling you how I . . . survived the Nazi concentration camps. . . . In my dreams I have stood before you and said these words a thousand times." His dreams kept him going when nondreamers died in despair.

In the United States Library of Congress, over an entrance to the archives, you can find these words: "They build too low who build beneath the stars."

Testimonials to the power of dreams abound. Many memorable quotes encourage us to dream—and do it on a grand scale. Few caution us to rein in our hopes and visions.

In truth, God has bigger dreams for our lives than we could ever think up by ourselves. Our limited human imaginations can catch just a glimpse of what Spirit has in mind for us.

We start, though, by identifying the life we'd like to be living, based on what we can see from our current position. As parents, we can help our teens articulate some elements of their dreamed-of futures—at least as far as they can identify them. There may be no conversation more worth having with a teen than one that starts like this: "If you could do anything at all with your life, what would you choose?"

It can be hard for teens—and parents—to distinguish passing fancies from bona fide, Divinely given dreams. To a certain extent, time alone reveals the nature and enduring power of dreams—they simply refuse to die.

However, there are some clues that what's brewing in your teen's heart and mind is a vision placed there by Spirit. Dreams seem, at first glance, impossible. "How could I ever be a writer/actress/artist/lawyer/doctor?" If a teen sees a clear path to making a dream come true, encourage him or her to think more grandly. "What if you didn't just do art as a hobby; what if you were a very successful artist?"

There's also an unmistakable gleam in a teen's eye when he or she connects with the life purpose born in his or her heart.

> "He looked so grounded when he decided what he really wanted to do. I could easily see him as an adult, writing for an important newspaper or going on a book tour." **—Susan, mother of one**

In my experience, dreams also make sense in terms of what you know about your child. As one mother of two teens puts it, "He thought he'd go into engineering, but when he switched to architecture, it made perfect sense. I flashed back on all the time he spent building Lego houses and drawing pictures of castles when he was a kid; he was fascinated with the places people lived."

To help your teen discover more about dreams that are waiting to be born, try or suggest one of the following:

* Write. Through writing, our unconscious minds sometimes reveal the truth in our hearts before we're consciously aware of it. In silent dialogue with a piece of paper, we may feel safe to articulate dreams we're not ready to share with another human being. And it's as if our words about our goals become magical messengers. As we write them on paper, they become more deeply inscribed in our brain. When we use this method to seek our goals, something amazing happens—*it works.* After working with this idea for awhile, a sixteen-year-old girl told me, "When I wrote it down, it seemed impossible. But here I am about to head off to the Nationals in fencing. I did it."

• Buy your teen a dreaming book—a place to record emerging visions of his or her future life. Then release the process, trusting that Spirit works perfectly in all our lives.

• Talk with your teenager about the people, living or dead, he or she admires the most. Augment your teen's awareness by looking for books and articles about other kids achieving their goals. What qualities in those individuals does he or she aspire to? Take the conversation a step further by asking your teen to imagine that she possesses these qualities in full measure. What would she do with her life?

• Listen for discontent, as that could be the source of a dream. We sometimes become aware of our unique gift to the world by noticing a wrong that needs to be righted. One young man, frustrated by what he perceived as biased reporting in his local newspaper, went to journalism school to learn how to do it better. While his dream is still forming, he's well on the way to living a life guided by a passionate sense of purpose.

• Remember that our human imaginations are limited, compared to the infinite possibilities of Spirit. As your teen sets intention, introduce him to a phrase that invites Spirit's full play: *This, God, or something better*. It goes at the end of a statement of intention. For instance: *I am an artist whose paintings are coveted by collectors and shown in the most exclusive galleries. I earn an abundant living from my artwork and have a rich family life. This, God, or something better.*

• Tap into the power of imagery. Anything your mind can conceive you can achieve! Cognitive scientist Stephen Kosslyn, who has studied mental images in his Harvard laboratory for twenty years, calls them "ghosts in the mind's machine." These images operate our actions and design our experiences. One of my favorite books is *Creative Visualization* by Shakti Gawain; maybe you and your teen could share a copy. This easy little guide can help anyone create what they visualize.

Incubating Dreams

On the way to making dreams come true, everyone—as far as I can tell—has a few experiences that don't feel at all dreamy. We stumble against fears, challenges, and often, failures.

FEAR

"I am afraid to act on my dreams because I know that my dreams are the keys to my success and the doorway to leaving my family and becoming someone. That's a scary prospect." **—Maddy, seventeen**

"If it doesn't scare you, it's not worth doing." That's what I told my friend Jackie as she was just about to step off the path she knew into the field in which her dreams could come true. Jackie was frightened of the unknown but compelled to head there. I reminded her that she wasn't alone, she had my friendship but more importantly she had God's help. I do believe that when we step off the edge of what we know, we either find solid ground or learn to fly! Jackie learned to fly and her life is now living proof of dreams come true.

When we align with Spirit's plan for our lives, we open the door that leads into a joy-filled life. But it doesn't always feel that way. Long held dreams are tremendously appealing and slightly terrifying at the same time. Adults and teens alike can find God-sized dreams overwhelming and be tempted to give up before trying.

As spiritual parents, our job is to help our teens navigate the fear-ridden territory that lies between having a dream and making it come true. Teens can express fears in a number of ways, in addition to talking about them. They can sabotage themselves or become ill. Fear can masquerade as anger and accusations, frantic activity or deep lethargy. For instance, when Seth, now twenty-four, got closer and closer to leaving for college at eighteen, he slept an increasing number of hours a day. The morning he was to check into his dorm room, his parents had to repeatedly shake him to wake him out of a deep slumber. Then there is Maggie, a high school freshman, who dreams of being a doctor, yet plays hours of Minesweeper on her lap-top computer, instead of studying for her biology final exam.

Fears are a natural part of taking a risk. That's what dreams call us to do—take leaps that require Spirit to bring us over the chasm yawning be-fore the far shore. And there are, as far as I can tell, two kinds of fears that arise during dream-building: healthy ones and the creations of an overac-tive imagination.

Healthy fears acknowledge the reality of any situation: the odds against getting a full ride to Harvard, the few number of high school baseball stars who go on to play professionally, the foolhardiness of living in a low-rent district in an unfamiliar city. These doses of reality are worth paying atten-tion to and investigating more fully.

However, fears that lack a real foundation are more numerous and troublesome for most of us. They often start with the words "What if" and gather steam quickly. What if I don't get into the college of my choice? What if I don't make the team? What if I don't score high on my SATs? What if I don't get my driver's license?

Our temptation as parents is often to reassure our teen that the what-if won't happen. However, the best way I know of to counter this type of fear is to do the very opposite. Ask your teen to imagine that she didn't get into the school of her dreams, make the team, ace the SATs, or get the li-cense. Then ask her to describe the worst thing that could happen if that were the case.

The same is true for us, as we examine the fears we hold about our children's emerging dreams. What if he doesn't get into the college of his choice? What if she can't find an apartment? What if he doesn't make the team this year? What's the worst that could happen in our own lives if the scenarios that our teens dread came to pass? Articulating the specific con-sequences of what-if scenarios brings them from the level of undifferenti-ated fear, to individual situations that we can imagine handling.

Our other responsibility as spiritual parents is to hold, for our teens, a belief in possibilities. Without dismissing fears and challenges, we choose to believe that our teens are capable, expanding into options, not defined by limitations. We hold a field of unlimited possibilities in which they can play and we communicate a belief in their strength that they crave.

CHALLENGES

"Moving away is so hard, but I know it's the right thing for me to do."

—Tina, eighteen

"It would be much easier to come home from school and plop on my bed, get my homework done early and not stress. But I know that being part of the swim team is ultimately the best thing for me, for my future, and even though I've forced myself to begin a new sport at my age, I'm finding I actually like it."

—Jen, fifteen

Here's to challenges. I love the quote, "No man knows what he can do till he tries." I don't know who said it, but I'd like to paint it on the walls of every high school in the country, or at least my own kitchen walls.

The challenges we all—adults and teens alike—face along the way to making dreams come true are a big part of what I call the "terrible richness of life." In the moment, these challenges can rock us to our core, yet, when all is said and done, they also contribute the most to our sense of satisfaction and self-esteem. Life's tough moments feel terrible—and the things we learn about ourselves while we face them are pearls beyond value.

Julie, the mother of three, talks about one such moment for her oldest child. "Emily chose to move to a big city far away to go to school. She worked sixty hours a week for two months, saving money, then flew out to stay with a friend and look for an apartment. She was only nineteen, but she's always been a few years ahead of herself on the road to adulthood.

"Her friend helped her look for a couple of days, but the market was tight, and rents were much higher than Emily expected. Not only that, but she got turned around on the subway once and ended up in a part of town that scared her to death.

"She called that night in tears, overwhelmed, afraid and very lonely. She ached to just fly home and call it quits.

"I told her she was too old for me to tell her what to do anymore, but that I really wanted to see her succeed at moving to the big city. I also told her that moving was one of the hardest life events, which was a surprise to her. She had no idea that most people find it very difficult.

"As we talked, she calmed down and before we hung up, she had a new plan for looking for a place to live. And, two days later, she found the perfect apartment: great location, small enough to suit her, and a real steal on rent.

"She worked really hard to find her apartment—and her success is even sweeter to her because she did. I'm really proud of her, of course, and *really* happy that she succeeded at what she set out to do. The hardest thing for me was to let her do it herself, to not insist on going with her in the first place or fly out and help when she panicked. If I had helped her in a more substantial way, she wouldn't have the pleasure of having overcome that huge challenge."

Therein lies the struggle for many of us as parents. We want our children to have success and we want to help them in any way we can. But doing so deprives them of the richness part of the terrible richness of life. Supporting our children's dreams doesn't mean solving their problems for them.

Julie continues, "For the rest of her life, she'll remember moving there and finding her first apartment on her own. She'll remember that we trusted her to do that. And her success at it will always be a part of who she is."

We support our adolescents as they face challenges by listening, commiserating as needed and framing difficulties in a way that normalizes them without diminishing our teen's experience, as Julie did when she told Emily that moving was inherently stressful.

And we pray. Julie has one more point to add to her story:

"On my walk one morning, I said a prayer of gratitude for Emily's perfect, safe, affordable apartment. I concentrated on feeling the same level of gratitude that I would if it had already happened. Less than eight hours later, it did. I know that her legs and my prayers worked together."

FAILURE

As parents, we may hesitate to encourage our teens to hold fast to an ambitious dream for fear of possible failure. It's a natural instinct to protect them from what we think may be a humiliating or uncomfortable experience. In truth, there are no guarantees in life—no matter how detailed our visualizations or how fervent our prayers.

Failure is part of the process of dreaming. There's a wonderful African proverb that goes, "If you're not living on the edge . . . you're taking up too much room." Unfortunately, we can fall off the edge, too. Every single individual I know—from family to friends to professional colleagues—has experienced failure in some form.

When our teens experience what seems, in the moment, like failure, we can give them the gift of believing in their dreams, *despite appearances to the contrary.* My friend Martin, who is senior pastor at a community church, tells a story about how his mother did just that.

When Martin was a young teenager, his father died. Like many young people who experience a sudden loss, Martin reacted with anger. His anger peaked during a time when social demonstrations were frequent in the community in which his family lived, and Martin used them as a venue for expressing his anger. He acquired a reputation as a troublemaker with the local police. Sure enough, before too long, Martin found himself, at fifteen, jailed overnight for disorderly conduct.

The following morning, his mother came to pick him up from jail. Instead of being angry, she hugged her son close and looked him lovingly and steadily in the eye. "I don't know who you're pretending to be, but I know this isn't who you are," she said.

Years later, Martin recounted this story as pivotal to his dream of becoming a minister. It would have been easy for him to allow himself to be defined by the social failure his arrest represented, but his mother's steadfast vision called him back to himself and to the dream in his heart. As spiritual parents, we must hold the high watch for our teens.

What looks like failure can also be a dream evolving. Sometimes, God lets us know that we need to make a slight course adjustment by putting up a roadblock. A teen can take steps toward the future he or she is currently able to imagine, only to find that an insurmountable obstacle forces a shift in plans. Soon, a whole, new, previously undiscovered dream springs into view. What may seem in the moment like failure is really the voice for God operating in a teen's life.

How can we help our teens pick themselves up after a disappointing experience and figure out a way to go after the essence of the goal? My daughter Elizabeth wanted badly to be her eighth-grade class vice president as this position was in charge of organizing community service activities. She ran for the position and wrote what I thought was a powerful speech, but she was not elected. She had a goal, she did her very best to achieve it, but, alas, it wasn't meant to be. I asked Elizabeth if there was another way she might combine her leadership skills with her strong views on the importance of community service. She's hatching a plan as I write.

Failure is, almost always, a blessing in disguise. In addition to seeking inner guidance about the nature of that blessing, it's also beneficial to learn from others who have followed their own callings. Mentors (who may be long dead or fictional) can offer invaluable inspiration and advice on ways to endure setbacks and recommit to a new path.

To explore your feelings about failure more deeply, try one or more of the following suggestions:

• One of the reasons we're uncomfortable with the prospect of our children failing is because we have painful memories of our own less-than-successful experiences in life. If you're squirming because your teen seems to be facing a roadblock, consider what it brings to mind from your own experience. Recall as many details of that experience as you can; perhaps writing about it will help you do so. When you've brought this experience in your own life as fully to mind as you can, identify the ways in which your teen's situation is different from your own. You're two different people, growing up in two different time periods, so there are bound to be plenty of differences. Try to identify at least three.

• Consider how much you really believe that your teen is capable of achieving the dream he or she seems inclined to pursue. Be honest with yourself about this. If your true level of belief in your child's ability to achieve the dream is less than you'd like it to be, ask for help in bolstering your belief with words such as:

Dear Spirit, I know that You can create in my heart a sacred space where my child's dream can lie safely sheltered from the world. Let my heart energy nurture this dream every moment. Let me hold this vision tenderly for my child. Let my child see only faith in my eyes.

• If your teenager seems dreamless don't panic. Instead, trust that there are dreams incubating but perhaps she isn't ready to share them with you. Ask yourself if her dreams are evident in ways you haven't noticed. Look beneath the cracks of your teen's life and see if there isn't a trace of an interest. Perhaps it's been there all the time, you just haven't validated it as a dream.

• Always remember that your children's dreams are so much more than vehicles to further glorify your own ego.

Take Action

"Twenty years from now you will be more disappointed by the things that you didn't do than by the ones you did do. So throw off the bowlines. Sail away from the safe harbor. Catch the trade winds in your sails. Explore. Dream. Discover."

—Mark Twain

Making dreams come true takes action. Prayer is an important part of the work of manifesting a dream, but it's not enough.

On the other hand, we needn't worry too much about the how of making dreams come true, either. When we commit to the what, God takes care of bringing it into being, often through perfect pathways we couldn't have imagined beforehand.

Taking action toward dreams is more a matter of moving our feet in the most obvious direction at the moment, rather than creating an elaborate road map that leads down a particular path. Martin Luther King, Jr., once defined faith as "taking the first step even when you can't see the whole staircase."

We take a step, then look around for the next step and take it. We don't need to know how many steps we'll need to take or exactly where we'll end up. This can be comforting for a teen to realize. It is also an area that many parents find challenging. Some teens are natural go-getters. Others aren't. Some teens process externally, letting you know about every detail of their evolving vision. Others prefer to plan alone, quietly imagining and rehearsing the future. You, more than anyone, know your son or daughter's temperament, strengths, weakness, and approach to adversity. How do we support our children—with such wide-ranging ways of being in the world—in nurturing and achieving their dreams?

One very important step has nothing to do with our teens—on the surface. Principle #8 will explore the idea of being what you want to see. As we honor our own dreams and take steps to make them happen, our teens see what's possible.

Show your teen with your own actions the difference between getting results and making excuses. If you believe that you're too old, busy, financially strained, or poorly educated (or any other excuse) to achieve your own dream, your teen is learning more about why dreams *don't* come true than about how to move into his or her envisioned future.

Are you also prioritizing your activities? Those who want to experience joy and deeper meaning in life let go of meaningless activities that drain away precious energy and distract them from their true purpose. The average teenager watches *seven hours* of television a day. Where is the room for soulful growth and goals when our kids are passive observers so much of the time? Remember your TV viewing habits are the biggest influence on your children's use and consumption of television. Demonstrate to your teen that enjoying a full life takes setting priorities: what comes first, what activity is most important.

Sarah, mother of two teenagers told me, "I so wanted to lose some weight and get into shape so I'd have better health and be around longer. My eldest daughter was complaining a lot about fatigue, and I could tell that exercise would help her as well. So we became exercise buddies, inspiring each other to walk four mornings a week. We worked out to an exercise program on Saturdays. We had a goal of sticking to this plan for three months and then rewarding ourselves with a weekend trip to the mountains if we stuck to it. We did! Not only do we both look and feel better but we had such a good time together that weekend."

Sarah gave her daughter more than just better health. She's helped her become clear on how to make a goal, stick to it, and then celebrate the success.

Another facet of supporting our teens in nurturing their dreams is to honor their style by pacing our support and encouragement accordingly. One approach I like is what I think of as "the two-step." As your teen takes a step toward realizing a dream, you take a matching step in support.

For instance, let's say your son finally registered to take the SATs. You then offer to get him a test prep manual. Two steps. You notice that he's poring over it during the weeks before the test. You offer to make his favorite dinner the night before. Two steps.

This serves at least two purposes. First, by gauging your response to your teen's motivation, you avoid overinvesting in something he or she doesn't really care about. Intense parental interest and support—even the most well-meaning kind—can overwhelm a teen's own inclinations and turn an exciting prospect into drudgery. Second, by waiting for your teen to take the first step, you yield the driver's seat from the get-go.

However, doing the two-step doesn't mean you have to play dumb until your teen takes the first step. If your teen seems to be avoiding taking any step in the direction of his or her dreams, resist nagging or pushing. Instead, sincerely ask if there's anything you can do to help, knowing that one of the possible answers is "No."

If your teen says "Yes," but doesn't know what kind of help to request, you could offer to help her set goals. Sit down together and create a list of goals she'd like to reach to create the field in which her dreams can come true. Next to each, write down what must happen in order for that goal to be realized. Taking action in small increments is a sure way to turn dreams into reality. Each step we take is important—even if it doesn't seem to pay off immediately. Include a timeframe for each step. Here are a couple of examples of specific action steps. "I will see the counselor at school to find out about available science internships for the summer by Monday." "I will read the novel for English class over spring vacation."

This is especially important when teens are facing big jobs. For instance, applying to college is a multi-step process. Help your teen break it down and assign him dates for specific tasks, such as: calling for materials, writing the first draft of an admission essay, rewriting and polishing it, selecting individuals to write recommendations, asking them to do so.

If you sense your teen going into overload, take a break and come back to the list of goals another day. Remember that the point of the process is to benefit him, so when the effort seems counterproductive, give it a rest. Many teens find the prospect of adult dreams and responsibilities daunting. Offer encouragement and positive reinforcement of your teen's ability to have the life he or she wants.

As you go along, talk about how much control your teen really has over each outcome. For instance, if she's applying for a summer job, she has 100 percent control over how she looks and whether she arrives at the interview on time, but she has no control over whether the job has already been filled.

Help your child decide if his goals are attainable. "I'll retake the SATs and increase my score" is an attainable goal. "On Wednesday I'll get in shape for the soccer season, which begins Friday" is not.

Help your teen determine if her list contains goals she really wants, not just things that sound nice or might get her into a good college or that a coach suggests. Mandy, a sixteen-year-old high school sophomore, said, "My mom insisted I join the crew team at my school. I hate the water and had no interest in crew but she claimed it would help me get into an Ivy League college. So here I am schlepping down to the school's boathouse every day after school, resenting every minute. It's no surprise that I stink at it, either."

Most of us, when we feel the wind swirling outside our comfort zone, rush back inside where it's nice and warm. Making dreams come true requires the courage to step away from the familiar and comfortable to face the unknown with no guarantee of success. Our ability to meet the cold wind of uncertainty, go the extra mile, and boldly move ahead is possible when we have a sense of being supported by spirit and a rich relationship with God. We have more energy when we link with this spiritual source and move away from limiting behaviors that keep us imprisoned in the comfort zone.

I'll end this chapter with a story about a boy who moved out of his comfort zone—in more ways than one. I heard it from Reverend Cathy George, Rector of St. Anne's-in-the-Fields in Lincoln, Massachusetts.

"Three boys live in Lincoln, Massachusetts, who have arrived from refugee camps in the Sudan. Some Lincoln residents organized a fund-raiser to enable these three boys to stay in Lincoln and to finish high school. It was a wonderful evening of food and great music. At the close of the evening, Kuol, one of the three boys, unexpectedly stepped forward and reached his hand for the microphone. Kuol has become a bit famous because he's a leading scorer on the Lincoln soccer team, which plays in the state finals this week.

"He told us how grateful he was that, now, when he is asked where he is from he not only says he is a 'lost boy from the Sudan,' but that he 'has been found and lives in Lincoln.' He beamed with gratitude. Then he said he wanted to thank his coach for giving him a chance. The middle-aged, medium-height coach came forward and stood next to tall, handsome, jet-black Kuol.

"Then the coach said that Kuol came to him in the middle of the season last fall and asked if the coach would let him just practice with the varsity team. He had never played soccer in the Sudan, but they kicked things around a lot at the refugee camp. The coach told us that Kuol did not have a birth certificate, doctor's permission slip, or registration fee, so what could he possibly say? He said, 'Yes, come practice with the team.' The season ended, and Kuol kept playing. He played in the spring, and through the summer, and then tried out for the team this fall, and he made it.

"'Most of my players have been playing soccer since they were six,' the coach said. 'Kuol has been playing two years now and he contributes a lot to the team.'

"Then he told us that in the beginning of the fall he asked each boy to tell the others on the team what their goal was for the team this year. He said the loudest boys went first, calling out that they wanted to win the Dual County League title, others wanted to make it to state, and around the room they went. The coach had to call on the quieter boys, and the last to speak was Kuol.

"'I hope,' said Kuol, 'that every boy on the team will come to believe in himself.'"

May it be so for all our sons and daughters.

Parents' Insight-Building Exercise

Find a quiet place where you won't be disturbed for a few moments. Remove your shoes and settle into a comfortable seated position in a chair, making sure that your back is well-supported.

Place your feet flat on the floor in front of you. If you need to, place a book or another flat object underneath them so that your toes and heels are in full contact with the surface underneath.

Imagine a stream of energy passing through the soles of your feet, carrying earth's grounding essence up into your body. Flex and spread your toes, then relax them. Feel the energy moving up through your legs into your lower abdomen, then into your chest, and on up into your neck and head.

Now imagine that you're surrounded by a gentle white light. It's brilliant without being harsh, enfolding you in a warm, safe space. Imagine that a stream of this light passes through the top of your head, releasing the divine inspiration and loving energy within you.

When you're ready, bring your son or daughter to mind. Simply notice any thoughts that arise in your mind about him or her. Allow them to arise and dissipate like bubbles breaking on the surface of the sea. If you're tempted to become attached to one of these thoughts through worry, anger, or pride, return to imagining the streams of energy that pass through your feet and the top of your head.

Now, shift your attention to the area of your heart. Feel it open as you consider the miraculous honor of parenting. You are here to help Spirit express Itself more fully in the world by supporting your teen to understand and move toward realizing his or her unique, God-given dreams.

When the time seems right, offer words of gratitude for this honor. If the following words express your sentiments, use them—or use words that feel more comfortable to you.

Thank You, God, for the opportunity to witness and participate in the creation of the wonderful life that my child leads. Thank You for the gifts You've endowed her with.

Thank You for the seeds of possibility You've planted in her heart and mind. Thank You for Your ever-present companionship in her life and for the guidance that is always available to her.

Thank You, God, that I am an instrument of helping my child become who she is meant to be. Thank You that, as I listen to Your still, small voice, I am guided to do and say the things that my child finds most supportive. Thank You that I am able to see with Your eyes, listen with Your ears, speak with Your words.

Thank You, too, for the edges this takes me to. Thank You for my impatience and fear, for my attempts to control and direct, because they show me where I have room to grow my faith in Your Divine plan. Thank You, God, for the spiritual partnership my child and I are engaged in, each here to help the other become more of who You would have us both be.

Thank You, God.

Rest in the energy of gratitude as long as you'd like. When you're ready, take a deep breath. Gently stretch your arms and legs. If any ideas came to you during this process, jot them down.

Repeat this process at any time to return to the energy of centered gratitude. It is always available to you.

Parents' Check-In Questions

• Do I think that most people can achieve their dreams? If not, why not?

• What messages did I receive as a teen and young adult about my own dreams? Were they valued or discounted in my family?

• How clear am I about my own dreams? What can I do this week to increase clarity? Can I journal? Talk to a friend? Spend a few quiet moments alone?

• What step toward honoring my own dreams can I take today? What phone number can I call, what website can I visit, what few moments can I set aside to honor the seed that God planted in my heart?

- Who do I know who has made their dreams come true? What was that like for them?

- Am I overly attached to my own dreams for my teen's future? How so?

Conversation Starters

- What do you think are your greatest strengths?

- If you could be remembered for one thing after you die, what would it be?

- Do you think you are a goal setter? If not, how do you prefer to manage your life and your dreams? If so, how do you feel when you achieve a goal?

- Who do you most admire? Why?

- Do you believe that most people can achieve the things they dream of? What do you think it takes to make dreams come true?

- Who do you know or know of who has achieved their dreams?

- If you could change one thing about the world, what would it be?

Awaken Wonder and Spirit Flows

"Sometimes I think that there has to be more than just nagging my teenagers to fill up the car with gas and study for their SATs. I miss the enchanting moments of their childhood." —**Kelly, mother of two**

• • •

For younger children, magic is everywhere—in the spider's glistening web, a bubble bath, a puppy's soft fur. Such things can appear to be less special to our teens. We can, however, help them continue to find the extraordinary that hides just under the surface of everyday experiences.

Teens crave magic. For them, just like us, experiences and perceptions that go beyond the ordinary soothe a soulful hunger. Time stands still for a moment or two, and we're drawn outside our usual busy selves as we find something rich and peaceful.

But the teen years can also be when we learn to squelch the yearning for or appreciation of magic. Wide-eyed wonder isn't cool; teens have to turn off the ever-present internal critic in order to experience being fully present in the experience; it's hard to be in awe if you're thinking about how your hair looks.

Magic moments allow our teens, who spend so much time and energy hiding their selves, plans, fears, hopes, and dreams, to just *play*. We had our first snowfall the other day, and Elizabeth, my thirteen-year-old, dashed home from school breathless with excitement. She had made arrangements with Carolyn, a neighbor and her friend since birth, to come over for their annual snow frolic. They spent an hour howling with laughter as they made snow angels and snowwomen, had snow fights, and played with abandon. The snow gave them permission to become little girls again—it was a delight to behold!

Magic isn't about bells and whistles, big wallets, or novel experiences. We uncover magic in the most ordinary moments. Rather than concocting it, magic is ever present, just waiting to be experienced.

Teens seek thrills and there is a certain thrill in creating and discovering magic. When my daughter Whitney was fourteen, she broke her back in a horseback riding accident. Not being able to ride was a blow more severe than her painful back. When we talked about what she missed, she was able to articulate longing for the thrill of flying and the freedom she experienced when cantering on a horse. How, I wondered out loud, might we replace this craving? She continued to go to the barn to groom but that didn't duplicate the riding experience or quench the thrill factor. We decided together that taking more healthy risks in other areas of her life might assuage the longing. She and a friend boarded the train to travel into Harvard Square, a half hour train ride, for lunch by themselves. She had a wonderful time, and it opened the door to more discussion about other healthy ways that she might push out of her comfort zone.

Teenagers want magic in their lives and we have the wonderful opportunity to be a part of that magic instead of labeling their hunger a scary thing.

Turn Down the Volume to Find Magic

"When I need to get connected with myself, I have to turn off my phone."

—Jess, nineteen

We live in a wild world. When our children are young, we can still control the sensory stimulation they encounter. By the time they reach their teens, though, even if we insist on music at a reasonable volume and refuse to subscribe to the hundreds of available television channels, our children are inundated with auditory and visual stimulation.

Take the halls of a typical high school between class periods, for instance. I recently had occasion to pick up Whitney from class just as a bell clanged loudly, marking the end of the period. Teens exploded out of doors that formed parallel lines down both sides of a hall, the walls and floor of which were covered in tile. Steel locker doors slammed, adolescents shouted to each other, and books clattered to the floor as a sea of people swirled around me. The rush of energy was palpable.

Then consider the many screens in the guise of electronic visual stimulation our kids tune in to for recreational and educational purposes: television, video games, movies, handheld devices like Gameboys and personal digital assistants, computers for word processing, games, e-mail, instant messaging, and Internet access. Add in cell phones, beepers, and portable CD and MP3 players with headphones, and you start to get a sense of the amount of sensory input that our teens experience. These screens can filter out the recognition of simple magic.

There's no disputing the value of at least some of these devices. I'm grateful for cell phones that allow my daughters to reach me at any time, and heaven help me if I had to balance my checkbook by hand. But the constant presence of electronics can also have a negative effect. A number of experts believe that the radiant light of some devices can actually stunt intellectual and emotional growth.

From a spiritual perspective, all this input tends to numb teens out, disconnecting them from their hearts, minds, and intuitive wisdom. When overstimulation is a way of life, quieter moments may seem empty. Most teens haven't been exposed to extended periods of quiet so inactivity feels uncomfortable. Or, they might be used to zoning out and have a fear of stopping and actually thinking, feeling, and taking stock of their lives.

Our job as parents is to gently invite our teens to remember that quiet doesn't have to equal bored or asleep or deep thinking. We can help them reconnect to the extraordinary experiences that can happen in ordinary moments and reawaken what may seem like a sleeping sense of wonder. We can encourage our sons and daughters to "stop already" and "center down," as the Quakers call quieting ourselves.

The common rooms of your home can counteract the busyness of your teen's other environments, offering them a sanctuary. Factors like subdued lighting, relatively low noise levels, and a sense of order can contribute to creating peace. As one mother and stepmother of two teenaged boys says:

"When our boys go to their other parents' houses, they get a lot of stimulation. In one house, people interrupt and talk over each other. In the other, there's a TV on all the time, even during meals. We try to be more serene here with conversation instead of electronics."

Of course, with teens in the house, peace and quiet won't reign all the time. The phone and doorbell will continue to ring, and a teen's natural exuberance has to find expression at home. However, if your intention is that your home will be a place of peace, you'll find ways to make it so. Magic can be more easily found in a peaceful place—a cat purring, the soothing *tick-tock* of a clock, a new idea bubbling up to the conscious surface of a stilled mind.

Try even one of these strategies and notice a little more peacefulness in your home:

- Move the TV to a location other than the rooms where your family congregates for meals and/or conversation. You can take this a step further. I know several families who neither have TV reception nor subscribe to cable. They have one TV in the basement that is used for movies.

- Unplug the phone or let voice mail pick up during family meals. Turn the ringer down as low as possible during other times.

- If you like to listen to music in the background, experiment with the difference between music with vocals and instrumental recordings. Some people find that background instrumental music is soothing, while vocals can create tension unless you listen attentively.

• Turn off unneeded lights in living areas. Not only will this save energy, it can be relaxing. We often associate bright lights with noise and busyness, so try creating the opposite atmosphere in your home.

• Scents and smells affect our experience of an environment, too. Pleasant aromas invite us to draw them deeply into our lungs with deep breaths. Incense, scented candles, flowers and greenery, fresh air, wood smoke—these scents can add to an atmosphere of peace. Remain sensitive when introducing a new scent into your home, however, as what can be a pleasant smell to one can be an irritant to another.

• Create a room in your home where every family member can sit comfortably with lights conducive to reading. My family realized recently that our pets used the living room furniture more than we did. So, we invested in some great reading lights, rearranged the furniture, placed coasters around to accommodate drinks and dug out throw blankets to entice napping. The serenity I feel when the four of us are all together reading in silence, pets on the floor where they belong, is deeply grounding.

• Candlelight can turn an ordinary evening into a magical event. My family has collected a number of candleholders over the years and in using them we are reminded of the circumstances around their purchase— a special trip or meaningful symbol. We light a candle in the morning at breakfast and always have candles at dinner, regardless of the menu. I find that soulful conversations are spun within the peaceful ambience of candlelight.

Create Touching Moments

I first thought about how important touch might be for teens when my mother, a widow, mentioned that one of the aspects of life that was hardest for her about living alone was that there was no one to touch her. No hugs or neck rubs or hands to hold.

I realized that, once our children reach a certain age, we may touch them less frequently. They're busy, we're busy, and we might not know quite how to get physically close when a cuddlebug turns into a long-limbed teen. It may seem impossible to create opportunities to touch a teen who is withdrawn or pushes away our loving intentions.

Many adolescents assert their independence by refusing to be hugged by their parents but will accept a simple shoulder massage or hand rub. That act of touch communicates love in a powerful way. It will frequently break down emotional barriers and may even help teens to open up and talk about what is on their minds.

Touch is a conduit for Spirit. The healing discipline of *reiki* teaches that what passes from toucher to touchee is *ki,* the universal life force. This healing energy is just as important to teens as it is to the rest of us. Healthy touch feels grounding and safe and can be spiritually nurturing. As one fourteen-year-old boy says, "My dad rubs my back at night sometimes. It feels really good and relaxes me. I think I sleep better."

Some teens continue to seek out opportunities for physical nurturing throughout adolescence.

"My nineteen-year-old daughter comes home from college and sits on my lap. I suppose some people might think it was weird, but it makes perfect sense to me. She's just starting out as a young adult—why wouldn't she want to crawl back into her mother's lap?"   —Jennie, mother of two

Some parents find a way to make touch a habit.

"Whenever my kids hit a rough spot, I hold them close and remind them that as they draw love from me, they have it to call up anytime they need it during the day. My teenagers relax and lean into loving arms. Just sitting close together and watching a comedy or favorite old movie together seems to be the touch that transfers my calm presence to them."   —Carrie, mother of three

I recently read an Associated Press news story about a middle school in Minnesota that banned hugging between students. Teachers doled out reprimands to kids caught hugging in the hallway. They were punished with detention if caught hugging three times in a day or four times a week. School officials were quoted as saying, "Hugging is sexual and not appropriate." One twelve-year-old girl written up for hugging said, "But that's how people express their feelings. It makes people feel better."

Hugging does make teens feel better by connecting them to their peer group and providing an affectionate sense of belonging. Banning these spontaneous acts of mutually comfortable human friendliness and limiting kids' natural desire for human contact may encourage them to enter romantic relationships just to meet their needs for touch and connection.

If healthy touch increases the flow of Spirit in your teen's life, consider these suggestions:

- The repertoire of touch includes casual and more focused gestures. Pats on the shoulder, back, or arm as you pass your teen in the hall or kitchen can be as meaningful as extended neck massages.

- Start with long-distance touches when a teen seems withdrawn. If one of those size ten feet is within easy reach, touch it rather than closing in to give a backrub. Touch the tip of a teen's finger with one of your own. Blow a kiss instead of planting it on a cheek.

- French braiding a teenage daughter's hair can be the opportunity to visualize light and love going from your hands into her beautiful healthy hair and deep into her very being. Along with the braid you might give her the extra zap she's been craving but unable to articulate. Offering a manicure and including a gentle hand rub can provide the same opportunity for loving touch.

- Consider picking up a yoga tape or signing up for a yoga class with your son or daughter. Yoga provides peaceful opportunities to offer assistance through touch. If your teen is interested, you might even try some yoga partner poses.

- There's nothing like the loving touch of a parent when we aren't feeling well. If your teen comes down with the flu, don't hesitate to tuck blankets around him, place a cool cloth on his brow, and hold his head when he gets sick.

- Don't overlook the power of seemingly silly touch. High fives, gentle head nuggies, or safe wrestling can be just the remedy for an adolescent boy who is drifting away from his father or mother.

- Nurturing touch doesn't have to come just from parents. A fifteen-year-old remarked, after observing a salsa dance class at her high school's dance club, "There's a lot of healthy touch going on. It's different from the grinding dancing that goes on during most high school dances."

- It may seem like an indulgence, but consider giving your teenager the gift of a professional massage or another kind of bodywork. Of course, you'll make sure the masseuse or practitioner comes highly recommended and has had experience with teens. Studies have linked the use of massage with a decrease in aggression among teenagers as well as an increase in the ability to concentrate among young adults with learning disabilities.

Create more opportunities for your teen to experience the magic of healthy, healing, loving touch—doing so allows stress to melt away and sprit to flow more easily.

Celebrate Transitions

A teen's life is filled with important milestones on the way to becoming an adult: first date or dance, first time behind the steering wheel of a car, learner's permit, driver's license, first job, middle school or junior high graduation, entering high school, college entrance exams, applications and admissions. . . . The list seems to go on and on.

Judaism honors the transition between childhood and adolescence with bat and bar mitzvahs, but, all too often, other important markers in a teen's life pass in the blink of an eye. Acknowledgement comes mostly in the form of a piece of paper from the department of motor vehicles or the College Board.

Family celebrations of these milestones acknowledge the progress a teen is making on the road to adult life and honor the importance of each step. And they stay in our teens' hearts and memories for many years, as my friend Nora's favorite recollection from her adolescence illustrates. "The day I got my first period, my mother asked me to come into the kitchen. She took my hand gently in hers and dipped two of my fingers into a jar of honey. Then she said, 'May you always have a sweet life as a woman.'"

Celebrations can take many forms. Blessing special moments doesn't require much more than inviting Spirit to be present in a teen's life as he or she moves into a new phase. As one mother relates, "My daughter really struggled her first two years of high school, trying to put it all together—social life, homework, more responsibilities. When, in her junior year, her hard work paid off in her best report card ever, I bought her a sterling silver cross necklace to honor her effort and her willingness to partner with God to make her life work."

A teen taking to the road for the first time is a wonderful occasion for a spiritual marker. Instead of just handing the car keys over to an adolescent with a brand-new driver's license, include a moment of shared prayer. "May you always be safe, knowing that God travels with you. The light of God surrounds you each time you get behind the wheel. Wherever you are, God is and all is well."

You might present your young driver with your family's version of Rules for the Road and include a sacred icon of protection, a special crystal, or a religious medal.

Birthdays are another kind of milestone. At our house, a special tradition honors all birthdays. As we settle at the dinner table, we raise our glasses in a toast to the person whose special day it is. Then, in turn, we each identify one thing we appreciate about that individual and offer wishes for the coming year. The table's centerpiece is a gathering of items that reflect the birthday person's interests as well as photos from their life. It's a wonderful opportunity for sincere words of love and appreciation to flow between our family members—and for each of us to hear how much we matter to those with whom we live. When I was growing up, birthday dinners included much of this same ceremony. This ritual is a part of who I am and a touchstone I'm passing along to my children.

To celebrate transitions in the life of your teen and your family, you might want to try some of the following:

- Spontaneous celebrations are as memorable as those that are planned in advance. God is present whether you're in a car, a coffee shop, or a church. Offer acknowledgements and blessings when the Spirit moves you, rather than waiting for the right setting. "Thank you loving universe for this perfect parking spot."

- Letters make a wonderful marker and keepsake. A teenage girl recalls an important birthday letter: "On the morning of my eighteenth birthday, I woke up to a letter from my mom and a big vase of roses from the garden. I don't remember right now what other gift my parents gave me, but I still have the letter. I had never heard my mom talk about why she wanted a baby or what it meant to her when I was born. I felt so touched by her loving words and incredibly honored."

- Invite adults from outside your family to participate in acknowledging and blessing important milestones in your teen's life, too. Taking milestones outside the family circle underscores their importance. For instance, I invited women from around the country who receive my newsletter, as well as family and friends, to offer memories, thoughts, and advice about their teen years to Whitney for her thirteenth birthday. I received hundreds of touching stories from women as old as ninety-eight who have strong memories of their transition from child to teen. I bundled these together into a book, called it *13 Candles* and presented it to Whitney on her special day. These words from women who have "been there" are still cherished by Whitney. A few sample nuggets from this batch:

"My dad never sings as he is completely tone deaf. When I turned thirteen, however, he sang every song he knew the words to, LOUDLY, so I would always remember my thirteenth birthday, and I always have. Always remember your parents' unconditional love for you. I remember feeling my body would never catch up to my spirit—it does and then you really inhabit your skin fully and joyfully. I felt like an old, wise spirit in a young unformed vessel. Now I feel like I will be a young spirit in an old vessel! The balance you seek is coming."

—Tracy, mother of two

"A few tips I'd like you to know from a wise old 89-year-old:

You really aren't indestructible.

Other kids have the same questions that you do.

It's okay to ask your parents the questions that are on your mind.

Don't ever drop a boy cruelly. Use kindness at all time even when you have no models of that kind of behavior from other kids.

Don't ever let yourself be dropped by a boy. Get to know a boy before linking your name to his.

Respect your friends and don't say unkind things about them."

—Maggie, mother of nine, grandmother of twenty-five

Make the Ordinary Sacred

"Sunday nights are a big deal. I have to be home, no matter what."

—Tina, seventeen

Milestones are momentous, but ordinary days are more frequent. Making them memorable helps us and our teens remain more focused on the here and now rather than on the next big event. One of the key steps to spiritual awareness is the ability to be fully in the present moment. Ritual lodges us firmly in the now.

Maintain your simple family rituals as a way of staying in touch. Teenagers need to know that the family is still a place where they can come home to refuel. So continue to have a family dinner every Friday night or visit relatives after church on Sunday, even if your teenagers sit there in silence or insist on wearing their most outlandish outfit.

Don't hesitate to incorporate explicitly spiritual or religious rituals into your days. As one teen says,

"We hold hands and say grace every night at dinner. If we didn't do that, I think I'd feel a hole in my day." **—Abby, fourteen**

Gloria Wade-Gayles, author of *My Soul Is a Witness: African-American Women's Spirituality,* remembers her mother's routine when she was a child. "I thought my mother's daily list-making a boring routine, a mere habit rooted in her penchant for organization. But when I became a woman and, as the Scripture says, 'put away childish things,' I realized that the activity was part of a spiritual ritual: first the lists, then the meditation, and before turning off the light, the prayers."

Sometimes, our rituals for ordinary days are secular, but they have the same effect, to connect us as a family and to link the events of our lives across the years. For instance, in our family we make a big deal out of the first day back at school. The kids get to choose the menu, and we spend the meal discussing what's new—and what's comfortingly familiar—from one year to the next.

We also take a photograph to commemorate the day. When they were younger, Whitney and Elizabeth posed at the bus stop, backpacks and lunchboxes in hand. Now we catch them in candid moments—not surprisingly, a telephone is often part of the scene. The magic in this tradition is the flash of recognition that follows close behind the flash of the camera. "Oh yeah," I can almost hear them thinking, "we do this every year so I'll complain a little but not a lot." Where they might have been tempted to object to the picture because of hair, clothes, pose, or mood, they play along.

When I look back on the advice my mother gave me for living a full life, it's the practical tips that I seem to put to use in my daily round. When I use the following advice from my mom, I seem to bring simple magic into my family life:

- Drink peppermint tea to soothe the tummy and the soul. (My daughters find this invaluable advice and we make sure to have a big stash of decaffeinated peppermint tea on hand—particularly during exam time.)

- A long hot bath soothes all problems, physical or emotional. (Whenever trouble or stress creeps in you can hear one of our bathtubs filling up).

- Always make your bed first thing each morning. Doing so helps you know that at least one thing is in order during your day. (We continue to work on this one.)

Other families mark different days in various ways. As one fifteen-year-old notes, "On the winter solstice, we don't use electric lights in the front room when it starts to get dark. My parents light candles and a fire in the fireplace instead of turning on lamps. It's kind of weird, but I like it."

Rituals help us stay connected as families and to God. I know a teen who's actively questioning his relationship with God right now. He won't go to church, but he and his father play chess and have lattes at the local coffeehouse every Sunday afternoon. A mom and her adolescent daughter who are temporarily having a tough time communicating go to a movie many weekends. The mother comments, "It's hard for us to talk without arguing these days. I think of our movie routine as parallel play. You know how little children like to play different games side-by-side? That's what we do—we go and sit side by side. We may not be talking, but we're together."

Rituals depend on the familiar and expected, but we all love surprises, too. They're a great way to fit a more meaningful experience into an ordinary day. I leave surprises on my daughters' pillows from time to time: a note, a pair of funny socks I picked up, a library book I think they might enjoy. On cold mornings, I might toss their jackets over a heater baseboard to warm up as they eat their breakfast. On cold evenings, I might warm a lavender and flaxseed pillow in the microwave and slip it into one of the girl's beds as a toasty surprise when she crawls in. Consider surprising your son or daughter on a random day by picking them up at school and driving to the local pizza place for a slice or ice cream shop for a sundae. You might announce that no chores are required for the afternoon, just because it's a magic day or better yet, do the chores for your teen and don't say a word as they grumble their way to take out trash that's long gone.

Here are some suggestions to help make everyday moments more memorable. Remember, these are simply ideas you might try rather than more "to do's" to add to your list.

• If your teen, like so many, has to get up at oh-dark-thirty to get to school on time, how about handing him a steaming cup of tea in a special travel mug on his way out the door?

• Angel cards in a bowl on the table can invoke the spirit of forgiveness, joy, love, or another quality to accompany a teen all day long. Pick up a deck at your local bookstore, and watch the magic that follows these little angelic messages into your teen's life.

• Flowers, candles, incense, and music can all help create a sacred atmosphere when we use them with the intention of expanding our experience of Spirit in our lives on a daily basis. These elements can go a long way toward turning an ordinary moment into an extraordinary one.

• Encourage teens to make more magic for their friends. They might write a note to a classmate who is feeling down, pick up a can of chicken soup and deliver it to the pal home sick with the flu, leave an encouraging message on a teammate's voice mail, or pick up a particularly magnificent leaf and tuck it under the windshield of a friend's car.

• A family altar is a great way to honor the sacred in the ordinary. Martha, mother of two teens says, "On an old pine table in our living room, we have a constantly shifting collection of found objects to which we all contribute. From pine cones to crystals, each object represents a connection to Spirit that someone felt and brought home to share."

• Ordinary events become magical when you endow them with your creative enthusiastic spirit. Norman Vincent Peale, the wonderfully positive speaker and author once said, "There is real magic in enthusiasm. It spells the difference between mediocrity and accomplishment." Make an effort to turn your attention to how you might add more enthusiasm to your everyday family life.

• Include in your home literature that evokes magic and mystery. (I've included some titles in the Resources section at the end of the book.) The writings of Einstein, for instance, are full of his thoughts on the great mystery of life. He says, "This insight into the mystery of life, this knowledge that what is impenetrable to us really exists, manifesting itself in the highest wisdom and the most radiant beauty which our dull faculties can comprehend only in their more primitive forms this knowledge, this feeling, is at the center of true religiousness."

Laughter can transform ordinary moments into magical memories. Sacred moments don't have to be solemn. Teens, and all the rest of us, can take life very seriously. Leavening the atmosphere by sharing something humorous helps everyone remember how delicious it is to release energy through laughter.

Humor—Use It More Often

Humor can be magic, especially with teens. Humor helps us cope, taps into something bigger than ourselves or the situation at hand, and can transform the energy in the room in a flash. When we laugh, we breathe more deeply and release tension.

Your teen may find it a little harder to laugh during the years between fourteen and seventeen or so. Some teens are tempted to take themselves and their experiences very seriously for a period of time. Mistakes become grave errors, and every dilemma seems life-or-death. Our job is to help them remember the power of laughter, of looking at life with a lighter lens.

Depending on your family's unspoken rules about teasing or practical jokes, you can look for ways of helping your teen remember to laugh at him- or herself. Needless to say, kindhearted humor is radically different from teasing that's meant to hurt or belittle someone else. One mother of a seventeen-year-old shares a story about teasing: "My son is a terrible teaser. I can't tell when he's putting me on or being honest. Recently, though, I got him back. I pretended to have a conversation with his girlfriend's mother on the phone. I was listening to a dial tone the whole time, but I totally had him going. 'The mother' and I were talking about how cute they were together and how we couldn't wait for the winter social. He was writhing in agony by the time I let him know I faked the whole thing. Laughing together was a fun moment I'll remember always."

Because the teen years can be a time of increased sensitivity, follow teasing or practical jokes with straightforward messages of love and appreciation.

> "I remarried when my daughter was thirteen. Her stepdad has always teased her. Now, at seventeen, she dishes it right back, but there were a couple of years when he was careful to follow teasing with a hug or by telling her how great a kid she was for putting up with him." —**Annie, mother of one**

Monitor the kindness quotient in family teasing and practical jokes. While teasing can allow family members to diffuse tension, it should always feel more like laughing together than laughing at someone in particular. Everyone should also come in for their fair share of teasing; if not, it can maintain an unhealthy power balance. Expect to get your share.

As adults, we can continue to laugh at ourselves and each other, even if our teens have temporarily forgotten how. Turning a mistake into a joke reminds teens that mistakes aren't, in fact, the end of the world. Light, teasing banter between adults sets a tone of humor in the house that is healing and hard to resist.

Humor helps us as parents, too. When we can find something to laugh about in a distressing situation, everything seems to shift into perspective. One mother tells a story about humor transforming a situation that she and her husband initially found unsettling:

> "In his freshman year of high school, our son started bringing home some pretty odd-looking characters, guys who dressed in bizarre thrift-store clothing, weird shoes, and had purple or red hair. His grades and attitude around the house were okay, though, and these guys, odd-looking as they were, were also polite and very pleasant. Neither Dan nor I knew what to make of the whole situation.
>
> "One afternoon, Justin brought a couple of friends home. I was working in our home office and didn't see them come in. A few minutes later, my husband walked into the room and told me to go look in Justin's room. He wouldn't tell me why, and he had a really strange expression on his face. He just said that I should make sure that Justin opened his door all the way.

"I went upstairs and knocked. Justin opened his door, and I had to stifle a gasp. His newest friend was wearing two-inch platform boots and shiny black vinyl pants. But the thing that really shocked me was his hair: blond, it was shaved in the back and braided into two long braids that hung down on either side of his face, reaching the middle of his chest. Justin introduced us, and he, too, was a nice kid.

"Dan and I laughed together for a long time. Between the two of us, that kid was always 'Heidi of the Alps' because of his hair. He took things to such an extreme that we finally had to laugh about what a weird-looking bunch of friends our son had."

Humorous activities and safe practical jokes can link you and your teen and definitely create some silly magic. My daughter Whitney and her dad are ongoing prank partners with another father/daughter duo. They call themselves "Delta Force" and have a secret signal, late-night meetings with popcorn, and mischievous phone calls throughout the year. The harmless pranks they concoct provide knowing winks and closer bonds between fathers and daughters. Tacky lights strung up at midnight on the front porch of our decorator friend's house may not seem like spiritual activity. But the flow of magic when the switch was turned on and fathers and daughters dashed out of sight will be recalled by all four of them for years to come.

To increase the humor quotient at your house, you might try some of the following ideas:

• Pick funny movies to enjoy as a family. Life is naturally full of opportunities for tension and grief; choose more healing family experiences. Some teen movies are hilarious, and my family has shared belly laughs at some films that I would never have seen without my daughters' influence. Remember the oldies, too; Monty Python and Mel Brooks films are slightly racy and reliably silly.

• Remember, revive, or reinvent family jokes. My siblings and my mom recently gathered at our home for the holidays. We recalled some of the funny times we had as children. We were all wiping tears from our eyes by the time the memories were exhausted.

• Time can turn trauma into good material. My friend Janet's son backed the car into their house while learning to drive. The only major damage was to his self-esteem, but, after waiting a few months, even he could see the humor in the situation.

• Find out what your teens think is funny. Watching our children laughing over healthy humor is pure joy.

• Who hasn't heard the nasty voice of their inner critic? I think the inner beast is really born during our adolescence. That inner critic, lurking in the background of our minds, accessing what the outside world sees, can squash creativity. We can help our teens recognize this toxic "inner brat" by naming it. Humor around this sabotager helps: "I sat down to write a report for work today, and that nasty little inner critic lodged in my mind taunted me with doubt, whispering 'You aren't a writer . . . this isn't your turf . . . you'll probably fail miserably. Why not just go eat some cake?' Well, I told this voice to take a hike; I was going to write the report and there was nothing he could do about it. Ugh, have you ever heard a little doubting demon?"

Holiday Traditions and Rituals

Holidays offer an unparalleled opportunity for creating magic that transcends the calendar. As one stepmother says, "I kind of miss the days when the kids were wide-eyed with amazement. They're certainly much cooler these days. But I know they're better able to understand what the holidays really mean. And I figure that they'll remember these years, too, when they're making magic for their own children."

The teen years are a great time—and sometimes a challenging one—for family traditions. Even though adolescents are in and out of the house, attending to school, social events, or work, ongoing family traditions are important. It may seem like they don't notice or care, but they do.

Laine, mother of two teenage sons and a ten-year-old daughter, talks about the difference in her son's celebration of the holidays since they moved into their teen years. "When we light the Hanukkah candles, the boys barely mumble the blessings now. I used to think they weren't enjoying it anymore, but then I overheard them talking about lighting the candles at their friend's house. 'Ours is so much better,' Denny said, and his brother agreed. I thought they'd be more enthusiastic that evening, but it was just the same—they dragged their feet and mumbled. Still, I realized that what they were showing on the outside was different from what they felt."

Caren Prentice is the mother of four children ranging from middle school to college and the author of *The Advent Box: How to Bring Spirit Home for the Holidays.* For more than a decade, her family has engaged in a home-grown family ritual that expands on the traditional Christian concept of an Advent box or calendar to include experiences of connection to family, Spirit, and community. Each day of Advent brings a few moments where the family gathers to light Advent candles and share a brief spiritual reading and a prayer and open a door on the Advent box. Each door conceals an activity that focuses on giving—to each other, to their friends, or those in need—or strengthening their sense of family connection. *Fun* is the theme that ties all the activities together, and the Prentice kids are enthusiastic participants—most of the time.

"When my older kids were teens," says Caren, "They went through phases where they could barely tolerate the fact that the rest of us existed. They opted out of family activities and weren't much fun to be around when they did decide to join us. I would often feel like I was wasting my time doing the Advent box.

"When Alyce was a freshman in college, though, she called to ask, 'We're doing the Advent box this year, right?' And, as a young adult, she's one of its most ardent fans."

If you ask Alyce now what she remembers about the holidays during her teen years, she recalls the experience of family closeness and connection to Spirit that this ritual provided for her family. "It's so much about what Christmas *really* is—it's about God and giving to others. I looked forward to the activities in the Advent box more than I did opening presents on Christmas morning."

The principles of this ritual, based on the Christian religious calendar, apply to other traditions as well. Your teens know which holiday traditions are most important to them. Invite them to participate, but don't be put off if they choose not to. The freedom to participate in whatever way they can is a powerful gift of love and acceptance. You can still carry on.

It's never too late to start new traditions. My friend Janet started one when she remarried and became part of a stepfamily that included her two daughters and her husband's son, all teens. "Stepfamilies are a little tough, because you're trying to combine separate ways of doing the holidays. For instance, we had "theirs" and "ours" menorahs; we decided to use ours because it had been my grandmother's. My stepson simply opted out of lighting the candles altogether on the first night. I went out and bought a family menorah the next day and asked him to light it. I was so afraid that he'd laugh at me or refuse. He didn't. Now we use our menorah every year and all the kids want to be the one to light it."

Hanukkah and Christmas are just the tip of the holiday iceberg. Dewali, Ramadan, Kwanzaa, and the Chinese New Year are only four among the multitude of days that are sacred in various cultural and religious traditions. For each of these, the way your family celebrates may—or may not be—slightly different because you have teenagers in the house.

"My teens are not the center so they don't need traditions or rituals honed for them. They participate as the members of the family they are and add to the dimension of fun for their younger siblings."   —Ed, father of five

Try these suggestions for honoring holidays with traditions and rituals:

• Incorporate more giving opportunities into your holidays. Explore the fun of secret giving. Teens are quick to join in when we take the lead on this festive activity, especially if it involves one of their friends. In her book *The Advent Box,* Caren suggests a trip to the mall with a small stash of one- and five-dollar bills on which you've attached a sticky note that says, "This has been dropped as a random act of kindness. Happy holidays!" Each family member drops two or three bills and watches in secret as passersby pick them up.

- Consider inviting your teen's friends and their families to participate in your family ritual, whether it's Christmas dinner or a special *iftar* meal during Ramadan.

- New Year's Day lends itself to rituals about releasing the old and welcoming the new. Some people burn the previous year's calendar. Invite your teen to share his or her most significant memories from the year that's ending and goals and dreams for the new one.

Remember that, in the moment, the sacred can feel anything but. Younger teens, in particular, can find it challenging to sincerely engage in rituals. Patience and perseverance are the order of the day, as the impact of rituals and traditions comes from repetition and accumulated history. Whether you're celebrating holidays or infusing a memorable moment into an ordinary Thursday let your teen guide you to what's magic for her. Feed your own soul by learning more about what feels like magic to you and incorporating more of it into your life.

Miracles

At a time when religious differences are at the root of much world conflict, belief in miracles is common to most world religions, including Christianity, Islam, Hinduism, Judaism, Buddhism, and Ba'hai.

Despite the fraud of psychic healers and televangelists, miracles do indeed unfold in our teenagers' lives. Divine reality is not passive and works through the world in extraordinary ways. Many teens are intrigued by the idea and the reality of miracles.

More than eight in ten Americans agree that "even today, miracles are performed by the power of God," according to a survey conducted by the Princeton Survey Research Associates for the Pew Research Center. Slightly more than one in three adults—36 percent—say they personally "experienced or witnessed" what they considered to be a miracle, according to a CBS news poll in 2002.

Miracles can draw worldwide attention, the apparitions of the Virgin Mary at Medjugorge or crop circles that appear mysteriously. Miracles also happen every day in less newsworthy, but no less significant, ways.

What some people call coincidences, others recognize as synchronicities: instances of the Divine energy working with us to provide the answer, personal contact, or guidance we crave. As we start to pay attention to synchronicities, they multiply and we understand the many and miraculous ways God has to communicate with and support us.

For instance, you may be wondering about how to handle a particular situation with your teen. What would God have you do to nurture your child's spiritual growth? Tired of mulling things over, you turn on the radio—only to hear a song that answers the question you'd been pondering. Your teen might mention that he or she has been missing a friend who moved out of the area—and receives a letter or a phone call that very day.

The following story from my friend Mary Ellen, whose website www. AngelScribe.com is full of angelic miracle stories, illustrates the miracles our teens are not only ready to embrace but initiate:

"My daughter Ariel and I made the decision to drop some groceries off at a local battered women's shelter, to make a positive difference in others' lives. Before we left the house, we asked a few neighbors and family members for used clothing to take to the shelter. We were given four large plastic bags of clothing. We then drove to a drug store and asked if they would give us a discount on sanitary supplies and diapers for the battered women's shelter. We were given a great discount and all we had to do was ask. We then went to the bread outlet store. I bought dried soup mixes and oats for breakfast, nourishing foods that lasted a long time in the tummy, would be the wisest to buy. I was thinking that one of the hardest parts of being homeless was being hungry all the time. We asked the bread store manager if she would give us a discount, and she gladly said yes.

"As I was reaching for the oats, Ariel blurted out, 'Take them bread.' I explained, in my Mummy way, that oatmeal for breakfast would be better. Ariel said the angels were whispering, to her, telling her to take bread instead. Who am I to argue with angels? So we bought a few bags of wholesome wheat and grain bread, at a discount. When we walked into the Shelter, there on the counter stood two of the hugest jars of peanut butter we had ever seen. The person before us had just delivered the jars of peanut butter . . . and as you know . . . peanut butter goes better on bread than on oatmeal. We smiled all the way home."

Some other ideas for drawing miracles into your teen's life include:

• The *Chicken Soup for the Soul* series offers many stories of everyday miracles that transform the lives of those affected; you can also find wonderful miracle stories in one of my daughter's favorite books, *Expect Miracles* by Mary Ellen. (Her miracle story with her daughter Ariel is above.) Consider sharing some of these short tales with your family by reading them aloud.

• Many teens seem to be drawn to the mystery and magic of spirituality. Now might be a great time to create some sacred field trips—Catholic missions, beautiful cathedrals, yoga centers, Japanese gardens, Native American architectural remains, celestial observations, or labyrinths.

• The National Museum of the American Indian in New York City recently featured an exhibit called *The Uses of Enchantment*. This exhibition presented people from Native communities of the Huatulco-Huamelula region of Oaxaca, Mexico, speaking passionately about their lives, families, histories, beliefs, and dreams. Magic and enchantment is a major focus of the ordinary lives of these people. The teenagers in this culture are linked with enchantment which guides them through the passage to adulthood. What we might call a miracle they would name an ordinary shift. Consider drawing upon the magical traditions from other cultures to enrich these years with your children.

By acknowledging the magic in simple ordinary wonders, we are often surprised by joy. Rabbi Nachman of Breslov who died in 1810 said, "The only thing worth giving your children is joy." Take a moment to answer the question, "What is joy?" Is it: authentic happiness, freedom from wanting, wonder, glee, humor, free expression, love, playing with abandon, or no expectations? What was a joyful experience you had as a teenager? Do you recall laughing with friends, the arrival of beloved grandparents, riding a horse on the beach, a wide-open summer with no plans, or your favorite dinner served for no reason other than your mom loved you? How might you make each day contain a sliver of joy and magic for you and for your teen?

Allow your teen's energy and excitement to infuse you. Open your heart to the many opportunities for joy and magic in your lives together. Awaken the wonder and spirit has the momentum to flow more vividly.

Parents' Insight-Building Exercise

Think back to your own teen years. What was nurturing for your spirit? What comforted you? How did you find peace? Were there experiences that increased your sense of connection to God? Have you brought those activities into your adult life? If not, can you?

Ask for guidance about what forms of everyday magic your teen might be most receptive to embracing. Some tune into music, others are visual. What avenues for experiencing the Divine can you help open up for your teen?

What happened *this week* that seemed magical to you? Would you be willing to share this experience with your teen? Practice gratitude for the moments when life takes on a little more sparkle; it's the surest way to make sure they occur more frequently.

Reflect on your holiday and milestone experiences as a teen. When did they feel most soul-satisfying? What would you have liked to experience? Is this something that your teen would also enjoy?

Parents' Check-In Questions

• What can I do this week to make our home feel more like a sanctuary?

• What adds magic to my life? Have I allowed myself to have this experience lately?

• What adds magic to my teen's life? Does he have opportunities to be a kid again? How can I help create these experiences for him?

• How much healthy touch does my teen experience? Is his "touch tank" filled up or is he due for a neck rub? If a neck rub seems too intense, how can I physically connect with my teen?

• What milestones are approaching for my teen? How do I want to honor them?

• Does our family have enough rituals? Are there words or actions my teen likes that I could use more regularly?

• In what parts of my current family's traditions can I invite my teenager to take a larger role? How would I feel if he declined the opportunity?

Conversation Starters

Try starting with a brief story from your own childhood about stress or holidays or family traditions. As you relate the full gamut of your experience, the good *and* the not-so-good parts, your teen will understand that all of his sometimes conflicting feelings are valid.

Questions like these can also get the ball rolling:

• What's your earliest holiday memory?

• What things does our family do that you can imagine doing in your own future family?

• How do your friends' families celebrate Christmas/Hanukkah/Ramadan? Are there things they do that you'd like us to try?

• What's your favorite part about the holidays at our house?

• What's your favorite birthday memory?

• Is there anything we do that makes you feel like we're really paying attention to the fact that you're growing up?

Remain Flexibly Firm

"Just when I think I have my daughter figured out she moves into a new emotion, phase, or interest. She's completely different than her brother was as a teenager. My struggle is to be flexible in how I parent her as well as how I respond to her various moods." —**Mother of two**

"The greatest edge I can give my child is my constant love, tempered with discipline and routine." —**Ann, mother of three**

. . .

By the time our children reach their teen years, we've gotten comfortable setting rules and creating family guidelines. We've seen how these parameters provide important elements of safety and predictability so our sons and daughters can function freely. We also know how to shift the structure as a child matures. A four-year-old might only have the freedom to play outside alone in a fenced backyard, while a seventh-grader can walk to a friend's house several blocks away.

The pace at which we evaluate and readjust household rules and guidelines picks up during our children's teen years. How easy it would be if we could set "teen rules" when our kids are thirteen and never consider them again until they're removed entirely when our young adult moves out of the house!

However, for our teenager's spirit to flourish, allowing him or her to move into the world in positive and empowered ways, we have to create a flexible structure. We increase the contents on our parental plate as we take responsibility for constantly reevaluating guidelines, adjusting and read-justing them based on ever-changing factors: our children's ages, attitudes, our perception of their maturity, the circumstances around a particular activity, how well or poorly they handled more freedom the last time they had the opportunity. We take all these—and more—into account as we consider the wisdom of either expanding or contracting our teen's scope of freedom.

As we create a flexible structure, we allow teenagers many opportunities to integrate the quality of flexibility into their lives. In the outside world, the ability to adjust to changing circumstances is necessary for healthy survival. Creating a flexible structure helps us all handle unanticipated events, revised plans, broken agreements, and circumstances over which no one has control. As someone once said, change is the only constant. In our interior or spiritual world, flexibility to the divine flow within is necessary for living authentically.

Cultivating a flexible structure also allows us, both parent and teen, to benefit more from our limited free time by being open to spontaneous opportunities. "Let's get in the car on Saturday and practice your driving. We'll just head east." "On Sunday, rather than going to church, how about we create sacred space and time by being quiet at home with no technology usage?"

Some parents worry that flexibility is too easily confused with inconsistency—rules that change for no apparent reason. This is a valid concern. Teens need predictability at home now more than ever. So much else is changing and whirling around them. Some adults have told me they recall their teen years as a blur they walked numbly through, physically fatigued and emotionally and mentally exhausted by their preoccupation with self and self-assessment.

However, as we consciously take on the task of creating a flexible struc-

ture, we have one central goal: to flex in the way that truly serves our adolescent's spirit. Sometimes, that means we give them a little more room in
which to spread their wings. Sometimes, it means we ask for proof that
they're really ready for more freedom.

> "Parenting my teenaged son and daughter seems like fishing sometimes. I give
> them some line and they run with it, then I reel them back in for awhile."
>
> **—Tom, father of two**

If we expect that our teens will sometimes make mistakes and act in
ways that are inappropriate, then we won't be knocked to our knees when
it happens. We can prepare for these mistakes and this behavior by involving our kids in creating limits, rules, and consequences for their lives. This
allows us to experience more joy in the journey of parenting rather than
being dashed when perfection is not achieved by our sons and daughters
along the way.

Creating a flexible structure also means that we look consciously at
love in action, the boundaries we have in place, and how we allow and encourage our teens to express their emerging power. It also means that we
assess our relationships with our spouse or partner—and our teen.

Pal or Parent?

> "It matters less that my daughter likes me than that she turns out to be a re-
> sponsible adult." **—Mother of one**

My mother and I are great friends. In the years since I was a teenager,
our relationship shifted from parent-child to adult friendship. Don't get me
wrong. I still occasionally forget I'm a grownup and long for my mom's
hand on my forehead when I'm sick or her praise when I've had a success.
But we now enjoy a friendship free from the constraints of parental responsibility.

As parents of teens, we can be tempted to make that shift too early,
turning our teens into buddies. This can happen for many reasons. We nat-

urally want to feel accepted by our children. Their approval feels good, so we hesitate to upset them. We may want to avoid seeming too old or rigid, or we may feel guilty about the lack of time we spend together.

The energy and enthusiasm of the teen years is invigorating and fun, so being "one of the gang" when our teen's friends come over can be tempting. If their friends like us, too, the approval and acceptance we feel is multiplied. Maybe we enjoy re-creating our own fond memories of a high school gang. Conversely, perhaps we feel we've finally found the teenaged acceptance that eluded us all those years ago.

Some adults tell me they want a relationship with their children that is different from the one they had with their own parents. If we felt rigidly controlled or emotionally distanced, we may adopt a friendship model for parenting our own teens.

If we're recently divorced or widowed, we may put our adolescent into the role of adult companion to fill the hole we feel so acutely. If we're in a new stepfamily, we might think that being a friend to a teenage stepchild is the only way to keep the peace.

In short, the reasons we fall into the friendship trap are many. And none of them are sound.

Teens need a caregiver who consistently enforces rules, boundaries, and expectations while providing clear direction. To help our sons and daughters develop into responsible, dependable, mature, and honest adults, we set limits, create structure, impose consequences, and accept that they might not think we're the coolest parent in the neighborhood.

But that doesn't mean we're always at odds with our teens. On the contrary, it's often easier to have a warm, close relationship with our kids when we're committed to providing a flexible structure. Of course, I love my daughters—but I also really like spending time with them. They are interesting people, and sharing enjoyable time together now is my delicious payoff for the years of wiping noses, interrupted sleep, and sibling squabbles. And as much as I love being with my children, I also have adult friends and don't rely on my daughter's companionship to fulfill my needs in the pal department. I'm clear about who's an adult and who is not. This is not always taken so well but that's part of my job.

Another part of my job, one that I might find hard to do if I were more friend than parent, is to make decisions with an eye to their possible impact on every aspect of my teens' lives. Studies about the intellectual development of teens suggest that their decision-making abilities, while significantly better than younger children's, are not on a par with those of adults.

One gift we bring to our teens' lives is this broader perspective. We've probably weathered challenges to our values over the years. Many adults have had the gratifying experience of working hard to achieve a goal. Most, if not all, of us have faced circumstances that made us quake in our boots and know that courage is when you're scared—and do it, anyway. As we matured, we learned that certain things about life are important, and others aren't.

The value of the perspective we've lived so long to acquire is invaluable, yet we can be tempted to deny if what we want is friendship or approval from our teen.

Try some of the following to explore more about the differences between being a friend and a parent to your teenager:

• Hone your perspective by creating a parental mission statement. In a single sentence, capture your most heartfelt, deeply held goal as a parent. Is it to raise loving adults? To encourage your children to live out their dreams? To support them in finding unique ways of contributing to the world we all share? Whatever your mission statement, the odds are that it's not about being friends with your teen. Rely on your goal in relationship to your son or daughter. The deepest longings of your heart are the most perfect way to parent your teen.

• Notice if you find yourself consistently avoiding conflict with your adolescent. While some minor sources of conflict are better left unmentioned, if you choose to overlook important issues or explain them away, you may be doing your teen a disservice. What feelings does the thought of disappointing or angering your teen inspire in you?

• Do a premature-adult check on your teen's life. Have you put her in a role meant for someone older? I know of one divorced father whose son often accompanies him to dinner parties. He both charms the adult guests and consumes his share of the evening's wine. This pattern began when he was just fifteen years old. Do you confide in your teen the same way you'd share with an adult confidante? Does your teen take on undue responsibility because you're overburdened? When was the last time you heard your teen laugh out loud, giggle, or act silly?

• When your teenager's friends spend time at your house, do you generally join in the fun? There's a difference between creating a welcoming environment and getting down on their level. Familiarity may not breed contempt, but it can certainly hinder the development of respect; a little distance is a good thing.

The Many Faces of Love

"When I was a teen, I got away with more than my siblings did. I was the youngest of four children, and my mother was in her sixties; I think she was tired of raising kids. But I felt like she cared less about me than she did about my older sisters."   —Mother of three

Kids, no matter what their age, are love-seeking beings. Your love is a powerful force in their lives.

There are no substitutes for your affection. I once heard a school counselor explain her reasons for leaving a position at an expensive and exclusive private school. She was taking a job at an inner-city public school. "I'd rather," she said, "deal with kids who are neglected because their parents are working three or four jobs to make ends meet than work with children whose parents give them cash instead of love."

When we love someone, we pay attention to them. We keep agreements and listen attentively. We spend time with them, honoring their individuality and recognizing their accomplishments. We don't necessarily wear a blissed-out smile or coo in their ear. One of the most loving acts we can perform as parents is to say "No" or "Enough" when a teen needs to hear it.

"When I stand up to my son, I feel both bad and good. I feel badly about denying him something he wants, and I feel strong, like the power of the universe is
moving through me." —**Mother of one**

It takes commitment and strength to be a force for real love in your
teen's life—the kind of love that distinguishes between what enhances self-
and soul-development and what doesn't. A friend of mine recently said,
"When my older daughter reached her teen years, I realized that one reason why human children mature into teens over the course of thirteen years
is so that we can be firmly bonded with them by the time they get there!"

Love is honest. We don't placate our teens by telling them that we agree
with their choices if we don't.

"Both of my teens experimented with their appearance: dyed hair, weird
clothes, that kind of thing. I didn't forbid it, but I didn't lie about what I thought
about it. I pointed out the effect that it might have on other people's opinions
of them. I told them that I loved them even though I wouldn't give them a job
if they looked like that." —**Mike, father of two**

When we are mindful of the power of parental love in a teen's life,
we're also careful not to withhold it when we're less than delighted with
their choices or behavior. In a loving parent-child relationship, love can coexist with anger or hurt or disappointment. The latter emotions are transient; the love is a constant.

Truly loving someone means that we open ourselves to the possibility
of great pain, too. When we're committed to sustaining a heart-to-heart
connection with our teen, we embrace the possibility that we will feel both
love and grief.

"I've raised two teens so far, with one to go. Each of my older children has broken my heart once. They've betrayed my trust in them in very different ways. It
occurs to me that heartbreak may be a necessary part of them becoming who
they really are. My job is to bounce back from it."

—**Betsey, mother and stepmother of three**

Heartbreak comes in different forms for different parents: breaches of integrity, failing grades, substance abuse, teen pregnancy, or rejecting family values. Our pain can be just as real when a child doesn't make the varsity basketball team or get accepted to Dad's alma mater. Some parents are devastated because their kids chose to become chefs rather than lawyers. Or draw cartoons rather than hit tennis balls. The pain is very real, no matter what causes it. The mother quoted above talks about what happened in her relationship with her stepson. She goes on to say:

"When he was sixteen, he lied to me. I'd always believed I could trust him to tell the truth, and he stood in front of me and told a bald-faced lie.

"I was devastated. Perhaps I overreacted, but I felt like our whole relationship was undermined by his betrayal of my trust. It took me a day or two to be able to talk to him about the situation.

"When we talked, I told him that I was hurt because I loved and had trusted him. I told him that I was so upset because I cared about him so much. I told him that I wanted to trust him again, but that I wouldn't be able to do that right away. Over time, our relationship healed, but it had definitely been damaged."

It's a natural impulse to withdraw when we've been hurt or disappointed. As we're committed to spiritually parenting our teens, we do what we need to heal ourselves so that we can step back up to the plate. I believe that one of the reasons teens suffer parental neglect is because their parents are mired in pain and disappointment, unable to reach past their own heartbreak to their child.

To explore the many faces of love in your relationship with your teen, consider the following:

- Make a date with your teen this week. Just the two of you can go out for coffee, on a run, or to a movie—whatever activity you both would enjoy. Go without an agenda, ready to be with your son or daughter precisely where he or she is. Consider making it a regular event.

- Be honest with your teenager about what you really think. If there's an area where you aren't being completely forthright, figure out why and the next time it is appropriate, speak your beliefs.

• Consider whether there's something you're uncomfortable with in your teen's life. Is there a "No" waiting to be said? Teens, particularly before age fifteen or so, have an amazing ability to shoot for the moon; that doesn't mean we need to provide the rocket fuel. Remember that "No" can be a powerful way of saying, "I love you too much to let you do that."

• If you're in the middle of an upset involving your teen, commit to communicating love, no matter what the upset is about or what the consequences may be. Simple affirmative prayer can help. *Dear Spirit, bring Your words to my lips as I speak to my child.*

• As always, make time to recharge your parental batteries by doing whatever restores you: yoga, reading, a long bath, a hike in the woods. Sustaining a heart-to-heart connection with a teen takes lots of energy. It is *emotional* energy rather than the physical exhaustion that came with being up late feeding a baby or on alert constantly to a toddler's safety. Make sure you take time to care for your relationship with your self and your spirit.

Know the Bottom Line—and Hold It

From the time our children are babies, we learn to let go. The process accelerates during the teen years. And yet we mustn't let go of too much too soon.

Boundaries and structure provide elements of stability in a teen's life that are critical to healthy development. Clear expectations and limits create the predictable framework that teens crave—even though they resist it verbally.

What I've come to see as the central paradox of the adolescent mind is the degree to which teens both need and resist boundaries. If we fail to appreciate this paradox, we might take the arguments at face value and withdraw the boundaries. One of the hardest things to hear about teens is that many of their difficulties arise from a lack of close parental supervision.

The challenge in parenting adolescents is to see past the arguments to the basic need for boundaries and structure. Here's a perfect example from Jane, a mother of three teenage girls:

"When my oldest daughter was fifteen, a friend of hers who was two years older invited her to attend a concert in a nearby city. The friend, who I knew only casually, would drive, and my daughter asked to have her curfew extended to one a.m. They wanted to have time to get something to eat after the concert.

I said no.

My daughter argued her case. You can probably imagine her script. *"But it's only one time. I'll call you when we get there. My other friends get to go."*

I said no.

She continued to argue for another ten minutes or so.

I kept saying no.

Suddenly, she stopped arguing and smiled.

"I don't really want to go," she said. "But I can tell Michelle that we had a fight about it."

Had I listened to her argument instead of my gut, I might have allowed her to go. She depended on me to keep her out of a situation she knew she wouldn't be comfortable with."

Boundaries keep our teens safe, and they communicate the strength of our love in a way that nothing else can. Positive limits are the road map our child can refer to time and time again on the journey to adulthood. Even a teen who resists rules needs them. Perhaps, the most resistant teen craves boundaries more than her siblings. She may be asking, in effect, "Do you love me enough to keep me safe even when I'm fighting with you?"

Naturally, the boundaries for a thirteen-year-old middle schooler aren't the same as those for a seventeen-year-old high school junior. The boundaries for a legal adult, age eighteen and up, who's still living at home are even more different.

Yet, for all ages, certain expectations apply: making a positive contribution to the household, being accountable for one's whereabouts and activities, demonstrating respect for family members, taking care of personal responsibilities. As parents of teens, we define the categories that make up our bottom line, and then we adjust the criteria according to the age of the child.

When we hold boundaries firmly, we tolerate disagreement and disappointment without changing our minds. We don't waste energy negotiating expectations that are non-negotiable. And we allow the magic of natural consequences to work in our teens' lives.

Perhaps adolescence is a period of time during which kids should make every possible mistake they can. While they're still living under our roofs, we can allow them to experience the consequences of their choices without suffering lasting damage. Each lesson they learn before they leave home—about money, trust, integrity, effort, relationships, and on and on—is one that they won't have to learn alone, out in the world.

Might your goal as a parent shift from wanting your children to make choices you would deem right to wanting them to experience the consequences of whatever choices they make? That doesn't mean hands-off parenting. Rather, it means that you make your expectations clear, offer advice, and allow teens to choose.

This shift goes against our grain, given the achievement-oriented culture we live in, but allowing a teen to experience the consequences of his or her actions means that the teen, not the parent, owns the problem. Of course, stepping in to rescue a teen from a problem is our natural impulse. It's also important to note that there are exceptions to the idea of natural consequences. I wouldn't allow my daughters to bike without helmets or ride in a car without seat belts, for instance, because the natural consequences of those mistakes are fatal.

My neighbor Peggy's son flunked the first semester of algebra his freshman year. Peggy contacted the school to arrange for Jake to retake the class the second semester; he flunked again. Peggy contacted the school district, signed Jake up for an online version of the class during the summer, drove Jake to the learning center to meet with the responsible faculty member, and paid the entire cost of the class.

Jake flunked algebra for the third time.

At the end of the summer, Peggy realized that the world wouldn't end if Jake had to spend five years in high school to pass algebra. She told him that she didn't know what he was going to do about it, but she'd entertain any suggestions he had about how he was going to get through the basic math required to graduate from high school. If his ideas involved extra expense, she'd pay part of the cost—but not all of it.

During his sophomore year, Jake took algebra again. He signed up for peer tutoring—and passed the class.

When we resist stepping in to rescue our teens and allow them to own their problems and experience the consequences of their actions, we can use our energy for compassionate support. We don't have to use it to manage our own anxiety or problem-solve. As this mother and stepmother of two teens says, "When my stepson got in a car accident, he was so overwhelmed and upset that I called our insurance agent for him. That was the only thing that had to be done right away. After that, he took care of the details. When the claims adjuster called, I handed the phone to him and went for a walk. Justin filed the paperwork with the state and came up with the money for the deductible."

I recently heard author Ross King interviewed. He was talking about his book *Michelangelo and the Pope's Ceiling* and explained how Michelangelo was basically forced to paint the frescos on the ceiling of the Sistine Chapel. He was a sculptor and wasn't eager to attempt fresco painting. Michelangelo went ahead, however, as he didn't have much choice in what he felt was a hopeless task. He had scaffolding constructed and despite technical and health problems, he completed a masterpiece.

Sometimes as parents we must insist our teens build their scaffolding. We will supply the wood and bring them a hot lunch as they work but our imposed structure and no-turning-back insistence may just allow the fresco of all times to emerge from a reluctant master.

Boundaries, bottom lines, and firmly held limits work magic in a teen's life. To further explore the issue of boundaries and structure in your teen's life:

• Review your adolescent's responsibilities around the house. Do they fairly represent his or her abilities, time constraints, and level of maturity? Consider adjusting them, welcoming your son or daughter's input. Teens who drive can support your home and family in new and different ways. Does the privilege of driving come with responsibilities that reflect this expanded capacity? How does your young driver see his responsibility to the family shifting?

• Review your teen's privileges as well. Do they, too, fairly represent his or her abilities and level of maturity? How do they compare to the privileges that his or her friends enjoy? Is there a good reason that your teen should be less or more restricted?

• If you find yourself resisting the changes that your heart is prompting you to make, think of the wisdom of Maya Angelou: "If you don't like something change it. If you can't change it, change your attitude. Don't complain."

• A challenge in setting boundaries is to relax them in an appropriate progression as your teen ages. I've found it helpful to think of what privileges and responsibilities I'd like my teens to have a couple of years down the line, as well as at the present time. For instance, if I can foresee a midnight curfew for a sixteen-year-old, a 10:30 curfew may be appropriate for a fourteen-year-old.

• You may also have to set boundaries for other teens who are in your home. Numerous times, I've traipsed down to our family room to enforce a departure time with firm humor. The time by which friends who aren't spending the night need to leave depends on our rules, not their curfews. In fact, that's one of the gifts you have to offer your son or daughter's friends—the presence of an adult who follows through on house rules.

• Maintaining boundaries requires a parent who's awake. Literally. When I was a teen and went out at night, my mother always stayed up or woke up for a conversation with me when I came home. No matter what I was up to, I knew she'd be there when I came in the door, sleepy but present. While it isn't easy at the end of a long workweek to do the same for my daughters, it's an important part of communicating for me to be serious about the rules they live by. The same is true when they have friends over. The presence of an awake and aware adult in the house is always important.

• Avoid negotiating on the fly. One-time exceptions can turn into standing rules all too easily. Instead of making exceptions under pressing circumstances, offer to sit down with your teen to review his or her boundaries and rules within the space of a few days.

• The most helpful parental attitude toward boundaries can be summed up in the old saying, "Trust God but tie your camel." Trust your teen to live within the structure you create, but keep your eyes and awareness open to the possibility that he or she will test them.

• If you are reluctant to use the term "rules" for fear of being too rigid, create a Family Respect Code. This code can articulate how you treat one another, in very specific terms.

• According to a study released by Public Agenda, 33 percent of adolescents say there is no adult at home when they return from school. It is my opinion that this amount of freedom is unsafe for our sons and daughters. Their power of discernment is simply not advanced enough to handle the options. Another study by Snyder and Sickmund found that the after school hours are when, "Violent juvenile crime peaks and when youth are most likely to experiment with alcohol, tobacco, drugs, and sex." Come up with a creative solution for after-school hours. Some possibilities are an ongoing babysitting job, volunteer work in the community, after-school programs, or doing homework in the local library. A group of parents in my town have arranged a casual but well supervised situation for their high school boys. They take turns supervising, once every two weeks for each parent, from the hours of three and six p.m. The boys hang out, play basketball, do homework, play chess, and are all accounted for. Expect your teenager, who thinks he is autonomous and self reliant, to rebel against this after-school monitoring. I urge you not to allow this to be the area in which you become too flexible.

• When creating a new limit or rule, ask yourself what exactly you are trying to teach your teen. Then, when you introduce the new limit, make sure to do so with casual conversation rather than heavy lectures. "You seem exhausted in the morning when I try to wake you up. I think we had better go back and discuss your evening commitments so you aren't dragging yourself to school." Or "Your math grade isn't looking so hot. I think we had better keep that car in the garage on weeknights and you with a math book open." Then follow through consistently with the limit you've established.

• Make an effort to understand and remain sensitive to your teen's temperament. Extroverts focus outward to gain energy—this is the kid who is jazzed by interacting with others. Introverts focus inward to gain energy—this teen might come home from school exhausted by the effort it took just to negotiate the halls of high school. It's tough in this culture for an introverted teenager to thrive as there is precious little time to pull away from the world out there and refuel. This teenager needs understanding parents. We might be inclined to say "Why are you wasting time just hanging out? Get out there and achieve something." What the introverted kid is doing is achieving balance—a necessity given his temperament, not a frivolity. We live in a world structured for extroverts yet studies show that there are three introverts for every one extrovert. Studies also show that extroverts do better in high school and on exams but introverts do better in college and graduate school.

Power and Consequences

"I wish my dad would punish me. It would be easier than having to live with what I did wrong." —Matt, fourteen

Natural consequences are different than contrived ones. Natural consequences always allow our teens to learn from their choices; the consequences we provide as parents may or may not teach our teens what we intend them to. It may depend on the age of the teen or the situation.

Ray, a father and stepfather of two, talks about his approach to consequences. "I don't ground Andy, who's seventeen, or take away privileges. If he makes a poor choice, we talk about it. I let him know that I'm disappointed in his decision and how it impacts our relationship. Last weekend, he spent the night at a house other than the one he told me he was going to. I only found out when another parent called me to see if her son had spent the night at our home. It slipped his mind, he said, to call me and let me know where he was going to be. I told him that didn't work for me and 'slipping his mind' wasn't an option in the future. He could tell me the truth or lie, but he'd never again 'forget' to call me. I'm lucky because the integrity of our relationship is really important to Andy. I think if I punished him, he could divert some of his own disappointment in his choices into being upset at the punishment I imposed. This way, he has to resolve his choice on his own, without being distracted by a consequence that I inflict."

Some parents find that imposing consequences is effective or necessary in certain circumstances. Another parent, the mother of a daughter who's now a young adult, puts it this way. "During her sixteenth summer, Annie really blew it. She threw a party in our home while my husband and I were out of town. She was supposed to be staying at her dad's house, but she told him she was sleeping over at a friend's.

"When I found out what had happened—the neighbors told me—I grounded her to her room and took away her phone privileges for a week. I forbade her to speak to any of the kids who'd come over until they apologized to us in person. They were old enough to know better, and her poor judgment didn't excuse them.

"She had to pay to have the locks changed, too, because I didn't know if she'd given a key to someone else. She had to quit her job, because I didn't trust her to be where she said she was going to be. After a week, she could leave the house for brief periods, but she had to be back exactly when we'd agreed on or she'd lose that privilege.

"It was really harsh and very hard for me to discipline her like that. I'd go in my room and cry. But I felt like I didn't have any choice. Her blatant disregard for the sanctity of our home was shocking."

Annie, now twenty, talks about the experience from her perspective. "I remember sitting on my bed in my room after my mom grounded me. I was so furious at her for taking my whole life away: no phone, no friends, I couldn't even go for a walk without her. Then I realized that it had been my entire fault. She didn't make the choice to have a party; I did. I had nobody to blame but myself.

"That was the low point for me, when I realized that I was to blame for the situation. But I had to get there to see that I needed to make different choices. My life started over that summer.

"The hardest thing I've ever done was to ask my mother to forgive me after I realized how big a mistake I'd made. What if she said she couldn't? But she just put her arms around me and held on tight. When she forgave me, I knew that I could eventually forgive myself."

The lesson Annie learned—that each one of us is responsible for our own behavior—is an important key to a happy and productive adult life. Depending on their temperament and the experiences of their lives, some teens learn this lesson more easily and some struggle with it for a little longer.

As teens mature, they're able to exercise more power in their lives. They flex their intellectual power inside and outside school, and they exercise their physical power in sports, recreational activities, and chores. It's an awesome thing to behold, the beauty of a fit young body at work.

Teenaged boys and girls struggle with their emerging personal power in different ways. Girls often aren't sure how powerful it's socially acceptable for them to become. They may dumb down or pretend to be less physically capable than they are.

"When I went to college, I realized that it was okay for me to be really smart. I can just say what I think straight out." —Maggie, nineteen

We do our teens a disservice if we dismiss or diminish their growing power. We can support their emerging capacities by acknowledging them and creating new and appropriate ways for them to express these new dimensions. By allowing them a greater role in household decision-making, for instance, they also gain insight into the realities of adult life, which include juggling multiple responsibilities.

"I make dinner once a week. I decide what we're eating, shop for the food, and cook it. Now I know what it's like for my parents to put dinner on the table after working all day." —**Heather, eighteen**

Yet the growing power of our teens can also make us uncomfortable.

"My oldest daughter and I both run. I used to have the edge in mileage, while she outpaced me. Not long ago, she upped her mileage past mine while maintaining her pace. I felt a definite twinge of jealousy as I realized she'd surpassed me, and I'd never catch up." —**Mother of three**

"My son's always been opinionated. As he got older, he started ranting. The topic didn't matter; he'd get red in the face and loud and invade my personal space." —**Jane, mother and stepmother of three**

Fathers and sons often grapple with power issues, too. Jane, the mother of three young adults quoted above, has more to say: "At fourteen, Brice tried the same behavior on his dad. His father asked him to settle down, but he didn't listen. So Jack got very loud and intimidating; I'd never seen him like that before. He kept walking toward Brice, who had to back up to avoid physical contact. Their faces were inches apart. He never touched Brice, but he literally backed him into a corner by yelling things like, 'Don't you talk to me that way.' I'd never seen that kind of behavior before, and it scared me to death. Later, Jack said he was letting Brice know that he was still the alpha dog."

I've heard a similar exchange described as "the old lion roaring back at the young one." Teenage boys begin to assert their male dominance as they mature. As their power increases, they naturally test the dominant adult in the household.

Jane concludes, "The young dog learns that they're going to have to leave to be top dog. Until then, they'll have to suck up."

A father who had a similar experience with his teenage son says, "I want my son to grow into a strong man. The best way for me to show him how to do that is to remain in charge until he leaves home. I'll roar louder than him every time."

To further explore the notions of power and consequences in your teen's life, consider doing one or more of the following:

- Examine your relationship with your teen for the presence of power struggles. Are you and your son or daughter at odds over a particular area of his or her life? Consider the possibility of disengaging from the power struggle and allowing the natural consequences of your child's choice to work in his or her life. Take a look at how you may be micromanaging or controlling your teen's behavior in order to see an end result that is your dream, not your child's.

- If it is necessary for you to impose consequences—"No going away for the weekend with your friend if you don't complete the overdue History homework," then be thoughtful about the arrangement so that it is logical and seen as something other than a punishment. Not going away for the weekend means that he can spend that time completing the homework.

- Ask for Divine assistance as a parent. *Dear God, help me make the right decisions here. Help me to see how I can parent my child most effectively right now. I trust in Your Divine, ever-present support and help, and I commit to following Your guidance.*

- As parents, we often have to discriminate between reactions that are based on our own unresolved emotional issues and those that are founded on the realities of our teens' lives. Are you uncomfortable with some of the ways in which your teen is exercising his or her power? If you're unsure whether to support particular behaviors or not, ask for help. Talk the situation over with your Spiritual Parenting Group, phone a friend whose parenting skills you admire, set up a quiet time to talk about this issue with your partner. Include prayer in your daily life. *Spirit, I release this situation into your hands. You move through me, providing the awareness and inspiration I yearn for. I rely on You as my partner in parenting my child.* And, if you are still feeling confused, make an appointment to speak with a therapist or counselor. Having a professional at the ready to support you as you raise a teen is a wonderful resource.

Flexible Spirituality

We can also give our teens the benefits of flexibility in terms of spirituality. My friend Caroline insisted that her younger daughter, who was fourteen at the time, attend one organized religious service each week. That structure was important to her. However, she let her teen pick where, when, and with whom for a year or two. Her daughter Lindsey attended the youth group at a church where one of her friends attended. Caroline would have preferred that Lindsey attend church with their family, but she recognized the value in allowing her daughter to forge her own spiritual path. Eventually, Lindsey rejoined the family.

One father of a teen who was uncomfortable with the religious services of his family said, "Gregg, when you're sixteen-years-old, you can decide if you want to come to church with us." Not surprisingly, Gregg decided he didn't want to continue attending. After six months or so, he rather sheepishly admitted that he missed seeing some of the kids from his youth group who attended schools other than his. Gregg's attendance was sporadic, but when he was given the freedom to choose, he decided to come at least part of the time.

The Amish have an interesting and extreme way of creating a flexible spiritual structure. In the film *Devil's Playground,* documentary filmmaker Lucy Walker highlights the flexibility the strict Amish society gives their teens in a rite of passage called *rumspringa.* At 16, Amish teenagers are allowed the freedom to explore the customs of the outside, non-Amish world before deciding whether to be baptized in the Amish church, which takes place as a young adult and is a lifetime commitment. Reneging on this commitment invokes the punishment of shunning, in which all members of the Amish community, including parents and spouses, scrupulously avoid contact with the individual.

Rumspringa is not a choice that Amish teens make lightly. And they have the opportunity to explore all that the outside world offers, including sex, drugs, and alcohol. One teen ends up addicted to crystal methamphetamine; another lives for months in a trailer. The parents of these teens are unaware of the extent to which their children are experimenting with English life.

However, Walker also captures the struggle that these teens undergo; they're not partying just for a party's sake. They're involved in an experience that will determine the course of their lives. Teens must decide what they want to believe and how they want to live. Some leave the church. But, somewhat amazingly, the vast majority of the teenagers—85 to 90 percent—return to the close knit communities from which they came. *Rumspringa* ends when a teen decides to rejoin the Amish community for life or live in the English world.

I'm not comfortable with the unlimited freedom that *rumspringa* gives to sixteen-year-olds, and I doubt it's a model that applies outside a community as cohesive as the Amish. However, there's wisdom in allowing teens to make their own spiritual choices—to being spiritually flexible.

My daughter Elizabeth is deep into writing a "Taking a Stand" paper for her English class. She's been thinking about, researching, and discussing capital punishment. She listens to NPR, reads the newspaper, launches into dinner discussions with us, and debates with her friends during carpool. I, a supportive observer, happen to be deep into my own thinking about this chapter, creating a flexible structure with our teens. Our processes mesh synergistically, proving once again that there are no coincidences.

Elizabeth wants to use religion as a basis for defending her stand against capital punishment. To do so, she explored religious beliefs as expressed in sacred texts. She looked in the Bible, then the Torah, then the Koran. We became engaged in numerous discussions about sacred texts and the nature of our freedom as spiritual seekers and thinkers.

From a fundamentalist perspective, regardless of the text, holy words are sacrosanct in themselves and literally interpreted. An eye for an eye surely means that murder justifies the taking of a life. Yet, I watch Elizabeth grapple with how inconsistent this is with the fifth commandment that Moses received on Mount Sinai: "Thou shalt not kill."

We both have great respect for the sacred texts of Christianity, Judaism, Islam, and other world religions. What we have grown together to understand, launched by this writing assignment, is that we find meaning not by automatically accepting sacred words, but from hewing our own thoughtful interpretations and drawing on the wisdom of many authors who share their inspiration with us. I watch my teen begin to think deeply on her own; bolstered by her research, to fit the sacred texts to her personal morals.

Elizabeth won't experience *rumspringa*. But she does have the freedom to decide what she wants to believe in, and, like the Amish teens who run wild for a few weeks or months, she's in the process of choosing the beliefs that will underlie the rest of her life.

To further investigate the notion of spiritual flexibility in your teen's life, you could:

- Consider if your teen's interest is flagging in certain spiritually related activities. Is he or she slow to get up for church and sullenly silent on the way there? This is pretty typical behavior for many teens. Do evaluate, however, your stance on religious attendance. Mandating religious participation isn't necessarily the best way to ensure that your child's spirit is nurtured. Consider options. Perhaps you might work with your religious community to allow kids to create an alternative service, or encourage your adolescent to invite a friend to join her at church or temple. Is there a way that your teen could become more involved in the service such as reading or singing in the choir?

- Discriminate between your fears about your adolescent's spiritual growth and the reality of his or her life. While church or youth group can seem like a lifeline to a parent, many teens have a well-developed sense of spiritual identity and will enjoy an occasional break from regular attendance.

• Discuss with your teen alternatives for meeting his spiritual needs. There's truth to the power of two or more meeting for a spiritual purpose—we often find the richest experiences in community with others. For that reason, some type of group experience often brings the greatest benefits. A yoga class, a meditation seminar, attending youth group with a friend, or regular community service can offer powerful spiritual sustenance. Your teenager may benefit more from an activity that he chooses than from compulsory family activities.

• There is also great comfort in a weekly religious service. If we've helped our teen develop a spiritual habit, even when it sometimes might be tough to show up, we give them the tool of discipline and perseverance. In turn, they will have that spiritual habit to fall back on when their spirits sag.

• Articulate your spiritual bottom lines. These beliefs can include specifics such as "I believe in abstinence until marriage because I think that sex is a beautiful act between husband and wife and because our religion states that belief." Or "Because I believe that our bodies are sacred vessels for our spirits, I don't think it's okay to overindulge in food or alcohol." Many teens have told me that using their religious beliefs as their excuse for not partaking in alcohol or drugs is a great out. Fifteen-year-old Susan remarked, "I just say, 'No thanks, I don't do weed because of my religion.' Kids are cool with that."

Provide a Solid Springboard Together

"In marriage, being the right person is as important as finding the right person."
—Wilbert Donald Gough

Teens—and all children—thrive in the presence of a stable, loving relationship between the adults in the household. We nurture their souls when they feel a happy partnership between two biological parents, a biological parent and a stepparent, two adoptive parents, one adoptive parent and a partner—any of the myriad combinations of adults who shelter and rear teens.

As with every other aspect of family life, the relationship between adults serves as a powerful model for a teen. He or she learns what adult love looks like by watching us interact with our partners.

When teens know that their parents' emotional needs are being met through adult relationships, they feel more free to fully separate, to move into their own lives unburdened by worries about the parents they're leaving behind.

While these are good reasons to pay attention to your marriage or relationship for your teen's sake, they aren't the most important reasons to do so.

You have more to give to your life when your own needs are being met. Also, your children will eventually move out of the house, leaving you and your partner alone together again. The busy-ness of raising a family is compelling, but it can't substitute for a strong and vital relationship between adults.

As a mother of four sons who are now adults puts it, "Once the boys were raised, we had to come up with activities that we could do together, it wasn't easy. Our lives had been so full with four sons that we had to find ways to be together when we weren't focused on them. It was either that or grow apart."

Life with teens is full of activities. Our houses may seem overrun with youthful energy and enthusiasm. Now, more than ever, we have to carve out time for each other and create a structure flexible enough to sustain our adult relationships. Following are some ideas for sustaining your romantic relationship while parenting teens:

- Laugh together. Humor is a healing elixir, drawing people close and clearing the air. Share a joke, rent a comedy on DVD, or attend a funny play. The teen years are particularly important ones for cultivating a shared sense of humor with your partner.

• Set up times to articulate your shared goals and dreams. Don't think of these meetings as dates, because it's too easy to erase a date from your calendar to create more time. Think of these times as planning sessions.

• Take the long view. During the years we raise children, we're also building careers, homes, and financial security. It's easy to get caught up in the moment-to-moment drama, but lasting relationships are best viewed over the long haul.

• Banish the television. Many couples find more time for each other when they eliminate the mindless evening entertainment that the tube provides. Scale back distractions and use the quiet time to be together.

• Learn the fine art of tolerance. My husband is a master at this. He rarely criticizes me and, believe me, there is plenty to criticize. If you must draw attention to your spouse's behavior, do so lovingly and without making it a personal issue. 'I' statements, rather than 'you' accusations, are a good basic strategy.

• Many readers over the years have written to say that they've used the principles in my book *10 Principles for Spiritual Parenting* with their spouses, turning it into *10 Principles for Spiritual Relationships*. You might be inspired to go through this book with an eye for how you could apply each principle to your adult relationship.

• Remember and nurture the feelings you and your partner had for each other initially. It's all too easy to forget these in the face of laundry to be folded, college financial aid forms to fill out, and fallen leaves piling up on the lawn. What was it about your partner that first attracted you? Look for the presence of these endearing qualities in the face that's grown as familiar as your own.

• Every family experiences challenges: financial pressures, illness, job loss, in-laws living with you, or any one of a number of other stressors. Despite the images portrayed by the media, no family is perfect. Avoid placing blame when you're feeling the pressure. Pull together to move through the pain.

• If you share a hobby or interest, you're blessed. If you don't, find one and schedule time to enjoy it together. A friend of my daughter's says she knows there's trouble between her parents when they don't play much golf together.

• When we have been in a marriage or partnership for some years, our reactions to our partner might become habitual. Try to see your significant other in a fresh new light. By doing so, you give your teenager a wonderful example of how to live fully present in the moment with someone they love. Also, by shifting your behavior towards one member of your family, you will begin to let go of old assumptions and reactions within all your relationships.

Parents who are flexibly firm have clear expectations and set clear limits for their teens. They provide a stable foundation for their child to develop into a loving, responsible adult. The effort and time it takes to follow through consistently in our teens' lives pays off in ways we may not fully appreciate at the time. We—and they—will definitely appreciate our efforts many years down the road.

Parents' Insight-Building Exercise

Find a quiet place where you won't be disturbed for a few minutes. Unplug the phone and settle into a chair with your back well-supported. Take off your shoes and place your feet flat on the floor.

Inhale deeply and exhale slowly several times. Notice the chair supporting the weight of your upper body and thighs. Spread your toes and relax them, allowing your feet to be supported by the floor they're resting on.

Imagine yourself as the trunk of a great tree, a majestic oak or redwood. Your body from the waist up is the beginning of an enormous system of limbs and branches that extends far above you, hundreds of feet into the sky. Imagine the sun warming your leaves and the rain gently cleansing them.

Your body from the waist down is the topmost part of a huge root system that extends far into the ground below you. Imagine each root spiraling down into the earth, drawing nourishment and strength from the soil. Breathe deeply into your belly and feel it fill with the earth's strength.

Pay attention to the grace and power that infuses your limbs. Around you, life moves at a blistering pace, but you stand serene, a compassionate witness.

Now bring your teen to mind. Notice his or her youth—a sapling compared to you. The years have given you strength that he or she doesn't yet possess. You have wisdom that he or she has yet to understand. Your strength and height give you a majestic perspective.

Notice how your branches sway in the wind, easily adapting to the changes around you. Notice, too, how your appearance changes with the changing seasons as you move gracefully through the years.

Now notice that your teen cannot move you, no matter how hard he or she pushes. You provide shade and shelter for your child in your strength.

Feel this strength infuse you fully, your arms and legs, back and shoulders. Simply rest in this awareness for as long as you'd like.

When you're ready to return to the room around you, take a deep breath and release it. This experience of strength is available to you whenever you like.

Parents' Check-In Questions

- This week, when have I pulled back from my role as parent in order to keep my teen's approval or acceptance?

- How much does my teen know about the part of my emotional life that doesn't pertain to him or her? Do I share confidences about things that are beyond what he or she needs or wants to know?

- What does my repertoire of loving behaviors include? How have I spent time with my teen this week? Do I substitute material things for affection? Am I placating my teen with words or actions?

- What are my true bottom lines for my teen's behavior? Are his or her boundaries consistent with them? Am I overlooking or tolerating behavior that I don't like?

- Have I negotiated a boundary that I didn't want to? Under what circumstances can my teen convince me to change my mind? If there are other teens there? If I'm preoccupied?

- Are there areas where I'm ready for the natural consequences of my teen's behavior to take effect? What do I need to do to support myself? Can I discern between consequences that teach and those that might be too damaging?

- What rules did I push against as a teen? How did my parents handle that rebellion? Was it effective? How did the rules influence my relationship then with my parents?

- What have my partner and I done this week to nurture our relationship? What can I do today to strengthen our sense of connection?

Conversation Starters

Teens are so busy that it's hard to find time to talk. However, working side by side in the house or yard can provide a chance to find out more about what your son or daughter thinks. Start a conversation with one or more of the following:

- What do I do that most communicates that I care about you?

- If you had a teen your age, what would you do differently than I'm doing?

• What are you most looking forward to about being an adult man (or woman)? What are you least looking forward to?

• Who among your friends do you think has the shortest leash? Who has too much freedom?

• What privileges do you feel like you're getting ready to take on? What responsibilities will you take on at the same time?

Be What You Want to See

"My parents are the most spiritual people I know. They never forced me to believe anything, but showed me the truth with their lives. They didn't just idly believe in something, they lived it." **—Sophie, nineteen**

"My dad tells me to be home on time, but he's never anywhere when he says he's going to be. He can't get that mad at me." **—Matt, seventeen**

• • •

We've heard it a million times: Actions speak louder than words. Whoever coined this phrase must have been the parent of a teen. We have no greater influence on our adolescents than through our own actions and reactions.

Carl Gustav Jung, one of the great thinkers of the twentieth century, who developed a new vision of the human mind, said, "If there is anything we wish to change in the child, we should first examine it and see whether it is not something that could better be changed in ourselves." We do have to take a big dose of responsibility for our teen's behavior.

A study by Teenage Research Unlimited found that 70 percent of teenagers name their mom or dad as the person they most admire. I've found, from my own experience and in talking with hundreds of teens, that *who we are* is much more important than *what we say* during these years. Our children may be less willing to listen to our words of wisdom, but they learn volumes from observing us, even when we think they're not paying attention.

In particular, when we value our own spiritual development by carving out time to nurture our souls, our children see spiritual discovery as a way to live. Parents who are grateful, prayerful, kind, and attuned to the sacred tend to produce kids who are much the same.

We may find that it is easier to be attuned to the sacred when we're sitting in meditation or relaxing in a warm tub. Life, though, has a way of throwing us curve balls—and how we handle those is key to what our teens learn about managing the inevitable conflict in their everyday lives.

Nonviolence and Forgiveness

Nonviolence has the potential to transform our world—and it starts in our own hearts. Mahatma Gandhi and Dr. Martin Luther King, Jr. were avatars of nonviolence, and their teachings have inspired millions of people around the world.

Nonviolence on the individual level is the practice of bringing Spirit into interpersonal conflict. We have ample opportunities to explore this concept. According to an article in *Science and Health* magazine, Princeton sociologist Robert Wuthnow found that 37 percent of adults have recently had serious conflicts with a spouse or partner, 36 percent are moving past something painful in their upbringing, and 32 percent face serious conflicts at work.

How we handle strife is an important learning experience for our teenage children. They, too, have countless opportunities for conflict—with us, siblings, friends and acquaintances, teammates, teachers, and others—and they learn how to handle these tensions by observing their parents.

How often we're tempted to struggle! Wanting to be right, to win, we choose to push on, escalating conflict to the point where it threatens to become all-consuming. Or, more subtly, we invite others to side with us, validating our sense of injustice or being wronged. These responses often arise as naturally and unconsciously as the impulse to breathe. And, in innumerable ways, our culture validates our primal impulse toward retaliation.

However, in his wise book, *The Parent's Tao Te Ching*, William Martin reminds us that difficulties are overcome only by yielding. He suggests that we become like water and embrace the hardest things of life, enfolding them with our hearts. Many of us already take this approach. In the article mentioned above, Wuthnow also found that 60 percent of adults are trying to forgive someone else and nearly half are trying to forgive themselves.

There is no lesson our teens can learn from us that is more important than avoiding the self-inflicted pain and suffering of anger towards others. As we accept that conflict is part and parcel of human existence and forgive actual or perceived wrongdoing, our breath comes more easily and our hearts beat more steadily. Our teens clearly see the difference between a parent who's at peace and one who's perturbed. We create the opportunity for them to witness the truth of a lesson they might not often hear in the world outside our homes—that conflict is a time to engage the soul's qualities and detach from the ego's desire to win or wreak vengeance.

Bob, father of seventeen-year-old Justin, reflects on the challenge of modeling nonviolence to his son.

"Frankly, my first impulse isn't always to let things go. Particularly if I think someone's mistreated my son, I want to get right in there, loud and strong. But that isn't the way I want my son to grow up—taking offense at everything and fighting back. If I had to choose between Justin being right as an adult male or feeling peace, I'd choose peace.

"I know nonviolence and forgiveness are the only way to really find peace. So I turn to God when I have a problem with someone. I *want* to forgive them, for my own peace of mind and for what my son is learning from me about being a man. Right now, I don't see much evidence that Justin gets it, but I hope he will someday."

Teens and adults alike can confuse forgiving with being weak. Reverend Michael Moran, cofounder of the Spiritual Life Center in Sacramento, California, notes the difference between forgiveness and being a doormat. "You can simultaneously forgive someone and take steps to make sure that something never happens again. Forgiving a behavior is not the same thing as condoning it."

The responsibility for creating a parent-child relationship that is relatively relaxed and respectful, rather than tension-filled, rests primarily on us, the parents. The best way to stop constant negativity, nagging, fighting, and yelling is to not allow it or engage in it. When our teens are consistently angry and unable to practice forgiveness the first thing we might do is look within ourselves and adjust our own behavior. We can accept that we have a part to play in his dance with anger without becoming immobile with guilt. We can take action and focus on the opposite of anger—peace, forgiveness, and nonviolence.

To increase your repertoire of nonviolent and forgiveness skills, you might try some of the following:

- When you notice you're ready to jump into the fray of an active conflict, pause and go to higher ground. A subscriber to my parenting newsletter told me the following story: "I was once stuck in a long fast-food drive-through line because I was driving a large SUV filled with friends and family, adults and children. Our order was complicated and completing it took a long time . . . and the Super Bowl football game was due to start in about ten minutes. The guy in the car behind mine looked so angry, I thought he might have a stroke before he got to the window. He made a rude gesture toward our car. I mentioned to my friend that *his* response was making *me* angry. She suggested that, instead of getting angry, we pay for his order as well as ours when we got to the window. We did, then watched as he pulled up to the window. His jaw dropped open, the girl in the window pointed to us, and we waved. Where I had been feeling really angry a few moments before, I was laughing with sheer joy."

- Look for alternative explanations for behaviors that strike you as unjust or hurtful. Since we all see the world through a highly individual lens, we seldom accurately perceive what might be happening to cause another person's actions. We simply don't know what is going on in someone else's life, and their actions aren't always about us. Another story from a newsletter reader: "A couple of years ago, my younger daughter ran next door to invite a neighbor to come over and hang out. She returned in tears, hurt because her friend had ignored the ringing of the doorbell. When I suggested that Kylie might not be allowed to answer the door if she was home alone, Emily relaxed, recalling the lack of cars in the driveway. A simple example, to be sure, but one that made me wonder how often I take offense when none is intended."

• Affirmative prayer is another tool for moving toward nonviolence. *I know that You, Dear One, are infinitely loving. As I turn my attention to You, I experience a willingness to forgive. I find peace by embracing that impulse.*

• Acknowledge your own struggles when handling conflict. No one said just because you were a parent that you weren't allowed to feel angry. Teens have acutely tuned antennae, and they know when a calm facade covers up a seething interior. Handling conflict, for many of us, is a lifelong struggle between our lower and higher selves. Teens benefit from knowing that they're not alone in experiencing the pull from opposing internal forces: one that leads us deeper into strife, and one that leads us to peace. Because teens can be self-absorbed, they may mistakenly assume your gurgling anger is a result of something they did. Remaining honest and communicating with our kids shows them how to be in relationship with those we love. Part of that honesty is letting our teens know when they make us angry and assuring them that regardless, we will always love them.

• Forgiveness isn't a final state; it's a fluid practice. I'm grateful that, as yet, I haven't had to apply it as many times as the Bible suggests I might: seventy times seven (Matthew 18:21, 22). However, it is true that I often have to repeatedly forgive the same people for the same injuries to find peace.

• Often the hardest person to forgive is ourselves. We are ruthless when evaluating our role as parents. We willingly believe that our children's pain or faults are caused by our shortcomings in the parenting department. What kind of message does this give to our kids? Remind yourself that you aren't responsible for satisfying your teenager's every whim or wish. You are enough, just as you are, even when you say "No" or "Not now" or "Do it yourself" or "You'll have to pay for it." Have a frank discussion with your teenager and let him know that what he sees is what he gets—a parent who loves him and can only give so much. Show your teen a parent who forgives herself, then moves on.

• It often helps to get your hands quite literally on a problem. When you are ready to release old hurts, grab some index cards. Write on each one the name of anyone who has caused you pain in your lifetime. Put the cards in three piles arranged from least hurtful memories to most painful. Now, beginning with the pile that has the least emotional zing, go through and hold each card. Can you forgive and let go? If so, rip up the card and symbolically let it go. Take the remaining cards and determine if there is any action you might take to resolve the friction. If so, make yourself a list of "to do's." Next, place those remaining cards in a spot where you can see them when you have quiet prayer time. As you pray, include each person on the card in your prayers.

Acceptance

"I think of life as terribly rich. At times, the experience of living it is terribly painful. But it seems to me that those moments also open my heart to the wonder of how rich it can be." —**Larry, father of one**

Let's face it. No matter what prayers I pray or intentions I set, I've never been able to control the events of my life. Disappointment is inevitable. Heartbreak happens. I can only control how I respond.

We choose whether we view chaos, disappointment, or pain—over relationships, money, career, health, to name just a few—as booby traps, catastrophes, stumbling blocks, or bumps in the road. We can bemoan our fate or give our teens the gift of an adult who finds serenity within the sorrow and remains grounded when the ground seems to quake beneath us.

Even in the middle of a conflict, we can choose to accept what's going on, rather than fight back. As one mother of two teens puts it, "My whole life as a parent changed when I realized that my oldest son just wanted to argue. He mostly wanted to express an opinion that was different than mine. I thought he was trying to get me to change my mind, so his arguing caused me all kinds of stress as I tried to come up with more and more reasons to justify my position. Now I know I can just listen. I don't have to change my mind or convince him to see things my way. The stress evaporated."

Sometimes, we're called to accept situations that seem more permanent or important than transient disagreements. As our teens mature, their personalities and preferences can run counter to our expectations. A father with an extremely successful career speaks eloquently about his nineteen-year-old daughter's choices: "We sent Shelby to a very competitive and well-regarded prep school. She struggled to maintain a B average; I was proud of her efforts. She was turned down or wait-listed at all her first-choice colleges, though, which was a shock.

"She entered a state university. Her GPA wasn't great, and she became increasingly miserable. She even developed relatively severe physical symptoms. I discounted this for almost a full year, until I finally acquiesced to her request to transfer to a community college closer to home. Even before she transferred, her grades improved and her illness resolved. The irony here is that I'm prepared to send her to any college she chooses. I thought she'd be more ambitious, like me."

I know of a woman, Jean, whose youngest daughter became pregnant during her sophomore year in high school. Teen pregnancy is definitely not a pattern in this devout Catholic family. Jean is a high school math teacher who's been married to her attorney husband for almost thirty years. Ashley, the young mother, is the youngest of five children; her siblings all graduated from college and embarked on successful careers.

This family's response to what was most definitely a heartbreaking disappointment is inspiring. Ashley's family—as well as the baby's father and *his* family—helped with childcare and expenses while she finished her GED and worked full time to build up savings. She enrolled at a state university, where she was able to take advantage of subsidized child care and start classes. She actually entered college the same year that her high school peers did, albeit under very different circumstances.

It's a spiritual discipline to simultaneously hold a vision of the potential we believe our children have and honor the reality of their lives. This family did it beautifully.

How might you find serenity and accept difficulties that threaten to turn your life upside-down? You can begin by dipping into your spiritual well, simplifying your life, focusing on keeping your words kind and honest, and allowing the love and essential innocence of your teenagers to fill your heart. These choices mirror a powerful message to your sons and daughters.

You can also try some of the following:

• Cultivate a "response-meter mentality." When you begin to feel angry or fearful that the emotional meter is moving toward "Hot," pause before responding. Make this a little longer than the old count-to-ten trick you used with your toddlers. Wait for your immediate reaction to dissipate and allow other interpretations or implications of the situation to reveal themselves to you. This approach takes practice when you're parenting a teen. Once you've developed it as a habit, however, you will find a subtle sense of calm seeping into your household. Share this response-meter habit with your teens. This is a time in their lives when big emotions can rule their feelings and their responses can have lasting consequences.

• Act "as if." We often wait to feel calm or loving to take calm or loving actions. In truth, though, feelings *follow* actions. This tactic isn't about denying our feelings; rather, we assume an attitude to experience the feelings that would accompany it. So engage your imagination in a stressful situation. How would you act if you *weren't* upset, fearful, or angry? What would your body language be like? What would you say? Where would you find the humor? Throw this suggestion your teen's way when she is feeling left out or "less than." How would she act, for example, if she had as many meaningful and enjoyable friendships as she wanted? Where would she find the humor in life if failing to make the basketball team didn't matter?

• Keep things in perspective. If you are apt to fall apart over the little things, your teen might also face problems in this way. One version of an old joke about keeping a healthy perspective goes like this:

Dear Mom and Dad,

I'm very sorry for not having written before. I'll bring you up to date about my life at college, but before you read on, please sit down.

First, I'm doing much better. The skull fracture I got when I jumped out of my window during the dorm fire healed well. My doctor assures me the blindness is temporary. In fact, I think I saw a little light just this morning.

Fortunately, a clerk at the convenience store across the street saw the fire and my jump. Rick called the ambulance and came to visit me at the hospital. One thing led to another, and we fell in love. I'm engaged! Of course, we're putting off the wedding until I can see. We haven't set the exact date yet, but it will be before I start to show.

Yes, we're expecting, too! I know how much you're looking forward to being grand-parents, and I know you'll give our baby the same tender care you gave me when I was a child. As soon as I graduate, Rick and I will be ready to be full-time parents ourselves.

Now that I've brought you up to date, I want to tell you that there was no fire, I did not have a concussion or skull fracture, I was not in the hospital, and I'm not pregnant, engaged, or blind. However, I am getting a D in History and in Biology.

Love,

Me

Compassion and Consideration

"If I could change one thing about my life, I'd take back all the hate I've 'distributed.'" **—Ellen, thirteen**

"I realized I couldn't lecture my kids about kindness. They had to see it in action. I try to go the extra mile to reach out in my daily life."

—Betsey, mother of four

Everything we do in relation to another person informs our teens about how they relate to people now—and in the future. Everything we do with and to each other is a spiritual act. How does our teen see us acting toward our life partner, our parents, our friends, neighbors, our boss or employees, and strangers who cross our path? How do we treat the hundreds of people we encounter in places like shopping malls, grocery store check out counters, or airport security lines?

In a recent workshop I gave, a woman attendee expressed sorrow over the lack of respect her nineteen-year-old daughter showed her. "She doesn't call or write or even seem to care that I exist except to pay her college tuition," my new acquaintance said. When I asked her about her own relationship with her mother, she launched into a litany of her mother's innumerable faults and the ways she had been wronged by her mother. No surprise, then, that this lack of regard is exactly the treatment she received from her own adult child.

Conversely, nothing gives me greater joy as a parent than seeing my daughters being kind to one another. I feel deeply moved when I watch them share secrets, clothing, and respect. When they compliment each other, snuggle on the couch and chat, surprise one another with a cup of hot cocoa on a cold New England morning, my heart soars.

In relationships of all kinds, between parents and children and among siblings, in adult friendships, loving relationships, business partnerships, and lifetime commitments, compassion and consideration are hallmarks of strong character. They are the natural outgrowth of deeply respecting the people, the ones we know personally and the ones we don't, with whom we share the experience of life.

With compassion, we suspend judgement on the words and actions of others, trying instead to imagine what it feels like to be in their place. We focus on the similarities between human beings, rather than the differences.

Compassion is an important quality that we can bring to the lives of our teens. They struggle with so much on a daily basis, trying on new responsibilities and grappling with new pressures; we don't need to compound their stress by being cold or unkind.

Take a moment and think back to yourself at your teenager's current age and your compassion level will inevitably go up. The old saying "These teenage years are the best years of your life" is not always true. Sitting alone at lunch, feeling out of place in class, lacking a date for the prom, suffering through acne, being the focus of jokes, missing the winning basket are just the short list of painful situations teens may face. We aren't able to take our children's pain away or make their environment less hostile, but our compassion for them is a key to making these years a little better.

When we mirror compassion for our teens, we emphasize kindness. I believe there are no circumstances that require unkind words. Compassion is compatible with mistakes, even grievous ones.

> "My stepson ran a stop sign while adjusting the radio in his car and broadsided another vehicle. I thank God no one was hurt. He'd been pretty cocky about driving, and, frankly, I think he was due for a lesson about humility. However, one of the only things I said to him about it was, 'Well, I guess we all make mistakes. That could have been so much worse.' I knew he'd have to pay for the ticket and the damage, and he didn't need me to rub it in." —**Stepmother of two**

Like nonviolence, compassion may not get much "air time" in the world our teens inhabit outside our home. Our role as parents is to demonstrate kindness rather than just talk about it. How do we respond when we learn that someone's in need?

> "My boys know that if the school asks for assistance for a family who's experienced a hardship or starts a food drive for the family shelter in our town, we'll participate. They don't even ask anymore. They just tell me what they'd like to take to help." —**Jane, mother of two**

Compassion is a necessary component of setting boundaries with our teens. When we hold a bottom line, steadfast and loving, they learn volumes about how to maintain their own boundaries with others. Firm doesn't have to mean unfriendly.

When we learn that our teen's friend is going through a tough time and respond appropriately, with words of sympathy, a hug, or a warm meal, our kids learn that we care about people who are important to the people we love.

"The parents of one of our son's friends are going through an ugly divorce. Whenever Rob comes over, even when Sam's out, we invite him in, offer him something to eat, and listen to what's on his mind. I figure it's important for him to have a place to go to and to see a home where the adults really care for each other. Maybe, years down the road, he'll remember what he felt here when he's thinking about starting his own family." —**Ann, mother of two**

Consideration is the partner of compassion in relationships. Compassion helps us understand how someone else might feel; consideration means we act on that awareness.

For instance, when I go out, I call home to say I arrived safely, as does my husband. We don't want anyone to worry. As a result, our children thoughtfully do the same. They check in often to let us know their schedules, where they are, and when they'd like to be picked up. Cell phones make this kind of ongoing communication easy.

We may need to remind our teens of the impact of their choices on the rest of the household. At the same time, we can let them know that we're aware that *they* experience the effects of some of our choices. "I'm trying to write a letter and your music is distracting. If you'll turn it down, I'll let you know when I'm done so you can crank it back up."

No parent is perfect. We've all had moments of standing at the top or bottom of a flight of stairs and yelling, "Turn it down!" or mumbling under our breath or grumbling to our partner about what an inconsiderate so-and-so that teenager is. In my experience, that's exactly the moment to check into my own recent behavior toward my teens.

If I've been harried or impatient, focused on what I need or want in my personal or work life, chances are I'll shortly see that same kind of self-absorption reflected in my daughters' words and actions. On the other hand, if I'm aware of how my behavior impacts my family and adjust it or explain it accordingly, I can expect that my daughters will follow suit.

At times, parental behavior can facilitate a teen's ingratitude attitude. The kid who rarely expresses gratitude or consideration is generally the one for whom the parents have willingly stepped into the roles of servants. Examine your life and determine if you have allowed yourself to become all things to your son or daughter—chef, laundress, bed-maker, computer technician, taxi driver, homework helper, and bank—without expecting reciprocal behavior. Your child isn't thankful, because he hasn't been taught that what you do requires gratitude.

There's only one key to consideration, and we all know it by heart. "Do unto others as you would have them do unto you." It's as true between a mid-forties parent and one or two teenagers as it was way back in kindergarten.

To explore the idea of mirroring compassion and consideration for your teen, you could:

• Embark on a family service commitment. Our friends the Wilsons serve a holiday meal at the downtown homeless shelter every year. Far from resenting giving up their afternoon, the Wilson teens wouldn't miss it. Another family we know returns each year to the same village in Honduras to offer help. The people in that village have become a part of their extended family.

• Choose a nonprofit human service organization to sponsor as a family. Particularly during the late fall, requests for donations often fill the mailbox. Collect them, spread them out on the kitchen table, and invite the whole family to participate in choosing one to support consistently. Let your teen make the checks out and contribute some of his own money if appropriate.

• Give an anonymous gift to someone you're having difficulty with. Leave a care package, a plant, or a bunch of daffodils on their front porch. Encourage your teen to consider how he or she could help, in secret, someone from whom they're feeling estranged.

• Consider sharing readings on compassion with your teen. The Dalai Lama, Mother Teresa, Pema Chödrön, and Gail Straub have all written eloquently on developing compassion.

• Identify an inconsiderate behavior on your teen's part. Does he or she do something that bugs you a lot or a little? Now, get scrupulously honest. Where did he or she learn it? I once heard the following story from a workshop participant: "One day my daughter, who was then thirteen, spoke to her dad in the most inconsiderate way I could imagine. Her tone of voice was terrible; she spoke to him as if he were an idiot. He dealt with it at the time, but I later went to her and asked the perennial parent question, '*Where* did you learn to talk to your dad like that?' In all honesty and innocence, she replied, 'From you.' I had to admit that was true—she did learn it from me. From that moment on, I vowed to never speak to anyone like that again, especially not my husband."

• Adolescents can often act as a barometer of how their parents' relationship is functioning. Observe how this might be true in your life and make an effort to show more compassion to your partner.

• Think of yourself as an instrument of God. Allow the qualities of a loving God to demonstrate through you as compassion, peace, and patience in your relationships with all the people in your life. Include these words in your daily round: *God, make me an instrument of your peace. Move through me as compassion, empathy, peace, patience, and love.*

Integrity

"Kids look for honesty, so I try to be honest in all walks of life."

—Chuck, father of four

"Lots of adults are hypocrites."   **—Justin, seventeen**

Teens crave models of integrity. Unfortunately, what they find in the media are stories about adults who lack it, from executives who misuse corporate funds to politicians who use semantics to evade personal responsibility and religious leaders who abuse their power.

Poor integrity among their peers surrounds them, too. In a recent *Campus Life* magazine survey, 80 percent of the readers admitted to cheating. Most acknowledged having done so only once or seldomly, but only 6 percent of respondents said they'd never cheated in school.

Integrity is the backbone of the trust that makes for solid relationships. As we model integrity for our teens, they learn how to build character into their connections with others as well as their reactions in all areas of life.

This character building has to come from us, because there's a character crisis in our culture. Character building is not tied to success, so we dismiss it as irrelevant. We might even back away from imposing consequences on our teens when they do something wrong because "They already have so much stress in their lives" or "It might impact his chances for the right college" or "How would others view me?" But character is formed by making mistakes and experiencing hardship, not by observing your parents working behind the scenes to manipulate events. Life is confusing enough for our kids. It used to be clear what was right and wrong; now there are lots of shades of gray. Fostering kids with strong characters means taking a stand for what is right, regardless of the personal embarrassment.

Integrity is a cornerstone of self-esteem. Most of us at one time or another have told a half-truth or an outright lie. I've experienced my own choices to deceive someone as a separation from who I know God planned me to be, from the person I know I'm capable of bringing to the world. I'm disappointed in myself.

As parents of teens, we can help our loved and lovely young people avoid adding the burden of disappointment in themselves to the self-esteem challenges they face every day. As we show them what it means to live a life of integrity, they can choose that path, too—and reap the rewards of living a life aligned with the truest impulses that God creates in all of our hearts.

Culturally, we recognize and honor integrity in people who blow the whistle on shady corporate practices or return found money. Integrity is expressed by thousands of small decisions rather than a single newsworthy choice.

Do we return extra change or pocket it as a windfall from the universe? Do we tell our teens to say we aren't home when someone we don't want to talk to calls? Are we quick to suggest that our high school senior hire a writer for her college application essays? When it comes to income taxes, are all our deductions strictly legal or do we fudge a little? Do we pretend to be sick when we need a day off from work? The list of situations in which we can choose to act with integrity—or not—goes on and on. Our teens are watching us make these choices.

A situation that many parents of teens find perplexing is how to address risky behaviors in our teens when we've done the same things ourselves. Many parents experimented with underage drinking, drug use, or premarital sexual activity during their own adolescent years.

Mary, the mother of a teenage son and a preteen daughter, talks about her response when she became aware that one of her son's friends smoked marijuana. "I go on a walk in the park every morning, and there's a certain area where high school kids go to smoke dope. One morning, I saw Neil there with a group of kids I didn't recognize.

"I didn't *think* my son was smoking dope, but I knew that he'd know Neil was. There was a good chance he'd be thinking about trying it, if he hadn't already. I had to address it.

"I couldn't honestly tell Jasen that I hadn't smoked pot myself. I first tried it during my junior year of high school and smoked dope occasionally during college. I'd never lied to my son, and I wasn't going to start now. I couldn't say, from my personal experience, that trying pot was the end of the world.

"What I had seen, however, was how stupid it made my friends who smoked more regularly than I did. All those stereotypes about stoners are true.

"That's one of the things I told him. I said that I'd seen Neil at the park getting stoned, and that lots of kids are tempted to try pot. I commented on Neil's potential to land in jail. I said that one problem with dope was how dull it made you, and that pot and school don't mix at all. At that point, he asked me how I knew dope made you stupid, and I told him that I'd had friends who smoked a fair amount of it. He asked me if I had.

"When I said yes and told him about my experience, I could see him start to take the conversation more seriously. He was all ears when I reminded him that possession meant automatic expulsion from school. I also told him that, because possession was a criminal offense, there would be no marijuana in our house, ever. That meant it was his responsibility to make sure that his friends, including Neil, didn't bring it here. I also reminded him that if police found pot in a car, they automatically confiscated the vehicle.

"He was pretty quiet the whole time. I didn't ask him if he'd ever tried pot. I did notice that he started making excuses to Neil about why they couldn't get together, and it's been several months since Neil's been over here. I take that as evidence that Jasen's making good choices."

Sometimes, as this mother found out, being honest about our own experiences makes us more of an authority on a subject and deepens our relationship with our son or daughter. I'm not, however, suggesting we hang all our dirty laundry out for our teens to examine. Doing so would be inappropriate. It might be oversharing for our kids to know the details of our alcohol usage in college, for instance. But if the situation calls for some sharing of your own mistakes, share away.

If you'd like to increase your integrity level, consider one or more of the following:

• Make note of the physical feelings that arise in you when you're being less than fully honest. Many people feel it in the area of their throat, heart, or belly. Paying attention to these physical feelings can clue you in when you need to edit or add to something you've just said in order to make it the full truth. Teach your teen this "honesty body scan" habit. It's often tough to tell the truth, but when we get that doing otherwise lodges negative energy in our bodies, we have even more reason to practice honesty.

• Remember that one of the essential spiritual teachings is that the truth sets us free. In all traditions, honoring the essence of who we are, our thoughts and feelings, beliefs and desires, is key to freeing the Divine within us.

• Make peace with past breaches of integrity. It's never too late to make amends. I have a friend who, at fifty-four, contacted the owner of a small store he shoplifted from in his early teens to apologize and make retribution. The burden that was lifted from his heart far exceeded the value of the compensation he offered the store owner.

• Take a good hard look at the excuses you make for any "slight breaches of integrity." I read an article about college admissions recently, and it featured interviews with parents who expressed the sentiment that their kids needed to cheat because everyone else was cheating. One father felt that the only way his son could succeed in life was by going to an Ivy League college, something this man had failed to do and credited with his strife in life. In order to get into that level college, the father unabashedly told the interviewer, his son needed to blur the lines of honesty a little and he, the father, would look the other way. His son was indeed caught plagiarizing on an English paper and, yes you got it, his father hired an attorney to fight the boy's fight with school administrators.

• Be aware that kids are swamped with messages about drug and alcohol usage and it's all pretty confusing. "There are so many mixed messages that kids think everybody is lying," says Mike Gray, the author of *Drug Crazy: How We Got Into This Mess and How We Can Get Out*. Your adolescents probably know that illicit drugs are dangerous and they should *never* do them. But then they are also aware that prescription drugs are fine and can be counted on to put you to sleep if you are having trouble or make you happy as long as a doctor has prescribed them. And alcohol is great after a stressful day for unwinding and relaxing, as long as you are of legal age. What messages are you mirroring? As Jamie quoted in the Introduction, "What I'm figuring out is how do I *do* my life?" Jamie is figuring out how to deal with stress and how to be happy. If you were Jamie's parents, what models for this behavior are you exposing him to?

Materialism—or the Lack Thereof

My friend Lynn's sons are several years older than my daughters. When they started high school, I didn't believe the stories she told me, so I asked her to take me on a field trip through the school's student parking lot.

There were a few classic "kid cars," older Hondas and Toyotas, the occasional American-made sedan with a healthy coat of rust. However, the vast majority of cars in that lot were new and shockingly expensive. Acuras, SUVs, brand new Volvos and Saabs glistened in the sun while their owners finished up algebra or English or social studies.

"Yeah, well, it's a private school," I said to myself. Imagine my surprise when I found only slighter fewer new luxury cars at the public high school my daughter attends. One recent graduate was known for the silver Jaguar he drove every day.

Gucci and Prada go to high school now, only slightly less frequently than Tommy Hilfiger, Steve Madden, and the inseparable Abercrombie & Fitch. Of course, these particular labels aren't the issue, nor are the new cars lining the parking lots of high schools all over the country. These are just two symbols of a cultural relationship to material goods that's overdue for serious questioning.

Time and time again, parents complain to me that their teens define themselves and others by the material goods they own and wear. Inevitably, if I ask a few more questions, I learn that the parent who is complaining admits that she prefers to carry a designer bag or he is comfortable with some credit card debt in order to "afford the finer things in life."

Certainly, our teens encounter daunting social pressures about the "right" kind of backpack, clothes, car, and so forth. But we must examine whether our own behavior contributes to the power of these messages or acts as a counterbalance.

Many of us work too hard at jobs we don't love so we can afford bigger houses, new cars, and exotic vacations. Little wonder that we see teens who are all business and no fun—they've learned that the only thing that's important is how much you make, not how you make it. If this rings a bell for you, maybe it's time to have an honest conversation with your child, to step in and give him permission to scale back. *"You know, I've noticed that you aren't getting much sleep. You've got an awful lot going on. I'm concerned about you. I think it's time to reevaluate your schedule."* You might find that your teen is just waiting for you to let her off the hook.

One of the things that disturbed me about the parking lot full of parental-provided luxury cars was that the teens who were driving them had little to look forward to. When you're driving a BMW at sixteen, what's next, a Learjet at twenty-one?

Delayed gratification provides two kinds of pleasure: the long-savored anticipatory pleasure involved in working toward a goal and the short-lived pleasure of achieving it. As we model setting material goals and then working towards them, we show our teens that there is pleasure involved in waiting for what they want, whether it is a new car or sexual intimacy.

On the other hand, immediate gratification divorces acquisition from effort. It gives our teens the wrong message: "I just *had* to have it!"

It's not surprising that shoplifting is a common problem among teens. A recent study of 116 shoplifters between the ages of twelve and seventeen, conducted by Dr. Paul Cromwell, a criminologist at Wichita State University, found that teens had three reasons for taking something without paying for it: the thrill and excitement of beating the system, peer pressure, and simply not wanting to pay for an item they wanted.

The last reason these teens gave concerns me the most. Cromwell also found that teens usually had the money for the item they wanted; they just didn't want to spend their own money on it. They felt entitled to take the object and keep their cash. I have to wonder where these teens learned that to expect *someone else* to pay for what they wanted; in this case, the store they stole it from.

If you want to explore more about nonmaterialism, you could also:

• Ask yourself the following questions about any purchase you're considering: "*Do I really need it?*" "*Will I still want it next week?*" "*What do I have that I haven't used for a long time that's just like this?*" You can also ask your teens the same questions about purchases they're considering.

• What percentage of the items in your home, roughly estimating, haven't been used for a year or more? Go through your closet, for instance, and simply count the items you haven't worn since a year ago. You don't have to do anything about them right now; just consider becoming more aware of the material goods in your home. As you do, your teen will take note.

- The next time you have the impulse to make a purchase, don't. You can put the item on hold if you choose. Simply build in a 24-hour pause between the decision to buy something and the act of making a purchase. For the next day, notice how many times you think about that item and how you feel about not purchasing it. After 24 hours, if you still want it, make the purchase.

- Consider giving—and asking for—gifts of the heart, instead of material goods. I had great joy in putting together a fortieth birthday scrapbook for my husband, complete with pages of poems, memories, and photos created by family and friends. Our children saw the meaning and joy that came along with this gift of memories. A newsletter subscriber recently shared her most meaningful gift. "One of my favorite gifts of all time is a steel sculpture of Kokopelli, the Native American icon of fertility. My husband made it for me when he decided he needed to learn how to weld. The welding has gone by the wayside, but Kokopelli stands guard over the backyard."

As parents, we need to know what behaviors, attitudes, and lifestyle standards we want our kids to develop, then live our lives accordingly. It's never too late for us to identify the specific standards we want them to embrace, instead of hoping they'll learn to make "good choices." We must pause and examine what we are mirroring in our lives and what we want to tweak in order to model standards that are in line with our beliefs. We don't need to expect perfection—from ourselves or our kids. Taking steps in the right direction, however, is a powerful way to begin.

We can also be comforted with the knowledge that we have the ability to hold up a mirror to our children and reflect their true selves, providing them the encouragement to go for the possible in their lives. When we hold up a reflection of our teenager's potential we not only give them hope, we remind them of what they, in turn, can mirror to the world: a person who is confidently going towards a future, fully engaged in the now, being all that they can be.

Parents' Insight-Building Exercise

Find a quiet place where you know you won't be disturbed for at least several minutes. Unplug the phone and settle into a comfortable position in a chair, with your back well-supported and your feet flat on the floor.

Take several slow and deep breaths and feel yourself relax. Allow the chair to receive your full weight.

Visualize a brilliant white light cascading over you from above. It surrounds you completely, extending well beyond the chair in which you're sitting. As the light contacts your skin, it goes beneath your skin to fill your entire being. From all directions, the light moves toward your center, your core.

Notice the quality of the light as it moves within you. Feel your heart soften. Notice your belly relax. Become aware that the light is both relaxing and empowering. Invite the light to dance fully within you, radiating from your heart and infusing your whole being.

Now, mentally bring your teen into your presence. Allow the light that you radiate to gently wash over your child, surrounding and embracing her.

Rest in radiant relationship with your child as long as you'd like. No intentions are necessary during this time; simply rest in the awareness of being connected to your child with brilliant light.

As you're ready to return to the room and your life, take a deep breath and release it fully.

Parents' Check-In Questions

- What spiritual quality do I feel drawn toward increasing in my life? Nonviolence? Forgiveness? Acceptance? Compassion? Integrity? Something else?

• What spiritual quality am I most resistant to increasing in my life? Am I resistant because it's the quality I most need to increase in order to experience more peace?

• Who exemplifies a spiritual being to me? What qualities are the hallmarks of his or her existence?

• What spiritual quality do I notice is lacking in my teen's life? Is there a way I can increase the degree to which I am an example of this quality?

• What step toward compassion can I take today? Who or what situation can I open my heart to in a new way?

• What am I struggling to accept in my life? Where can I act "as if?"

• Who do I need to forgive today? What anger or resentment is smoldering in my heart?

• When have I been out of integrity this week? What can I do to correct the impression or situation?

• Am I mirroring an image of the kind of adult I'd like my teen to become?

• What was mirrored to me at this age?

• How might I hold a mirror to my teen so she sees her inherent worth and amazing inner self?

Conversation Starters

During a moment of quiet togetherness with your teen, consider introducing one of the following questions. You can also engage the entire family over the dinner table. Make sure that everyone is allowed to express their opinion without disagreement.

• Who's the holiest person you know? What do you admire about them?

• If you could do one thing over in your life, what would it be?

• Who do you think has the hardest time at your school? Is there an individual or a group of teens who really find it hard to be there every day?

• What do you think kids at your school would think if a teenaged Jesus or Buddha or Muhammed or Krishna was a student there? Who would be their friends?

• What's the worst thing that happened to you this week? How did you respond? Would you do anything differently if it happened again?

• Do you think I practice what I preach?

• Is there anyone in our family that you look towards as a model for you in life? Why?

• Is there someone that looks up to you—a sibling, neighbor, younger friend? What behaviors do they emulate?

PRINCIPLE NINE:

Let Go and Trust

"Things really started to improve when I stopped letting my sixteen-year-old daughter set the tempo for the family, when I stopped criticizing her and quit trying to force her to do things my way." —**Cathy, mother of three**

• • •

We can hit rough patches in our parenting, and they often come during adolescence. But, and this is an important "but," it is during these times we have to release the struggle of shame, guilt, frustration, and pain to remember that we are in a spiritual partnership with our teenager. Once we release our firm hold on struggling, we can finally rest in the peace of trust. A loving God partnered us with our child and will support us as we move through these teen years.

I often think of the story about a woman named Jane who went out for an afternoon hike in the mountains. Jane was enjoying her solitude, praying quietly as she often did, when the path she was walking on gave way, and she began to slip down the steep mountainside. As she fell, she managed to grab a branch of a young tree. Hanging on with both hands, Jane began to scream, "Help me, oh please help me! Is anyone out there?"

With that, there was a loud clap of thunder, a bolt of lightening and the voice of God rang out: "Jane, I will save you. I have heard your cries and with all the love possible I will save you. Let go, Jane; I am here to catch you. Just let go."

Jane thought for a moment, still clutching the branch, and looking up to the top of the mountain she yelled, "Is there anyone *else* out there?"

Letting go is one of the most difficult challenges we face as parents. This process requires that we change from having the tight grip of a closed fist to an extended open hand. When we take this attitude, we are free to follow the pathway of Spirit and experience true peace. Our peace translates to our kids and, inevitably, struggles begin to wane.

The more we resist, it seems, the more our teen will fight. Think of adolescence as a time when you work *with* your son or daughter to move through their evolution to adulthood. Perhaps the purpose of adolescence is to correct the belief that we are separate from God while smoothly separating from our parents. This is not an easy endeavor for anyone, much less a teen juggling constantly shifting rules and changes.

These teenage years are your child's birth into adulthood. The birth of any new life is messy. A baby being born is accompanied by effort and pain. A seed pressed into the ground pushes aside and disturbs the dirt around it to grow roots. The old gives way to new life and it may come with some turbulence.

Along with angst, however, comes humor, abundant energy, enormous excitement, and the potential for great joy. Take in the positive rather than focus on what might go wrong or the mistakes your kids make. Relax and enjoy this time—after all, you've worked hard for thirteen-plus years to get here.

Teens, too, may struggle during adolescence. Yes, many teens are truly in crisis during the passage into adulthood for a variety of reasons. In addition, many are dealing with their new perceptions of really big concepts such as death, their own mortality, spiritual transcendence, and the soul. Young adulthood can be a time of loneliness, emotional turmoil, struggle, and confusion. However, it can also be a time of spiritual growth, introspection, and values clarification, especially when teens have a strong support for this journey.

When parents focus less on the daily struggles, their teenage children are better able to cope with their own rocky emotional terrain. Each thought of peace centers the thinker in a calm assurance. That assurance inevitably moves out into the family.

Parental Struggles

I see many parents expend huge amounts of energy trying to change their children when the only person any of us can really change is ourselves. As we add more acceptance to our relationships, we become less fettered to our disappointments.

Acceptance is sharing unconditional love—with ourselves and with our kids. Acceptance of ourselves exactly as we are empowers us to become that which we have dreamed of and brings us, less burdened, to the final stages of parenting our child. Accepting our teens exactly as they are gives them the power to shift in ways that we call miracles. The only way to move out of judging our kids is to accept and love them as they are today.

Take a moment right now and bring your teenager to mind. Think of any ways in which you have not accepted her for who she is and tried to change her. Say the following right out loud, "I love and accept _____ exactly as she/he is." Make this out-loud acceptance statement a habit and notice how the weight of control and tension lessens. Rather than stressing and straining to change your teen, trust that God is guiding you as you lovingly guide her. This doesn't mean you are abandoning your child but rather unlocking the cuffs of control.

Many of us are afraid to let go of the struggle. We avoid slowing down to examine our lives and our relationship with our teens for fear of what may become painfully apparent. Taking inventory can make us afraid of what we might find, so we move through, hanging on to our struggles for all we're worth. When our energy is so focused on the struggle, we miss this fleeting window of time when the child we love is still living under the same roof.

Lucy is the mother of three kids. She was locked into a battle of wills for a few months with her oldest daughter, Erica. One evening at dinner, Erica was acting angry and disruptive. Rather than reacting in her usual way by matching her daughter's screaming, Lucy took a deep breath, feeling her connection with God. As she exhaled, she looked directly at Erica and imagined that all the love, compassion and calm healing she felt was being sent to and received by her. Erica immediately calmed down. Lucy relaxed and was able to finish her meal.

Even when your relationship with your teen is damaged, especially when your relationship with your teen is in trouble, you can move out of the struggle. First, get honest and ask yourself, *How did things get so bad?* Many parents I talk to want desperately to repair their damaged relationship with their kids. When I offer suggestions and strategies, however, their faces seem to go blank and their responses run something like this: "Nope, I tried that, and it won't work." Or "You don't know my son." And "Maybe that would help for a parent who doesn't work full time, but I'm just flat out with my job responsibilities."

When we want to make a change, often the first thing we must change is our thinking. Our thoughts, trapped in a rigid way of viewing, defining, and replaying circumstances often prove to be our greatest obstacles. When Ralph Waldo Emerson said, "Stand guard at the portal of your mind," he was speaking directly to those of us who allow our thoughts to carry us down a negative road. We often go over and over a specific uncomfortable thought, reopening the wound each time. We pick at the mental scab of anger, frustration, and limitation. We can, instead, choose to release these negative thoughts and find new ways of viewing our teens, ourselves, and our lives. We can control our thoughts.

A tendency that many parents experience is the temptation to suppose, or assign meaning to a teen's behavior. When we do so, we can create tension and misunderstanding.

For instance, your son seems rather quiet and remains in his room longer than usual. You wonder if he's viewing pornography on the Internet or hatching a plan to quit school and so ask casually probing questions. He resists, and your anxiety increases. "If he's hiding it from me, it must be bad." In reality, he is writing love poems to a girlfriend and would be mortified if you found out.

Your fourteen-year-old is acting secretive. You knock on her bedroom door and she asks you to wait a few minutes before she opens it. You catch a glimpse of a notebook shoved hastily under her bed. You suppose that her behavior reflects the inevitable pulling away of a teen, and the notebook contains private thoughts. "It's bound to happen—she's writing about how much she hates her parents." Then, on a bright spring morning a few days later, your child presents you with a collage of mother-daughter photos she made for Mother's Day. "Geez, Mom, you kept coming in my room. I had to hide it under the bed."

If you feel hurt by something your son or daughter has done, take a moment to evaluate the situation. Might you have imposed assumptions over facts? What alternative explanations can you imagine for your teen's behavior? Assume your teen's best intentions and avoid jumping to conclusions. Believe the best and notice if anything shifts.

Let go of the negative images of teens and release your son or daughter's activities into the highest light possible. Of course you want to take action if there is trouble afoot, but don't dally in doom.

Choosing not to struggle with your teen doesn't mean withdrawing, although it might be tempting at times. Releasing means rising above the occasions when your teen tunes you out and your natural response is to retreat as well. Matching their behavior only lowers your energy. Now, more than ever in your life with your child, stop the struggle and love even more.

"When my son is surliest, I try to remember to act as though he isn't. I don't coddle him, but I'm extra careful to treat him politely, as though he were a guest in my house. It's so much more effective than yelling at him. He can react to my yelling, but it's hard to stay mad at someone who asks if you'd like butter with your bread." —Janice, mother of two

"I work to try and sort of forget that my teenage daughter has been screaming and slamming doors only half an hour before appearing to be her old sweet and friendly self. I make an effort to ride the waves—up and down with the flow. I used to try and figure out what I had done to upset her. I now realize that her mood swings usually have nothing at all to do with me. I was exhausted blaming myself for every little dip my daughter had. But I now know that what's around the next turn might be a surprise, but I'm in it for the long haul. I'm starting to enjoy the ride a lot more." **—Sharon, mother of one**

Sharon helps remind us how important it is not to hop on the emotional roller coaster with our adolescents. It's so easy to feel the devastation when our child is unhappy, "Life sucks and I have absolutely no friends." Emotional highs and lows can be typical behavior; their emotional development is open full throttle. It's our charge, however, as spiritual parents, to remain centered and solid rather than weave into the feeling mode of their upset at any particular time.

In our house, the old saying, "If Mama ain't happy no one's happy" should be "Mama's happy when everyone in the family is happy." I feel deeply when my husband and children are unhappy, disappointed, or angry. I also feel deeply when they are jubilant, optimistic, and joy-filled. Separating my feelings from theirs is a constant effort but one worth making, so that I might stay more grounded and support my family rather than living their lives by feeling their feelings.

To let go, release your struggles, and trust in the strength of spirit, try any of these additional ideas that resonate for you:

• Find a quiet place and time in your day, get out your journal or a piece of paper. Make a list of all the struggles you would like to release—problems, worries, fears, past mistakes. Write down even the little things that are causing you anxiety. Be honest and don't stop, as uncomfortable as this process is, until you are finished. Include everything from the constant ache in your left knee to your son's apparent lack of academic motivation. Then picture the paper surrounded by a beautiful and healing white light. Speak words of release to shake the negatives out of your life: *I disengage from these things or conditions, I let them go and move forward in my life. I know Divine Guidance seeps in to inspire me with ideas for appropriate action to take concerning these worries. I am ready to move away from stress and toward greater peace. With the power of the Universe guiding and assisting me*

*I am at peace now. I know all is well in my life and in the lives of those
I love.*

• Ask for help. Many of us find it easier to give help than to ask for it.
When we do, though, we benefit and so do our kids. When they witness
us seeking assistance from others, they can consider asking for help as
an option during their own challenges.

• Try to remember that the problems you tussle with aren't obstacles
to your spiritual practice—"My schedule is so crazy I can't find time
to meditate"—they *are* your spiritual practice. "I can embrace calm
centeredness even while balancing my workload and another load of
laundry."

• Remain focused on what you are *for* in life rather than what you are
against. It's easy to focus on our limitations as parents. However, what
we focus on grows, so when you're tempted to browbeat yourself, gently
turn your attention to your intentions as a parent. "I create a stable
ground from which my son can take flight as a responsible, caring adult."
Nurture yourself, treating yourself as the beloved being you are.

• Accept a bad day for what it is—a temporary glitch. Avoid allowing
minor ups and downs to stress you out in a major way.

• Stop and examine the patterns that have formed in how you relate to
your adolescent. Do you automatically bark out a command first thing
in the morning, "Take out the garbage" before giving him a chance to
do it on his own? Are you so used to struggles that you've come to expect them? If so, then that's how your day will unfold—with a pattern
of conflict. Choose to move out of the rhythm of tension with your
kids. Ask them for help. "Is there something I'm doing that causes us
to struggle and if so what might I do to stop?" Then be prepared to listen without becoming defensive.

• Does your son or daughter have to look or act a certain way for you
to love her? Can you drop down into the place of inner knowing for a
moment and ask yourself, "What is more important, the outfits she

dons or that she knows I love her?" I've often wanted to make flash cards for parents of teens that say, "It's not about me." Your son comes home from school, throws his backpack on the floor, grunts, and stomps upstairs. You can then gaze calmly at your flashcard, reminding yourself that his behavior has nothing to do with you. You avoid hurt feelings that might prompt a response such as, "Listen, young man. Can't you say hello when you walk in the house?" Instead, you shout up the stairs, "Hey, Dan, welcome home." Let go of the struggle of thinking your teen's rebellion, surly mood, low grades, or tattooed boyfriend are your fault. This is a time when your son or daughter is figuring out their behaviors, repeatedly asking and finding new answers to the questions, "What will I be today? Who am I? Where do I fit in?"

• Make a list of the topics that cause conflict in your household. Is it chores, late curfews, grades, bedtime, the car, dating, talking back, or any one of a million other potential flashpoints? Knowing in advance what might push the quarrel button helps us prepare as we enter into a touchy topic. After you've picked the hot spots in your family, grab a piece of paper and write down three strategies you can try to avoid this particular confrontation. Focus on actions you can take, not changes your teen should make. For instance, if you struggle with your teen over joining the family for dinner, perhaps you could tweak the dinner hour to accommodate her evening study group or excuse her before dessert is served. One father of a sixteen-year-old son established a certain number of weekly nonnegotiable show-up-at-the-table nights. The rest of the time, his son was free to choose when, where, and with whom he ate an evening meal.

• Releasing the struggles with your teen doesn't imply that you let go of what's truly important to you. Ask yourself if you've begun to accept language, standards, attitudes, and behaviors you don't like just because it's become too much of an effort to try to enforce what you believe. If you have, begin now to change things. Talk with your teenager about what behavior of his you have let go and what you will no longer accept and why. Then, stick with it no matter how inconvenient and uncomfortable it might become.

* Stop worrying what others think of you or your teen. This can be a powerful experience of release. Remind yourself that it's between you, your child, and God.

* Avoid mental and verbal comparisons between your teen and her friends, the teenagers living down the street, the sister who never stumbled during her teen years, or yourself at the same time of life. Let go of constantly judging your teen, her friends, her status at the moment, her potential. Our judgments hold our kids back from fully expressing their unique spark and finding their place in the world.

* Catch yourself if you fall into the "if only" trap. "If only my son were smarter, got into a better school, hung with nicer kids, hadn't discovered skateboarding." Teenagers are on a divinely guided path. Sure, we may need to step in and help them make minor adjustments, but their choices are part of their attempt to claim their place in the world. Skateboarding might be the metaphorical balance they are seeking at this stage of their journey.

* We are fully responsible for our own emotions and reactions. When we respond to our teens the way we'd like them to respond to us, we'll begin to see a change in their behavior.

* Professor John Archibald Wheeler, the noted quantum physicist, stated, "I do take 100 percent seriously the idea that the world is a figment of the imagination." How do you *imagine* your relationship with your teen? Think of your interactions with the overlay of Wheeler's quote. If it's all imagined, then our energy, intention, images, and thoughts create our reality. Thus, we create our own challenges and are fully empowered to release them.

* If worry has you by the throat, and for many of us it has become a chronic thought habit, soak in the words of author Melodie Beattie:

"What if we knew for certain that everything we're worried about to-day will work out fine? What if . . . we knew the future was going to be good, and we would have an abundance of resources and guidance to handle whatever comes our way? What if . . . we knew everything was okay, and we didn't have to worry about a thing? What would we do then? We'd be free to let go and enjoy life." Fill in the last line with, "We'd be free to let go and enjoy our teenager." Hang onto the won-derful fact that, according to studies I have read, 94 percent of all teens sail through adolescence without any trouble.

• Despite our best attempts to remain loving, we are human. We re-member past pain and respond to certain circumstances as if they were intended to wound us again. Our teen hurts our feelings by laughing at our choice in sunglasses and we are zapped right back to the teasing we took from an older sibling. Our reaction isn't appropriate. Ask your-self: "Where in my family am I holding a grudge? Is my past coming back to haunt the way I interact with my teenager?"

Very few of us can simultaneously struggle with hurt, anger, or fear and love without reservation. Let's make an attempt, as we parent our teenagers, to let go of everything unlike love. Living in love erases past hurts and oozes out into our teen's hearts. When we no longer keep score, we give our kids the permission to relax into our unbarricaded love. Loving deeply will help you to wipe the slate clean.

Loosen the Grip

Loving our teens means we nurture and nourish their spiritual growth and highest good. We offer them support, compassion, and understanding with-out expectations about the outcome. Controlling behavior, which we often aren't even aware we are involved in, is when we attempt to get something from our kids such as their love, attention, or ego gratification from their achievements.

We control our kids in many ways. We use threats, punishment, judgments, sarcasm, criticism, the silent treatment, money, shame, and suffocating affection. They, in turn, struggle for our approval or attention by giving in to our demands when it goes against their core beliefs, taking care of our emotions, getting sick, acting out, being overly sweet, becoming perfectionists, or taking control of what they can—their grades, whether or not they use drugs and/or alcohol, and their diets.

There is a delicate balance between guiding our children, acting as a kind of loving earthly coach, and taking on the responsibility of making them into the people we think they *should* become. When we operate from a spiritual perspective, our highest priorities are loving deeply rather than controlling and managing.

Martha, mother of three, says: "I felt an enormous pressure from my parents to perform, achieve, and fit into their plan for me. I wasn't able to follow my heart because I didn't know what I wanted. I vow not to do that to my kids but don't know how to remain objective."

Martha, like many of us, experiences conflict over the notion that teenagers are already who they are meant to be. We believe that, as parents, we should mold and shape them into our vision of their future selves. Teens can feel the pressure of this attention and it becomes a burden that often turns into anger and squelches their flow of Spirit. The harder we hold onto our version of how a teen's life should look, the harder Spirit has to work to flow the perfect outcome in. When we give sway to the creative flow of the Universe, releasing our rigid outlines, there is less push and pull for our adolescent and us.

As our kids become teens we are forced to embrace change. Some of us clutch tightly, grabbing for fleeting control. The problem with resistance is it's a losing battle—100 percent of the time. When we try to resist the inevitable, we cause ourselves and our kids, great pain, struggle, and sorrow, and we both miss out on potential joy.

Ironically, teens with the most controlling parents are often the ones who rebel and struggle the hardest. Letting go of your child as he seeks independence can be difficult. Releasing control seems to be harder than taking care of the details, no matter how busy our lives. We want to jump in and rescue our children from feeling unhappy, afraid, angry, sad, or anxious. If we become involved in and give our energy to their unhappiness, then it may turn into a powerful tool our teen uses for our attention. Think of the toddler crying in the checkout line for candy. We give them candy. They continue to cry each time we go shopping. When we reward our teen's manipulative behavior with our attention or model controlling behavior, we teach them the soul-deadening results of control.

We're also called upon to loosen the grip on the earthly adversities we're all bound to face. When we view unpleasant situations within the context of this lifetime only, we experience the suffering that comes with struggle. If, however, we let go and embrace a spiritual perspective, we see everything that happens to us and our family on an infinite continuum. Shifting to a spiritual understanding of our challenges helps us experience them as opportunities to evolve our souls by being more compassionate.

The greater the turmoil in your relationship with your teen, the harder you're holding on. Trust that Spirit can flow into the pain—you aren't in this alone—and release the struggle into the helpful embrace of a loving God.

Some ideas to help you trust and loosen the grip of control:

- Trust that your teenager is guided by a loving, all-knowing presence and that he was put here on earth for a reason. Think of yourself as part of his support team rather than his only lifeline.

- We strive so hard to make our lives and our teen's lives work out the way *we* envision them. I would like you to take a day, just one day, and give up struggling for the entire 24 hours. If you have to pretend you are releasing the struggle that is just fine. For this one day, trust that all of your needs and your son's or daughter's needs are completely met. Relax in the knowing that the natural flow of life will carry you through the day, effortlessly. Being in the moment without tension can be a very freeing experience. During your day of freedom from struggle, you might discover that you feel wonderful, your teen does just fine without your worry and control and it becomes easier, as time goes by, to remain in the flow of less tension. So, bite your tongue before issuing a snide comment about her parking techniques or choice in attire.

- I love Goethe's advice: "If we treat people as they are, we make them worse. If we treat people as they ought to be, we help them become what they are capable of becoming." When we embrace change and accept our teen as the young adult they are today, we open the door to a far more peaceful existence. We help them become what they are capable of becoming rather than what we choose to react to today or remember from their past behavior. Then life becomes more of an adventure—each step more special and important.

- Give up the concept of being right. The next time you're tempted to argue a point of fact with your teen, ask yourself how important it is. In my experience, surprisingly few facts are worth fighting over.

When our lives are complete and we are filled with our own spiritual connection, we won't need our children to fill a need in our soul. We can release them to their destiny without holding on, clutching to the need to be needed. We can delight in this person for who she is rather than who we've always hoped she'd be.

The Body Is a Car Driving the Soul Around

It's hard to find answers, inspiration, or balance when we're physiologically compromised. Taking care of his or her health isn't high on a teen's "to do" list, and yet so much difficulty can stem from this inattentiveness.

How much easier life would be for our teens if they'd eat healthy meals, take their vitamins, and go to sleep at a decent hour. My friend Megon Mc-Donough sings a great song with lyrics that include "the body is a car driving the soul around." Her song is appropriate for teens for whom food, energy, mood, and spirit are so tightly woven. Our teens could save themselves a lot of unnecessary struggle if they would be attentive to Megon's lyrics. We could, too.

Teens' emotions are affected by what they eat or don't eat. Vitamin deficiencies, an overload of sugar, fat, and caffeine, starvation dieting, and binging affect the spirit the body is driving around. According to the U.S. Youth Risk Behavior Surveillance Survey, fewer than 24 percent of the 1,270 teen participants consumed the recommended five servings of fruits and vegetables per day, and a mere 18 percent drank three or more glasses of milk per day.

What are our teens consuming instead of the recommended food groups? Data from the Centers for Disease Control indicate that soft drinks—soda and 10 percent fruit juice—and sports drinks make up 11 percent of the calories in an average teen's diet. Fast-food consumption has also risen exponentially in the last decade.

We have to help our teens take care of their basic needs when their schedules are packed with events, chores, challenges, and responsibilities. Here are some suggestions that you can consider:

- Sleep cycles change during adolescence. Help your teen begin to unravel the connection between fatigue and anxiety. When we're tired, fear looms large. Often, simply taking a nap will put things in perspective.

- Similarly, help your teen begin to understand the impact that dietary choices have on physical and intellectual performance. Ask questions such as, "How long does the energy from a can of soda or a cup of coffee last you?" We don't need to hammer home the point we're trying to make.

- We can't control the choices our teens make when they're away from us but, as parents, our responsibility is to offer them healthy choices at home. Go through the cupboards and pantry and see how many snack and meal options contain overloads of refined sugar and fat. Make different purchasing decisions the next time you go to the store.

- Eat a few more meals at home. More than 40 percent of family food dollars are now spent on food eaten outside the home. Research shows that kids who eat more meals at home eat more fruits and vegetables and are more likely to take vitamins. Home-cooking's reputation relies on more than just nutrition, too. A soul-sustaining quality infuses food that is prepared with care.

- Divide responsibility for family meals among family members. Turning out a family dinner is a great accomplishment for a teen, nurtures the soul of the entire family, and is part of preparing for independent living.

- Include gratitude for your physical selves in family prayers. Like the old commercials for Timex watches, our bodies take a lickin' and keep on tickin'. As our conscious awareness of the vehicle increases, we're more inclined to treat it well.

As we and our teens understand that taking good physical care of ourselves is part of spiritual practice and fundamental to enjoying life fully, we're less inclined to overlook the basics of eating well, sleeping enough, and taking good care of the vehicle driving the soul around.

It's Not Fair

Part of becoming an adult is realizing that life is not fair. Most teens pop in and out of the "it's not fair" thinking from childhood. Rather than search for a solution they become angry, tune out, complain, or become bitter. Kids still look to the adults in their lives to model this behavior. Do we blame the referee for bad calls when our child's team loses the game? Is it another driver's fault if we speed up on the highway?

Let's help our teen understand the pointless struggle in this kind of reaction to issues or events deemed unfair. Instead, what might we change in ourselves? Acceptance that life is not fair opens the door to resolving the mysteries of life. If we don't accept the reality of unfairness, we stay stuck in the reactive mode of the rebellious child, and our spirits aren't free to soar.

Teens find it easy to fall into the blame mode which then forms their daily experience. "The teacher doesn't like me." "My parents are too strict." "That girl dissed me." Blaming is disempowering and further alienates them from what they crave but might not be able to articulate—a dynamic connection to the spiritual power within. They become powerless and then angry or depressed when blame is their game.

Ted, a bright high school junior, sang me his sad song of being wronged, "I would be in Honors Math if it weren't for my freshman math teacher. He totally screwed me and my chances. If I hadn't had him, I'd be on a different math track." The truth is, if Ted pulled himself up, worked harder at math today than at the anger he has over yesterday, he could move into the honors course.

Blaming others for our circumstances erases any personal responsibility we might have—the exact opposite of a healthy sense of personal responsibility and power, the quality teens must learn to develop. Blaming others for our experiences is one way we—adults and teens—create a reality that is less than we'd like to experience. No one *wants* to be a victim, but it can become a familiar way of life.

Whatever we believe, we live. If we believe we make bad financial decisions, we do. If we believe that we don't know how to make small talk, we're tongue-tied at social gatherings. If we believe we'll never find the house of our dreams, we'll always find ourselves living in places we don't fully love.

Conversely, if we believe we're capable of anything we decide to do, that's what we experience. In this regard, our children can surely become our teachers. The other night at dinner, Elizabeth mentioned a test she was having the next day. Her teacher had been out sick and wasn't able to teach Elizabeth's section a particular element that was going to be on the test. "Well," I chimed in, "you should just point it out to your teacher. She's very understanding, and I'm sure she won't make you answer those questions. After all, if she didn't teach them to you, it wouldn't be fair." "Don't worry, Mom, I've got it covered," said Elizabeth. "I'm speaking on the phone to a bunch of kids in my section tonight, and we're going to just go over the area that the teacher missed by ourselves. We'll be ready for the test."

If we believe, like Elizabeth does, that we're responsible for what happens in our lives, we experience empowerment. If we believe we're never too old to learn new things, our life is an expanding universe. If we believe this is the year our relationship with our teenager flourishes, it will be. If we believe we can have a personal experience of and relationship with God, we do.

It's not just us, either. Our beliefs influence the way we perceive other people in our lives.

"One of my parenting epiphanies came on the day I first described my older daughter as 'enthusiastic' instead of 'overactive.' By changing my vocabulary, I changed what I had viewed as a liability into a great asset. Since that time, many people in her life have shared with me how much they enjoy her energy and positive attitude." —**Hope, mother of three**

If your teen expresses interest in a highly competitive endeavor, focus on his or her success, not the long odds against them. If he or she wants to be a musician, for example, focus on the large number of working musicians, not the stereotypical starving-artist scenario. Cultivate mastery of the can-do attitude. No dream is beyond God's power; some just take more time and energy than others.

We can break free of limited thinking and recraft our experiences. We can redraw our mental image of our teen. We can help our teens do the same. To explore more about this idea, you could try one or more of the following:

* Take some time to list your beliefs about yourself. Then, next to that belief, write how it is manifesting in your life. For instance, one of your beliefs might be that you don't make friends easily. How is that notion playing out in your life right now?

* Do the same with what you believe to be true about your teen. What do you believe about your son or daughter and how is it manifesting in his or her life? "I believe my son is a quiet, kind boy but will never be a leader." Chances are, even if he were interested in exploring a leadership role, you might not encourage him out of fear that he wouldn't succeed.

* Discuss with your teen what he or she believes to be true about him or herself. What impression does he make on other people? What difficulties does she routinely face? What are her strengths? Where does he experience challenge—intellectually, socially, physically, emotionally? Are there beliefs that your teen finds troubling or limiting? Listen for the black-and-white thinking that teens so often use, where "I didn't do

well in French this quarter" becomes "I stink at foreign languages." Discuss with your teen an alternative idea that could replace the limiting belief.

• One of the most powerful things we can do in the process of revising our beliefs is to ask someone else to help us believe. Often, others can see our unlimited selves more easily than we can. Offer to see your teen in a new way that he or she wants to experience. Cultivate wholehearted belief in the possibility that it can be true. Regularly visualize your teen experiencing exactly what he or she most wants.

As we explore our unlimited potential and that of our teens, life becomes a joyful mystery. We learn the artistry of God's touch in our experiences and the deep joy of allowing ourselves and our teens to become inspired and fueled by the divine power pervading the universe.

Peer Pressure

"Peer pressure" is one of those fear-eliciting phrases that send shudders down parents' spines. "Sibling rivalry," "terrible twos," and "rebellious teens" also invoke fear and trepidation. Believe that these phrases are true and they'll happen to you.

I urge you to abandon any old associations you have with the "peer pressure" phrase. Banish the picture of some terrible group of kids lurking somewhere out there waiting to lure your child into sex, drugs, and rock and roll. Research shows that you are more important in shaping your child's values than any group of peers.

Another often-overlooked truth is that peers can exert positive pressure: to stay in school, try out for the team, share a book, join the choir, and so forth. Shift your thinking to how friends might enhance your teen's ability to make connections, show kindness, stand up to hurtful behavior, express an opinion, define themselves as individuals, learn forgiveness, and develop healthy boundaries. Sure, friends may at times try to persuade your kids to do things they don't want to do or know are wrong. As challenging as these pressures may be, they are learning opportunities for teens to put into practice what they know to be right and how to stand up for those beliefs.

Teens solidify the ability to make connections with other people through friendships—friends are integral to a teen's sense of self. However, a critical reason for instilling in teenagers a sense of belonging to their families is so they won't hungrily seek that connection *solely* through peers. When faced with tough social choices—invited to a party where drinking or drugging might happen, asked by a friend to cheat on a quiz, encouraged to exclude someone—the sense of being a part of something strong helps kids make the right choices.

Here are some ways you can create a strong sense of connection to help your teenager weather the waves of social influence and experience positive peer interaction:

• Encourage participation in groups that are joined together for positive outcomes, youth groups at your church or temple, Scouts, Students Against Drunk Driving, 4-H, Amnesty International, and so on.

• Ahead of time, brainstorm with your teenager options for uncomfortable situations such as being at a party and the talk has turned ugly or a friend has had a few drinks before driving him home. Give him an out, such as a secret code he can use with you that means he wants to be picked up immediately. One family uses, "Is Paddy feeling better?" Paddy is their dog.

• It's important that we don't judge or criticize our adolescent's friends. It forces them to become defensive, pulled between parent and friend. My wise daughter clued me into this once when I made a statement about how her friend's behavior had hurt my feelings. "You need to take that up with Marilyn, not me, because you put me in the position of having to defend her," said Whitney.

• Keep it real with your teenagers. Our often out-of-reach expectations can crush them—they just give up. Don't overwhelm your kids with unattainable goals or they'll find acceptance among those with standards they feel they can meet. Applaud and accept your kids today—just as they are.

College Anxiety

Over the years, parents have asked me how to get their kids into a good college if he or she didn't excel at sports or take part in extracurricular activities. They, like me, are struggling with raising balanced kids who develop their interests, stay connected to their spirits and their families while branching out to embrace opportunities, all without being exhausted. Many feel better just knowing they're not alone in the quest for relaxed, mindful kids who have room to explore their spiritual selves without always keeping an eye towards what college admissions offices want.

In response to worried questions about "What will colleges think of a kid who isn't a star by seventeen?" I want to tell you about a young woman named Laney. Laney was raised on a farm in Virginia with parents who encouraged her to paint the hallways of their home with her vivid images and fill her afternoons making mud pies. Not one for talking on the phone during the adolescent years, Laney would beg her mom to tell the kids she wasn't home. She was busy painting. There were no art classes in her little town so Laney developed her own unique style. By the time she visited me last summer while touring colleges, she had quite a collection of small unusual collages. She also created a purple portfolio from hand-painted paper to feature photographs of her art. Laney had never played soccer or joined a club but some pretty fancy colleges sure wanted her during their admission selection. Laney had a passion, art, and low-key, yet attentive and loving parents who supported her as she explored her calling. In doing so, she discovered herself.

My email overflows during the spring months when college acceptance and rejection letters go out. There are questions, concerns, and tales from the trenches about getting into college, paying for college, not being accepted at the desired college, and the high price of it all on children's spirits.

It's almost impossible as a parent in today's world not to feel pressure to parent kids who achieve prestige, power, social status, and lots of money. We don't have much support for raising good kids who achieve happiness and personal understanding. Those qualitative aspects of success don't seem to show up on our cultural rubric.

Sarah, the mother of a high school senior, writes, "We are completely unprepared for the enormous pressure on my daughter. She has focused her whole high school career on getting into an Ivy League college, and, even with honor roll and high SAT scores, she has not succeeded. We all feel at a loss. My husband and I both work overtime to save for college and yet we haven't tucked enough away to pay for the school she was accepted to. We don't see much soulfullness in this ordeal."

Sarah, like many of us, needs to find some kind of balance to wade through this stress-filled process. As do our teenagers. A recent Nickelodeon/Yankelovich Youth Study shows that 58 percent of young people worry they won't ever get into college, up from 36 percent in 1998.

Some ideas to begin letting go of college stress:

• Pause for a moment and consider how you define success—not by our culture's definition, but your own deeply felt benchmarks for your child's achievements. Kids can't help but sense our disappointment when they don't quite measure up. You might spend some time redefining success. Peace of mind, lasting friendships, improving the lives of animals, and an education that feeds one's mind and spirit are all important qualities.

• Pray for guidance on how you might develop a more spiritual approach to the college admissions process. Doing so will bring you insights and synergistic opportunities. Prayer helps you let go and trust that God is guiding your son our daughter to their divine right place. *God, I understand You as boundless love and gracious grace that flows through my life. I ask You to help me loosen the fear that comes when I worry about my child's future. Help me to let go of stress around my preconceived ideas of how his/her education should unfold. Open the path for (child's name) to move easily to his/her next place in life. Thank You for the wisdom that informs all our decisions around this issue and for the rich opportunities we have to choose from.*

• Remind yourself and your teenager that college is not simply another "thing" we purchase with a definitive outline of what is and isn't the "best." Education is not a commodity, as much as the ranking services will tell us otherwise, but rather an opportunity to gain understanding and wisdom. Approached from this prospective, we can be assured that a loving God wants to open our paths toward deeper understanding. College is a link in that unfolding.

• Shift your focus to how a college education might enable your son or daughter to give more to the world rather than how a name college might up their earning potential.

• Explore financial aid options for your child. Check out www. savingsforcollege.com for some great ideas. Many high schools offer college admission and financial aid seminars—make it a point to attend. Don't forget your local library. There are many books that go into great detail on the ins and outs of college scholarships.

• Consider alternative paths to graduation from a desired alma mater. Transfer admission deadlines and criteria are different than for first-year applicants. A year or two of success at a university is excellent evidence of the potential for success at the school of your child's dreams.

• Infuse the college search process with questions about a school's spiritual climate. How does the institution address academic honesty, service, leadership, substance-abuse prevention, faith communities, and emotional support?

• Expose your kids to all kinds of career options and people who have paved unique paths to success. Ask people you respect how they got where they are, what role college had in their journey, what they wanted to be when they were young, then share those rich experiences with your kids.

• Continue to offer your teen tools for releasing the struggle even when they head out the door after high school. Write her a prayer for the college journey, help her articulate her life-after-high-school worries, find a yoga class in the town where he will live or a pool where he can swim off stress.

Don't let a lack of financial or spiritual reserves keep your family from living the life of your dreams. Take responsibility today and watch the stress, frustration, and anxiety diminish. See your child as being perfect, just as he or she is, with no validation from an admissions office needed to justify your love.

I'm So Mad I Could . . .

A toddler gives us clear demonstrations of uncontrolled anger and frustration—flailing arms and legs, howling, biting, and screaming. As our kids grow older, they express anger—from indignation and resentment to rage and fury—in many ways: snide remarks, swearing, sarcasm, clenched teeth, sulking, silence, and possibly violence.

Anger is another way teens express sadness, grief, depression, or embarrassment. "I failed another test," might become anger towards the "unfair teacher" or result in a punched-in bedroom wall.

Helping our children process and express their anger in healthy ways allows them to avoid saying and doing things they later regret or stuffing feelings that only surface in uncomfortable ways.

Mark is a sixteen-year-old who, like so many teens, moves in and out of rage as quickly as he flips radio stations. He says, "I get angry a lot these days because I feel like I have no control over my life and then my parents ask me to do something when I'm already tired and overloaded or my brother gets in my face and it's the last straw. I blow!"

He "blows" and then his parents respond with fear and anger of their own. They, in turn, blow and everyone ends up feeling deflated and spiritually void.

In *East of Eden*, John Steinbeck writes, "The greatest terror a child can have is that he is not loved, and rejection is the hell he fears . . . and with rejection comes anger, and with anger some kind of crime in revenge for the rejection . . . and there is the story of mankind." This allusion to the Cain and Abel story urges us to attend to our teen's anger, to accept them more and to take seriously any suggestion of or tendency towards violence.

We've raised our kids in a culture of violence that provides explicit examples of what to do with anger. Act out! We naturally have our own stressors and, overwhelmed, might allow our child's anger to wedge hurtful distance between us.

What we can do instead is strive for serenity and centeredness. Our child wants us not to falter. Remember that she is terrified by her own anger and pushes against you, but, more than anything, your adolescent doesn't want you to fall. Think of yourself as one of those punching dummies that has weighted feet. Wobble, but don't fall down. Think, too, of this: "Every oak tree started out as a couple of nuts who stood their ground."

Believe it or not, there is a positive aspect to anger. Like all strong emotions, it can indicate to both parent and teen that a problem exists. Paying attention to the true sources of strong emotion allows us to discern positive steps we can take to resolve any issues.

Anger is usually a response to unacknowledged fear. Once we acknowledge and name the various triggers to fear, we can move toward a resolution. Author Wayne Muller says, "When we are in fear, we focus all our attention on the point of danger and lose our capacity to find any courage, sanity, or peace within ourselves. . . . Perhaps this is why, in the Christian New Testament, the phrase 'be not afraid' is found so often."

Teens, like many of us, allow their minds to play tricks on them, fueling fears that might otherwise lie dormant. Someone once described FEAR in an acronym: False Expectations Appearing Real. Help your teen develop the practice of reining in his or her mind as it begins to imagine something awful that hasn't yet happened. How? By reining in your own fearful thoughts and doing so in the presence of your teenager. "I am worried about Grandma getting sick on this trip. But, every time I think about that, I replace the thought with the vision of her strong and healthy and enjoying her vacation."

Anger is not at odds with spirituality. "Many of us have been conditioned to hate our anger . . . to get rid of it because it is 'bad' and painful, or shameful and 'unspiritual,'"says Jack Kornfield in *A Path with Heart*. Later in the same book, he assures us that even Zen monks feel anger, and he says, "Transform the energy. . . . Turn [it] into useful feelings and useful action."

Sally, mother of two teens, told me the following story. "When a vacant lot in our neighborhood was earmarked for a huge apartment building, many neighbors were angry. We hated the idea of increased traffic, disturbed wetlands, and the loss of a great play spot for our kids. We lashed out for a week or so, blaming everyone we could think of. Pretty soon, it was clear that would get us nowhere. So we figured out how to come together as a group and best voice our opinions, as well as research all possible options so we were making smart moves, not emotional moves. We wanted everyone to win. Ultimately, the developer decided to build a smaller cluster of homes and designated a section of the lot for a playground. My teens saw me take action for something that affected our family that also made me so mad."

When we express anger by taking action, we can make a difference in ordinary neighborhood events as well as be a part of profound social change. Find books and articles that give your teen examples of those who used their anger productively. Your teen might join Amnesty International or take a Habitat for Humanity trip. They might run for class officer if they are angry at the way things are done at their school. One young woman I know, angry at the lack of *real* action teens are taking, is beginning a group at her large public high school she calls, SOFA, Students Organizing For Action. Encourage your teen to release the struggle of anger by fighting back peacefully through mobilizing into action. Her motto is, "Get off of your sofa and take action."

You can also help your teenager handle anger by trying any of the following ideas:

- Create a way for your teen to be heard within the family and to have a say in family choices without burdening them with adult decisions or handing over the family credit card. It's one thing to research and present his choice in your new automobile selection; it's quite another for him to have sole voting power.

• Articulate clear boundaries and acceptable outlets for aggression. Being mad is okay; being mean isn't. Help your teen figure out how to release the intense energy of anger. Maybe it is through physical release, shooting baskets, a punching bag, chopping wood, or yoga postures. Perhaps keeping a journal is a helpful way to express anger. By writing down feelings, your teen is, in effect, transferring the emotions onto the paper. Writing also might help her gain a deeper clarity about the situation.

• Take a look at how you handle your own anger. Does your teen become a scapegoat for your frustration? What do you do when your teen is frustrated or fuming? Has your child's anger taken a leading role in your household? Do family fights occur weekly? Do you scream back when your teen is raging or refuse to talk to her until she can calm down? These are tough questions, but they are essential when establishing this important principle of letting go into your family life.

• Many teens feel intense anger at God for the terrible tragedies they see unfold in their world. The writings of Harold Kushner or Viktor Frankl may help. I particularly like Kushner's *When Bad Things Happen to Good People* and Frankl's *Man's Search for Meaning*. Both books are accessible for teens, as the authors write from personal experience rather than a theoretical position. One particularly helpful idea comes from Frankl: While we may have no choice in the misfortune that we experience, we always have a choice with regard to the stance we take in the face of such suffering.

• If your teenager experiences frequent rages, get help. Repeated angry displays signal a problem that you need an expert to help diffuse. Pray about it, but also take action to find support so a catastrophe isn't the result. Do the same for teens who bottle up anger and experience ongoing depression or other manifestations of unexpressed emotions.

Author and Buddhist monk Thich Nhat Hanh says that anger is like poison, it can overcome us. Anger, however destructive, is a natural human emotion. It can harm us and others spiritually, physically, emotionally, and socially. Refining and transcending anger, however, provides us with a rich opportunity to become the type of human being we wish to be.

What most parents want for their kids is a peaceful life, rather than years tarnished and wasted by seething anger. When they see the world as a positive place in which they have a say in their destinies, teens will learn to release the struggle of anger and trust in their glorious potential.

Increase Your Family's Stress-Reducing Repertoire

"When I get nervous or anxious, I can usually pray and it all gets easier. Or I find it helpful to get away from people and just go to a quiet place and sit down awhile." —Tia, nineteen

"My parents cause me stress. I release it by doing something they wouldn't want me to do: sex, drugs, smoking, drinking. Knowing that it would piss them off is enough stress relief for me." —David, fifteen

It's hard to feel the presence of Spirit when we're stressed—and that's exactly when we need to feel it the most.

Stress is our body's signal that we need to get back to what's simple and important—loving ourselves and our kids. This doesn't mean the myriad activities and obligations will go away. We simply choose to embrace them with an intention to relax and be present rather than struggle.

Statistics confirm David's quote above. Stressed-out adolescents are at a higher risk of self-destructive patterns such as alcohol, tobacco, and drug use, depression, compromised immune systems, and anxiety disorders. In a recent study published by researchers at Murdoch University in Australia, forty-five kids with a history of ten or more infections in the past year were taught stress management and relaxation skills. Afterward, episodes of chronic colds were shorter and blood tests showed increased levels of infection-fighting antibodies.

As I write this, Whitney is facing high school midyear tests. Stress is high. I try to craft a home that eases her stress rather than adds to it: a hot mug of tea delivered to her room as she studies, handling a few of her chores so she is free from that responsibility for the week, picking her up from school, candles around the house, soothing music, an early dinner with lots of protein, and some affirmative words. This doesn't end her stress, of course, and a certain amount of stress might even be a motivator for her. However, it does show her she is loved and allows me to acknowledge her efforts and nurture her process. It also gives her ideas of how she might self-soothe when stress rears its head in her life. "Ah, a cup of tea might be the perfect antidote."

Many people escape from stress electronically. Carl, fifteen, says, "When I'm stressed, I play video games or get lost on the Internet." Adults and teens alike veg out in front of the TV or Nintendo.

You might want to suggest alternatives to your teen if electronic hypnosis is his or her stress-reliever of choice. One stepmother of a seventeen-year-old tells a story about how she was able to do so. "Justin used to hole up when he was stressed out, behind his door, with his music on. Then, out of nowhere, he had a panic attack at a friend's house. He was terrified when he came home.

"I ran him a warm bath, lit some incense and candles, and put a soothing CD on the stereo. Now, when he's had a really tough day, he does the same thing. He'd never talk about it, but I can tell that it's really soothing for him."

Regular physical exercise is another stress buster. Steve, nineteen, agrees: "If I don't run for a few days, everything seems more intense." Exercise benefits our bodies, minds, and spirits—and many American households include people who don't get enough regular physical activity. While many teens are involved in sports, others lead amazingly sedentary lives. Running, walking, bike-riding, swimming, aerobic exercise classes, going to a health club—there are as many ways to get active as there are personalities in your family.

Physical exercise not only relieves stress, it provides spiritual sustenance. In *Sweat Your Prayers*, dancer Gabrielle Roth says, "To sweat is to pray, to make an offering of your innermost self. Sweat burns karma, purifying body and soul. Sweat is an ancient and universal form of self healing, whether done in the gym, the sauna, or the sweat lodge. I do it on the dance floor. The more you dance, the more you pray. The more you pray, the closer you come to ecstasy."

To increase your teen's—and your—options for handling stress, try the following to outrun the demon that urges us to do more, more, more, and do it faster, faster, faster:

- Designate a quiet sacred space in your home for reconnecting and healing. If space is at a premium, even a corner of the couch will do. When it's occupied, others honor the person who's there by not disturbing them for a reasonable period of time.

- Exercise gets the endorphins zapping around and makes you feel more hopeful and less stressed. Invite your teen to take a walk or run with you. Offer to sign up the two of you for an aerobics, free weight, or pilates class.

- Help your teenager to identify her symptoms of anxiety. Maybe she has a nervous habit of twirling her hair, biting her nails, tapping her foot, eating at breakneck speed, or snapping at you for no apparent reason. If she has developed an "inner watchdog" that can recognize when overwhelm is kicking in, then she can better cope. "I'm biting my nails again. I guess I'm feeling pretty anxious about the chemistry exam. I'll make a schedule of study times between now and then instead of chewing my fingers."

- Assess family stress. Look at your whole household before you single out your teen as the source of angst or the one suffering from high levels of anxiety. Are you bringing home tension from the office? Are family dynamics causing friction? What, if anything, can *you* do to lessen these situations?

- I find that, for most families, higher levels of stress occur during the springtime. The year is wrapping up at school, bringing final exams, year-end projects, and papers. Warm weather sports are in full swing, and many kids are trying to find summer jobs or feeling anxious about leaving friends. Being prepared for stress to notch up in the springtime can help teens and parents manage expectations as well as devise strategies for balance.

• Encourage your teen to create an action plan to handle his worries and challenges. Divide the tasks up into manageable pieces. Anne Lamott in her wonderful book, *Bird by Bird* tells of how her father helped her brother handle a huge school paper on the topic of birds. Rather than become overwhelmed by the vast scope of the project, Annie's father encouraged his son to take it one bird at a time. A one-step-at-a-time approach divides and conquers anxiety.

• Dealing with failure or the prospect of failing is a huge stressor for most of us. This is particularly so for teens who are so full of judgment about their most interesting topic, themselves. Be aware if your adolescent consistently blames himself. Pessimists blame themselves; optimists don't. If you hear, "I failed the quiz because I'm stupid," call a time out. Help your teen articulate the truth behind why she failed. "I failed the quiz because I didn't study the right material." Doing so allows her to see that she is in control of changing the situation for the better next time. Berating herself serves no purpose except making her feel powerless when, in fact, she is not.

• Have you had fun lately? Have you laughed with your family? Has your teen had a good time or is she so caught up in grades, extra-curricular activities, college pressures, and job stress that she doesn't have time for joy. Laughter frees the spirit. Make sure, in this pressure-cooker environment, that you and your teenager have some healthy fun.

• Provide open-ended free time, apart from technology, so your teenager might cultivate her relationship with peaceful serenity. During the Christmas vacation this year, our family had a "no technology" mandate. It was wonderful. We had long conversations in front of the fire, read books in the same room, played games, and just hung out together. Not running to check our e-mail or growing silent in front of a movie gave us the space to create a cozy togetherness. I found it particularly liberating not to be at the mercy of my constantly calling e-mail. Our kids, surprisingly, never complained. They did, however, watch like hawks to see if I was going into my office.

• I have found that certain delicious smells help me to release the struggle and relax. In the spring I snip lilacs from our yard and place them next to our beds—we all seem to drift off easier with this luscious smell wafting into our dreams. The winter months call for a fire in the fireplace with pine cones thrown in for a cozy aroma. Sprinkle some lavender oil around your child's room, light a scented candle at day's end, or spray scented room mist in your teenager's study area. Use your imagination, but do make the effort to add some aromatherapy to your routine and notice if everyone's burdens feel a bit lighter.

• Part of the stress we feel comes from too many choices. There are fantastic books to read, movies to see, sporting events to attend, upgrades for our computers to install, trips to plan, flowers to plant, activities to take part in, tips in this book to try. With the plethora of options in our lives, we can always feel as if we are missing something. I encourage you to take a deep breath and bring yourselves fully to the present moment where the options available for right now are to breath, to love, to just be! Life is a buffet of options. Pick moment by moment without drowning in the opportunities.

Release the little distractions and trust that what truly matters is this human being you live with, warts and all. What is essential is your love for your teen and your faith in a loving Spirit to guide you both. How you feel in your heart during these years, not your judgmental mind, is the truth. Focus on the essential goodness of your teenager, and have faith that God guides her through her birth into adulthood.

"What is essential is invisible to the eye. It is only with the heart that one can see rightly." —Antoine de Saint-Exupery, *The Little Prince*

Parents' Insight-Building Exercise

Most of us don't have "relax" as one of the items on our daily "to do" list. I am encouraging you, however, to go against the norm and add that oh-so-important fifteen to twenty minutes to your calendar. Not only will your teenager figure out that relaxing and getting still is what allows you to connect with Spirit, but he will see that this time is really a healing technique for releasing the struggle. So, take some time now to relax and move into that sacred, serene place of still knowing within you. This is the place where you are safe with no fears or worries; where you almost feel that excited birthday morning kind of feeling in your tummy. Allow yourself to simply rest in this feeling as love wraps around you like a light fleece blanket.

As you settle into this place, bring to mind whatever worry or problem has been biting into your joy. Picture this issue, or experience you no longer want in your life, as being placed inside a glass ball that you hold in your hands. Imagine it as one of those paperweights that you shake up for the snow to swirl around. See your problem encased in this ball of glass. Feel the weight of the worry. It's heavy in your hands.

Now, imagine that you are shaking up the ball and rather than snow, beautiful white light fills the space. Watch this light of Spirit wash over your problem. Soon the ball is filled with white light—it is glowing and radiating and it drowns out your worry. You are now holding a glass ball full of effervescent light. It almost floats out of your hands. The light from the ball seeps into you and warms your very being.

Thank this white light for being here. Thank your problem or issue for dissolving and moving out of your reality. Let go and trust that all is well.

Parents' Check-In Questions

- What, if anything, am I struggling with the most these days?

- Is my teen part of this struggle?

- How might I allow God's light into this situation so I can release my grip?

- What stress reliever works best given my life today? (yoga, running, writing in my journal, a hot bath, reading a mystery, chatting with a friend)

- How might I add more of these options in my week?

- What assumptions have I made about my teenager that have caused me tension? (he's not trying hard enough in school, she is just moody)

- Is there a way I can rewrite this script so that I don't limit my child by my assumptions?

- Am I trying to control my son or daughter rather than act as a loving coach? How so? What would happen if I released the grip?

- Do I enter into the blame game? How so? How might I stop blaming others and take responsibility that what I experience in life I create on some level?

Conversation Starters

- What makes you feel angry?

- How do you think I express my anger?

- Do you think you have many choices in your life?

- If you could improve one thing about our relationship, what would it be?

- What would you like to have more control over?

- What causes you the most stress on a daily basis?

- What do you do to release your stress?

- Are there healthy ways your friends release stress you might want to try?

Each Day Offers Renewal

"My son hurt my feelings terribly in the past few years. I've struggled to forgive him and forge a new relationship now that he is eighteen and about to leave home. I have to make a big effort to be in the present day instead of allowing past hurts to color my responses to him." **—Anonymous, mother of three**

"Starting over every day is something you choose to believe in. It's a mindset."

—Ted, nineteen

• • •

The years when our children are between the ages of thirteen and nineteen are full of change. Many parents approach these years with fear, and their anxiety is often validated by a media that portrays teens in a negative light.

Certainly, you might not be able to control your son or daughter's actions or appearance. You can control your responses, though, and they can be informed by an understanding, open heart. These years are our opportunity to live in a sacred union with the teenagers we were meant to parent before they journey out into their worlds as adults. When we embrace this life partnership with our son or daughter, we can prepare for a new day full of harmony, rather than preparing for battle.

No matter what your relationship with your teen has been, what it's like now, or how your parents treated you when you were a teenager, you get the chance—*now* and in every moment—to begin again.

Beginning anew often means making small changes in the right direction, rather than quantum leaps toward perfection. It is truly the small changes that can shift our relationships and experiences over time. It may seem as though nothing is changing, but keep up the small stuff and in a month or so you will notice a whole new direction has taken root.

Ralph Waldo Emerson lived in my town of Concord, Massachusetts, and I draw upon his wisdom often. His views on the power of the present moment are among the most meaningful to me. He says: "One of the illusions of life is that the present hour is not the critical, decisive hour. Write it on your heart that every day is the best day of the year. He only is rich who owns the day, and no one owns the day who allows it to be invaded with worry, fret and anxiety. Finish every day and be done with it. You have done what you could. Some blunders and absurdities no doubt have crept in; forget them as soon as you can. Tomorrow is a new day; begin it well and serenely and with too high a spirit to be cumbered with your old nonsense. This day is all that is good and fair. It is too dear, with its hopes and invitations, to waste a moment on yesterdays."

Nature conspires to help us make new choices. Every day, we start again. We wake to a life that is both the same and radically different than what we experienced the day before. Sleep has a spiritual magic all its own. During the night, our subconscious mind continues to process events in our lives through dreams: reordering, shifting, inspiring, resolving. Sleeping on a decision or an issue can help us clarify options or put them in a new perspective. I've often found great peace and clarity by simply allowing myself to rest deeply.

Throughout the year, too, we're reminded that we can choose to leave the past behind and move into a new experience of life. Spring is a potent and obvious reminder of renewal, as new life buds and blooms all around us. In winter, the landscape can change dramatically in the space of a few hours; gray and brown hues become buried under sparkling white flakes. Fall shows us the natural wisdom of allowing withered aspects to fall from the tree of our lives. And, in summer, gardens and flowerpots can transform virtually overnight as water and warmth create exponential growth.

Making resolutions doesn't have to be confined to January 1, the start of a school semester, or Rosh Hashanah. Instead, we can begin our week with new resolutions, or write mini resolutions for each obstacle we face. We can make the most of each dynamic new day by making sincere and meaningful resolutions, letting go of our past mistakes and asking God to give us the courage and strength to follow our resolutions to change.

The power of starting over is always available, to us and to our teens. Life explodes with possibilities when we tap into this truth by letting go of the past, focusing on the present moment, and envisioning a future without limits.

Teens are particularly ready to benefit from making each day a new beginning, because their minds are wired that way. New studies reveal that teens' brains are developing and changing at an amazing rate. Dr. Jay Giedd, Chief of Child Psychology at the National Institute of Mental Health, conducted a study that showed, contrary to previous thinking, that the brain's prefrontal cortex goes through a growth spurt at the onset of adolescence until about the age of twenty. This area of the brain handles emotional control, rational decision making, and impulse restraint. No wonder life with teens isn't a predictable linear journey! As parents of teenagers, embracing the newness of each day acknowledges our child's developmental process and allows us to continually reorient ourselves to the true north of Spirit. We can be open to and delighted by *who* our teen is *now*.

No Regrets

In order to start fresh, we may have to leave a few things behind. One of our strongest ties to the past can be the things we did or didn't do that we wished were different. Perhaps we said or did something that we'd like to undo. Perhaps we held back, refraining from taking action or speaking when the opportunity was ripe.

Every day should bring a clean slate, a chance to start anew. If last night's argument was talked out and resolved, leave it behind. If your daughter apologized for the lie she told last week, believe that she's going to tell the truth today. It's never too late; your child is never too old to begin again. Each day is a new opportunity, a new chance to live with no regrets.

One perspective on regret, and there are many, comes from Katherine Mansfield, a contemporary of Virginia Woolf's. "Make it a rule of life never to regret and never to look back. Regret is an appalling waste of energy; you can't build on it; it's only for wallowing in."

When we're parenting teenagers, it's easy to say and do things we wish we hadn't. To find out more about the experience of regret in the lives of parents, I asked my workshop attendees if there'd been a time when they said something to their sons or daughters they now wish they could take back. Only about a quarter of these parents answered with a "No." The others mentioned incidents like these:

"Once when I was angry over my son's continuous slacker work ethic I yelled, 'Fine! Grow up and work at McDonald's! Do you think colleges let you in on your winning personality?' Yeesh. . . ."   **—George, father of one**

"Yup, I did it. I suggested my daughter forgo dessert as she was filling out a bit too much. I never wanted to comment on her weight and out it came."
—Bonnie, mother of two

"My nineteen-year-old was home from college doing nothing but using the phone or Internet. I asked her if there was a way she could go back to school a week earlier. Later on, I apologized."   **—Jen, mother of three**

Making amends can release us from the weight of regret. A friend of mine who travels the country as a corporate trainer and business coach is actually a spiritual guerrilla in the corporate world. One of the tools he brings to his interactions with individuals and groups is the power of what he calls "taking care of incompletes." These are the moments we regret from the past that linger as unfinished incidents in our hearts and minds.

When we identify the specific thoughts, words, and actions we regret hav-ing—or not having—we can complete them: by making reparations, an apology, even an anonymous gesture.

The process is remarkably freeing. I suggested it in a workshop for par-ents I lead a year or so ago and one of the participants called weeks later to tell me the following story. "Your talk prompted me to recall an incident with a college chum—well, I had actually thought about it hundreds of times over the years. I'd spoken careless words in jest to this friend and, even though I'd seen the wound they inflicted, I was too embarrassed to apologize at the time. The incident was never addressed, we lost touch, and a few decades passed. Nevertheless, I thought about it frequently, wincing each time.

"I decided to do something about it after your talk. I tracked down my old acquaintance over the Internet, a simple matter since he now holds a prominent position in the federal government. I drafted a brief and heart-felt apology and sent it by mail.

"Although I didn't hear back from my former friend, I have no reason to believe anything other than that he received and read my note. The process of apologizing—some twenty years too late—lifted a burden of regret I had carried for far too long. In an odd way, it's also freed me up to attend to the other areas of my life. My teens know the story, and I do believe they will be more careful with how they handle friends."

We can clear up incompletes with other people in our lives—and, most definitely, with our teens. If there's an incident from the recent—or distant—past that you regret in your relationship with your child, acknowledge and apologize for it. By doing so, you model the value of sincere apologies in healing relationships and allow yourself to begin anew as a parent.

Teens can have regrets that are just as painful as an adult's. Words said or unsaid, deeds done or undone eat at our teen's hearts. The following are some responses to the question, "If you could revise one thing you've said or done in the past and begin again, what would it be?"

"My friendship with my friend Allyson was a tad rocky for about 3 months . . . I would want to go back and correct that, since she is the best friend I have."

—Brad, fifteen

"I've done a lot I wish I hadn't and I wish I could just take it all back. All the stereotyping I've done and hurt I've put out there to everyone."

—Sara, fourteen

While Sara, quoted above, might not be able to take back all the thoughts, actions, and words she regrets, there may be specific people to whom she could offer an apology. Certainly, taking care of the "incomplete" that hangs over the head of Brad would be much easier.

To explore the possibilities of living a life free of regrets, consider the following.

- Make a list of "incompletes" for yourself. What past actions or words would you take back? What opportunities to speak or act in the past do you wish you'd taken? Choose one, and decide what you can do to complete it. Write a note of apology to someone? Express your appreciation? Do it, and then notice any difference in your energy and in the number of times you think about that particular past event. In particular, notice what happens to the energy of your memories of the situation.

- Don't linger in the pain of what you didn't do when your teenager was younger. It's okay to mourn the loss of his childhood, but begin today to embrace the stage he is in rather than missing the good old days.

- Suggest to your teenager, if she expresses regret, that it's rarely too late to do things differently. Encourage a deed or expression that will allow her to channel the wasted energy of regret into positive action. For example, she could slip a note of apology into a school locker, invite a friend with whom she had a falling out to lunch, or meet with the biology teacher to learn from her mistakes on the blown test.

- Sometimes, teens (and adults) find decision-making difficult for fear of future feelings of regret. We can find comfort in knowing that the vast majority of decisions can be undone if the need arises. "Just decide for today," my mother used to say. "You don't have to decide for the rest of your life."

• Don't look back five years from now and regret not really knowing your teenager. Many parents of teens begin to hold back during these years, purposely moving out of their children's lives. It's natural as teens seem to seek distance to retreat. But the distance becomes habit until a chasm is formed. Ask yourself if you are holding back from your son or daughter emotionally or with your time and how you might shift from coasting through the teen years—one foot on the brake—to fully embracing your teenage son or daughter.

• Most major religions include the practice of some sort of confession or reconciliation. If you are part of a specific faith, share this freeing element of your belief system with your teen.

Deep Regrets

"Make the most of your regrets. To regret deeply is to live afresh."

—Henry David Thoreau

Another perspective on regret is that we learn our most valuable life lessons from the things we'd do over if we could.

David, older at nineteen then the teens quoted above, expressed a more mature perspective when he answered the question about what he'd go back and revise: "There are many things I've said and done that I regret. But honestly, I would not change one thing. Each of those moments have taught me something about myself and others and life. Without experiencing them firsthand, I may have never learned those valuable things. Sure, I regret them, but I would much rather have learned something for the better and regret the situation that taught me, than have never experienced it at all."

Thoreau and this wise teen offer us sound advice. When past acts cannot be undone or the person to whom we need to speak words of apology or love can no longer hear them, we can look for the ways that regret can help us make a new beginning.

When we regret something deeply, we're often motivated to make a change that will prevent its recurrence. When we recognize that deep regret can catapult us into a more desirable future, we accept the gift that remorse has to offer us.

To understand more about deep regret and lessons of the broken heart, you could:

• Look at the lessons you've gleaned from situations you deeply regret and encourage your teen to do the same. Sometimes, these emerge only over the course of years. Encourage your teen to be patient and look for the learning that will reveal itself as time passes. Offer a prayer of gratitude for the as-yet-unknown education your son or daughter is receiving. As a teen, a pastor at a church in a neighboring town was the driver in a car accident in which his best friend died. Today, he offers a great gift of healing to teens who've been involved in accidents causing injury to others.

• Commit to yourself to begin living today in such a way that you needn't experience regret about a new situation. What one thing do you need to do differently to bring that about? Ask for human and divine help in making this change.

• Help your teen see the connection between regretting the past and making new choices. Gently explore with her alternative actions that can lessen the chance that she will feel remorse for the same situation in the future. For instance, a friend of mine lives in a state in which new drivers may not have teenagers as passengers. Despite this law, her son had a friend in the car when he was involved in an accident. The friend received minor injuries, and her son felt deep regret for being their cause. From that point on, he became a model driver in all regards.

Be Here Now

More than thirty years ago, Ram Dass coined this simple phrase that contains a key to seeing each day—each moment—as a new beginning.

Only the present moment exists. We remember the past and imagine the future; we only experience the *now*. Each moment is the now, and it is the only moment that is important. Each moment is a new beginning in itself, and focusing our attention on the present brings us peace. From this place of peace, we can choose to look at life differently—creating a do-over for ourselves.

If we look carefully, there is always good in the present moment, even though it may take us a little while to perceive it. This good is both the key to relaxing into the present and the foundation from which we create new beginnings.

Florence Scovel Shinn, author of *The Game of Life and How to Play It,* writes: "Thy will be done this day. Today is a day of completion; I give thanks for this perfect day, miracle shall follow miracle and wonders shall never cease." She reminds us that our thoughts govern our experiences each day. In the present moment, we can decide what kind of day we want to have. As we allow ourselves to notice the sun pouring in through the kitchen window or the spring in our sixteen-year-old's step, we can decide to lay down any loads—of resentment, fear, anger, sadness, or self-pity—we might be carrying.

This capacity is a great resource for all of us, regardless of our age. Parents and teens alike can center themselves in the present moment, letting go of the history that a particular event symbolizes and fears about the future that it can arouse. Help your teen trust in her power to live in the moment without the old baggage of yesterday.

> "I'm in the midst of a divorce and freak out when I start to envision where the kids and I will live or if I'll be lonely. When I focus on the here and now, it's easier to keep things in perspective and move forward with trust."
>
> **—Jeannie, mother of two**

As a culture, we gauge success by the ability to multitask, but when we're mindful, we do one thing at a time. Vietnamese Buddhist monk and author Thich Nhat Hanh gives the example of washing dishes. We can wash dishes in order to have clean dishes. We can also wash dishes to wash dishes: enjoying the feel of hot water on our hands and the smell of the soap, the smooth surface of dishes and the clarity of clean glass. I recently had a conversation with a woman who thought the idea of meditation was far-fetched, a kind of Eastern occultism. "I don't need that kind of silliness," she said. "If I get upset, I find that doing the dishes seems to get everything all straightened out."

For teens who might not leap at the idea of the spiritual practice of doing dishes, Thich Nhat Hanh gives another idea: eating a tangerine. We center on immediate experience and breathe more easily by paying attention to the heft and smell of the unpeeled fruit, to the burst of aroma when the skin is broken and the gentle tearing that parts peel from flesh. Eating tangerine sections one by one, we notice their temperature, texture, and sweetness—and find ourselves more relaxed and ready to see the world anew when the pleasure of eating has ended.

Chopping wood, doing dishes, eating a tangerine, applying lip gloss, or taking a thorn out of our toe—it doesn't matter what the experience is. In fact, at any given moment, we can move fully into the present by simply noticing what it contains. A teen in geometry class can notice the feel of pencil on paper, the smell of the chalkboard, the sound of pages turning, the texture in a sweater on the person sitting in front of her. A parent who's tempted to drag past experiences onto the interpretation of a current situation can notice his or her surroundings with the same careful attention—and gain some leverage over a reaction that may be brewing.

Moving into the present moment lessens the hold of yesterday's bleak feelings. Disappointment, grief, hurt, and frustration can't compete with the power of the present. They don't necessarily disappear, but we experience a reprieve from their intensity. Moving into the present moment also balances the high-flying wings of excitement, jubilation, and self-congratulations; it reminds us that these, too, are transitory experiences.

When teenagers are able to practice shifting into the now and experience the present, it will lessen the intense "What do they think of me?" thinking that is such a huge rock in their consciousness.

In the present moment, we have the power to create. Trust this power in yourself, and encourage your teen to do the same. You can begin again *right now, right where you are.*

To learn more about the power of being here now, try some of these ideas.

* Right now, pay attention to each of your five senses in turn. What can you hear? What noises are in the room and outside it? It doesn't matter if it's the hum of a computer or birdsong; noticing it is the key to coming into the present moment. What can you see from your current position? What's the quality of the light around you? Allow your eyes to rest on a single object and notice its color, contour, and size; let your eyes travel its terrain slowly. Similarly, what can you smell or taste? What physical sensations are you aware of? How does your body rest on the chair you're sitting on? How do your clothes feel? Notice if your breath pattern changes as you focus on what's in your immediate present. Invite your teen to do this with you; take turns noticing one detail and telling each other what it is.

* Commit to doing one thing at a time during a particular daily event. For instance, decide that you're going to simply eat breakfast instead of also reading the newspaper or watching the *Today* show. If your pattern is to continue working during your noon meal, commit to moving away from your desk. Invite your teen to do the same, perhaps by not listening to music, doing homework, and instant messaging at the same time. Know that there's time enough for everything.

* Alternatively, identify your most absent-minded multitasking moments and commit to finding a new pattern. I sometimes notice that I'm tempted to keep my hands busy at my desk or in the kitchen while I'm talking to my daughters. On those occasions, I try to remember to take a deep breath, relax my hands, and be fully present in the conversation with them.

* Gently point out to your teen when you notice multitasking that seems counterproductive. If he is trying to do too many things at one time, offer to help with sorting through priorities. Together, you can identify the right order in which to complete all the items clamoring for his attention.

• When your teen is struggling with disappointment or other negative feelings that seem to be lingering, invite her to practice the present with you. Remember that any experience makes a good focal point for centering attention on the present; simply sitting in your teen's room with her and paying careful attention to the sensory experiences available there is enough. Talk her through reining in her rambling thoughts and focusing on the now rather than all that's coming up or what happened in the past.

• Look at your son or daughter with a new awareness today. I find that my children evolve and change faster than my image of them morphs. Seeing my kids with fresh eyes often takes more effort than relying on my old definitions of who they are. But, when I bring myself to a conversation or interaction with a blank slate kind of awareness, I allow myself to get to know them as they truly are, in that moment. The truth is, they are changing faster than my ideas of them can keep up. So, I can joyfully come to know them day by day rather than by old associations and expectations. When I remember to do this, I'm always surprised at the young women I see.

• The "atmosphere" of your home is a subtle concept with a vast influence on those living there. It's the feeling someone gets when they enter your house and can be a sensation of tension, chaos, and disconnected emotions or of bustling goodwill, lightheartedness, and caring. You can shift the energy in your home anytime and in so doing shift how your teens feel when they are there. Do a quick assessment of your home's atmosphere. Are you walking on eggshells half the time? Do your teen's friends feel welcome? Are rooms disorganized and cluttered? Is there shouting and disrespect? It's hard to craft a soulful home when those who live in the house feel put down or insignificant. Make today the day you attend to your home's atmosphere. With God's help it's never too late to make one small change and reap huge results.

Infinite Possibilities

Focusing on the present is a tool for allowing ourselves to sink into peace, after which it's easier to look at the world around us with fresh eyes. Naturally, we get to choose what we see when we look through those eyes. To live as if each moment of every day contains the potential for a new beginning, we need to also cultivate the awareness that anything is possible.

Embracing infinite possibilities is more than being optimistic. Optimists believe that life will turn out well; those who embrace infinite possibilities believe that life will turn out well in ways they can't begin to foresee. Embracing infinite possibilities means that we act, think, and speak as if our past experiences have nothing to do with what the future holds for us.

Our responses to our lives and our teens are closely related to our spiritual convictions. In this new day, what do we believe? Do we trust in a power greater than ourselves that is lovingly guiding our teens and us through this time of change? How does this knowing shift our response to a teen who stays out past curfew, talks back, chooses friends we'd label "losers," changes her mind every two seconds, bursts into tears, or snarls his responses?

I learned a very useful phrase several years ago. It helps create possibility instead of a future determined by past experiences.

Up until now.

These words fit into sentences that could sound like these: "I've always been disappointed by my son's choices." "I'm easily frustrated by my kid's actions." "I work so hard, my life is a whirl, I don't give my daughter the time I should."

When the substitution is made, they turn into: "Up until now, my son has made some irresponsible choices." "Up until now, I've been an impatient parent." "Up until now, I haven't had time to do one on one activities with my daughter."

This is more than just semantics. By inserting these three words into how we speak and think, we acknowledge the truth that we can choose a new way of seeing and living at any time. The present moment marks the transition between what has been and what can be.

This can also be an important practice for teens. The primary goal of adolescents is to develop a comfortable and fairly complete picture of who they are and how they fit into the world. Their experiences create an important mirror in which they see themselves.

Sometimes, though, teens perceive an inaccurate or unproductive image of themselves in the mirror created by their experiences. "I'm not good at math." "I don't do well at sports." "I can't draw." "I don't have many friends."

One of the best tools we can offer them is the perspective that three simple words represent.

"Up until now, math has been challenging for you."

"Up until now, you haven't found your sport."

"Up until now, your drawing skills haven't been what you'd like them to be."

"Up until now, you haven't had as many friends as you'd like to."

As parents, we know the degree to which our experiences of ourselves and of life can change within the space of a few months or years. When we make a practice of replacing absolute statements with ones that include "up until now," we reaffirm the truth about life—that it is full of infinite possibilities. As we help our teens cut the ties between the past and the future, these possibilities become more available to them in every moment.

To expand the possibilities that lie just beyond the threshold of the present moment, try one or more of the following suggestions:

• Distinguish between knowing what and knowing how. When we have a clear idea about the future we want to move into, bolstered by deeply felt desire, the ways by which that future goal takes place can surprise us. Our chief job is to identify what we can see as our greatest possible future good; the universe takes care of the rest. The essence of what we want for example, might be a home full of beauty and serenity, a place our teens are comfortable hanging out in with friends. How our home gets to that point will become clear day by day as we focus on the image rather than a vision of what our home lacks.

• Share the power of personal stories with your teen. When my oldest daughter was in her early teen years, I told her anecdotes about my own adolescent discomforts and feelings of loneliness and read her a few entries from my thirteen-year-old diary. As I matured, those feelings vanished—and they will for her, too.

• Search out stories of teens doing truly inspirational things in the world and share them with your child. Just the other day, I read about an Eagle Scout in our community who organized a coat drive during the holidays. What began as an idea in a single mind turned into warmth surrounding hundreds of people during the chilliest part of the year. Stories like these abound and serve as proof positive of the power of new beginnings.

• "As if" your way into the future. If you're like many of us, perhaps your life as a person and a parent, your teen's life, or your relationship hasn't provided everything that you've longed for. Start today by acknowledging that the seed of what you most want lies within you. Act as if it's already the case, and you'll find yourself making steady progress toward living the reality.

• Consider adopting "just for today" as your mantra. *Just for today, I'll speak only loving words to those I love. Just for today, I will notice my fear-based thoughts without acting them out. Just for today, I'll spend more time listening to my teen.* The truth is, that's enough. Take care of today, and the rest of your life will take care of itself.

Begin Now

I dreamed last night that my daughter Elizabeth and I were having dinner in a crowded restaurant in some big city. A bomb exploded and panic ensued. Everyone was rushing and pushing out the front door, Elizabeth and I right along with the crowd. As we got to the sidewalk, flames following us, I desperately tried to pick up Elizabeth. I wanted to hold her in my arms so she would be safe, and we wouldn't become separated. I was having a hard time picking her up; Elizabeth is 5'9" and I'm 5'3". I realized, in the dream, as the observing onlooker character, that it would be much easier to protect this precious child if her body fit more snugly in my arms. I awoke feeling bereft and made myself complete the story. In my morning, semi-awake state, I pictured the end of the dream. I saw Elizabeth strong, fast, and running for safety, next to me but all on her own.

We may miss the sweet little boy or girl who snuggled in our arms, needed us for most everything, and was relatively easy to protect. But we can embrace today as a new beginning in our relationship. Let's see this relationship as a timeless connection in which we allow our child, now a teen, to safely move out on her own. We can rest in the comfort of knowing that she still needs us, just as much as ever, but in different ways.

It is my intention—and my deeply felt desire—that you will use the Ten Principles in this book to begin anew. That you will set goals to be fully present in your teen's life and enjoy the ride. The power of new beginnings allows you to set aside anything you haven't liked about the way you've parented up until now and start over in a new and loving relationship with your teen. It's never too late to begin again.

You can look for the magic in each day, trust your intuition to guide you, release the struggle of controlling your adolescent's behavior, and be flexibly and compassionately firm. You can acknowledge your power as a mirror in your child's life, making sure that you embody values and behaviors you'd like to see in your teen while listening and speaking with greater consideration. You can deepen your awareness that you—and your teenager—are deeply cared for by an infinitely loving Presence that connects all of life in a unified and glorious whole.

You can put down this book and dive into the ideas presented here. Make them your own. Adapt the thoughts in ways that feel right to you, add others that occur to you as you read, using your deepest intuition as your guide. Expect an almost magical shift to occur in your life as you begin to approach your days with conscious intention and attention. Your new beginning as a parent can't help but inform your teen's experience of

Spirit. Watch as this child of yours begins to blossom in the light of your love and God's care.

Blessings to you and the lucky teenagers in your life.

Parents' Insight-Building Exercise

Find a quiet place where you know you won't be disturbed for a few moments. Settle into a chair, making sure that your back is supported. Place your feet flat on the floor in front of you.

Breathe in deeply through your nose and release it slowly through your mouth. Do this a few more times and notice that your shoulders start to relax. Imagine that they are attached to your ears with a piece of string and mentally cut the string, allowing your shoulders to release more fully.

Imagine that you and your teen are standing silently, side by side in front of a closed door that is wide enough to accommodate two people passing through it at the same time. In your mind's eye, create a clear picture of this door. Is it heavy and wooden or graceful and glass-paned? Allow your mind to fill in the details of your current surroundings. Notice each in turn, allowing yourself to have a full imaginary experience. What can you see? Hear? Smell? Feel? Use each of your senses in turn, exploring your environment.

When you're ready, step toward the door. Place your hand on the knob or handle and turn it. It turns quite readily, and the door swings open easily and silently, revealing what it concealed.

You see precisely what it is that you most deeply desire in the future. Allow your imagination to create a vivid picture of the other details of your future. What does it look like? Sound like? Feel like?

You take a step forward, turning to your teen and silently inviting him or her to join you. He or she does so eagerly, with the energy of a small child excited to explore new territory. Together, you move through the door into the future.

Whatever the details of the situation, the light that surrounds you on this side of the door is bright white. Feel it cascading over you from above, and notice how it also washes over your teen, surrounding him in a cocoon of brilliance. What else do you feel in this new space? Notice what you see, hear, and sense. Breathe this experience into your body as deeply as you can. Remain here for as long as you like—and return whenever you wish.

Parents' Check-In Questions

• When in your life have you had a do-over? What did you leave behind to move into a new future?

• What qualities would you like to embrace more of as a parent? Patience, a sense of humor, more structure in your own life so that you have more time for your relationship with your teen?

• What did you do or fail to do *today* that you'd go back and revise? Can you do so?

• How much of the time do you multitask? What is this experience like for you?

• How much of the time does your teen multitask? How does it seem to affect him or her?

• During the past week, when did you feel most present? When was it hardest for you to feel in touch with your current situation? What could you do differently next time?

• If you could do one thing differently just for today, what would it be?

• What limiting thoughts can you transform with the phrase "up until now"?

• What limiting thoughts does your teen express that you can help him or her transform with the phrase "up until now"?

• What was the atmosphere in your home growing up? Are there elements of that energy in your home today? What small step might you take today to begin to create more positive energy?

Conversation Starters

A mother of a fourteen-year-old son says that the best times to talk to him are when he's helping her set the table for dinner or she's making dinner and he is in and out of the kitchen grabbing snacks. At a similar moment in your teen's life when he or she seems ripe for a heart-to-heart, start it with one of these:

- Have you ever felt like you wanted to start all over? When was it, and what was that like for you?

- Have you heard people say that "today is the first day of the rest of your life"? What does that mean to you?

- Do you know anyone your age who is doing something that seemed impossible?

- What would you really like to experience in the future that seems impossible right now?

- Does the atmosphere in our home support you?

- Do your friends like to come to our house?

- How might we make our home a place that feels nurturing to you and your friends?

Resources

Hotlines and Web sites

AIDS AND HIV

- AIDS Clinical Trials Information Service
  (800) 874-2572
- CDC National HIV/AIDS Hotline
  (800) 342-2437 (English) (24 hours)
- HIV/AIDS Treatment Information Service
  (800) HIV-0440
- National AIDS Hotline
  (800) 342-2437
  www.ashastd.org/nah/tty.html
- Project Inform National HIV/AIDS Treatment Hotline
  (800) 822-7422

ALCOHOL ABUSE

- ADCARE Hospital Helpline
  (800) ALCOHOL
- Al-Anon Family Group Headquarters
  (800) 356-9996
  www.al-anon.org
- AlATeen
  www.al-anon.alateen.org
- Alcohol and Drug Helpline
  (800) 821-4357
- American Council on Alcoholism
  (800) 527-5344
- Children of Alcoholics Foundation
  (800) 359-COAF
- National Clearinghouse for Alcohol and Drug Information
  (800) 729-6686
- National Council on Alcoholism and Drug Dependence, Inc.
  (800) 622-2255

AFTER SCHOOL ACTIVITIES

- Federally Funded After School Activities
  www.afterschool.gov

ANIMALS

- Animal Rights Groups
  www.worldanimalnet.com
- Humane Teen
  www.humaneteen.org/reclinks3.html
- Liberation Now
  www.defendanimals.org/libnow/
- Listing of Companies that Don't Test on Animals
  www.allforanimals.com

ANXIETY

- Anxiety Disorder Line
  (888) ANXIETY
  (888) 826-9438
- Panic Disorder Line
  (800) 64-PANIC
  (800) 647-2642

BOOKS AND TEEN WRITING SITES

- Merlyn's Pen
  www.merlynspen.com/college_list.htm
- Merlyn's Writing Sites
  www.merlynspen.com/links.htm
- Spiritual Themes in Young Adult Books
  www.scholar.lib.vt.edu/ejournals/ALAN/spring96/mendt.html
- Teen Writing Opportunites
  www.bettendorflibrary.com/teen/writers.htm
- YALSA—Booklists
  www.ala.org/yalsa/booklists/index.html

CHILD ABUSE

- CHILDHELP USA® National Child Abuse Hotline
  (800) 4-A-CHILD
  www.childhelpusa.org

CRISES

- National Youth Crisis Hotline
  (800) 448-4663

DISABILITIES

- Children and Youth With Disabilities
  (800) 695-0285
  www.nichcy.org
- Smart Kids With Learning Disabilities
  www.smartkidswithld.org

DRUG ABUSE

- Alcohol and Drug Issues for Teens
  www.child.net/drugalc.htm
- Drug Help
  (800) 378-4435
  (800) 202-2463
- Housing and Urban Development Drug Information and Strategy Clearinghouse
  (800) 955-2232
- Inhalants
  www.inhalants.org/

- National Parents Resource Institute for Drug Education
  (800) 279-6361
  (800) 853-7867
- National Inhalant Prevention Coalition
  (800) 269-4237 (Recording)
- Narcotics Anonymous
  www.na.org

EATING DISORDERS

- National Association of Anorexia Nervosa & Associated Disorders
  (847) 831-3438
  www.anad.org

ENTERTAINMENT

- Power Of Sound
  www.thepowerofsound.com/powerofsound.html
- Reel Spirit Movie Reviews
  www.spiritsite.com/forums/columns/reel
- ReelAppeal Spiritual Movies
  www.SpiritualParenting.com

ENVIRONMENTAL ISSUES

- Audubon Society
  www.audubon.org
- American Rivers
  www.americanrivers.org/
- The Forum on Religion and Ecology
  www.environment.harvard.edu/religion/main.html
- Greenpeace International
  www.greenpeace.org
- National Resource Defense Council
  www.nrdc.org
- Nature Conservancy
  www.nature.org
- Sierra Club
  www.sierraclub.org
- Union of Concerned Scientists
  www.ucsusa.org
- Wilderness Society
  www.wilderness.org

- National Wildlife Federation
  www.wilderness.org
- World Resources Institute
  www.wri.org

FAMILY CONFLICTS

- A-WAY-OUT
  (800) 292-9688
- Boys Town 24-Hour National Hotline
  (800) 448-3000

GIFTS

- Serrv International
  www.Serrv.org
- Blue Moon
  www.Bluemoon.org

GOVERNMENTAL ISSUES

- Nation One
  www.nation1.org

HEALTH ISSUES

- National Health Information Center
  (800) 336-4797
  www.health.gov/nhic/

INSPIRATIONAL

- Inspirational Teen Quotes
  www.motivateus.com/tquotes.htm

INTERNSHIPS AND JOBS

- Idealist
  www.idealist.org

INTUITION

- www.LynnRobinson.com

MEDITATION
- www.meditationcenter.com

MENTAL HEALTH
- National Mental Health Association
  (800) 969-6642
  www.nmha.org

MIRACLES
- The Miracles Page
  www.mcn.org/1/Miracles/

MULTICULTURAL ISSUES
- Minority Health Resource Center
  (800) 444-6472 (en espanol)
  www.omhrc.gov

ORGANIC CLOTHING
- Animal Rights Stuff
  www.AnimalRightsStuff.com
- A Happy Planet
  www.ahappyplanet.com
- Family Organics
  www.organic-cotton-clothes.com
- Maggie's
  www.OrganicClothes.com
- Now Sweat Apparel
  www.nosweatapparel.com

PARENTING
- Raising a Teen
  www.parent-teen.com
- Spiritual Parenting
  www.spiritualparenting.com
- Talking with Kids About Tough Issues
  www.talkingwithkids.org

PASTORAL COUNSELORS
- American Association of Pastoral Counselors
  www.aapc.org/centers.htm

PEACE

- Prayer for World Peace

  www.worldpeace.org

PRAYER

- Prayers for Girls

  www.Girlprayers.com
- Prayer Request

  www.lecworld.org/prayerrequest.html
- World Prayers

  www.worldprayers.org

PREGNANCY CRISIS

- America's Crisis Pregnancy Helpline

  (800) 672-2296

RAPE

- Rape Resources

  www.womensstudies.homestead.com/rape.html
- Rape, Abuse, and Incest National Network

  (800) 656-4673

  www.rainn.org

RELIGIONS AND DENOMINATIONS IN NORTH AMERICA (MOST MAJOR)

- Adherents

  www.Adherents.com

- Buddhism

  www.dharmanet.com

- Christianity

  American Baptist Church

  www.abc-usa.org

  Assemblies of God

  www.ag.org

  Church of Christ, Scientist (Christian Science)

  www.tfccs.com

  www.spirituality.com

  Church of Jesus Christ of Latter-Day Saints (Mormon)

  www.lds.org

  Episcopal Church

  www.ecusa.anglican.org

  Greek Orthodox Archdiocese of America

  www.goarch.org

  Jehovah's Witnesses

  www.watchtower.org

  The Lutheran Church

  www.lcms.org

  National Baptist Convention

  www.nationalbaptist.org

Presbyterian Church
www.pnbc.org

The Roman Catholic Church
www.nccbuscc.org

Seventh-Day Adventist Church
www.adventist.org

Society of Friends (Quakers)
www.fgcquaker.org

Unitarian Universalists Association
www.uua.org

United Church of Christ
www.ucc.org

The United Methodist Church
www.umc.org

United Church of Religious Science
(Science of Mind)
www.scienceofmind.com

Unity Church
www.unity.org

- Hinduism
  www.hindu.org
- Islam
  www.islam.org
  www.ias.org (Sufism)
- Judaism

  Rabbinical Council of America (Orthodox)
  www.rabbis.org

  Union of American Hebrew Congregation (Reform)
  www.uahc.org

  The United Synagogue of Conservative Judaism
  www.uscj.org

- JBahai
  www.us.bahai.org
- Shintoism
  www.shinto.org
- Sikhism
  www.sikhs.org

RELIGION AND SCIENCE

- Metanexus
  www.metanexus.net

RUNAWAYS

- Covenant House Nineline
  (800) 999-9999
- National Center for Missing and Exploited Children
  (800) 843-5678
- National Runaway 24-Hour Switchboard
  (800) 621-4000

SERVICE PROJECTS

- America's Second Harvest

  www.americassecondharvest.org

- Servenet

  www.servenet.org

SEXUAL EDUCATION

- Sex Etc.-For Teens by Teens

  www.sexetc.com

SEXUALLY TRANSMITTED DISEASES

- Centers for Disease Control and Prevention National STD Hotline

  (800) 227-8922

- Herpes Resource Center

  (800) 230-6039

- STD Hotline

  (800) 227-8922

  www.ashastd.org

SEXUAL IDENTITY

- Gay and Lesbian National Hotline

  (800) THE-GLNH

  (800) 843-4564

  www.glnh.org

- Making Schools Safe

  www.aclu.org/safeschools

SPIRITUALITY

- Beliefnet

  www.Beliefnet.com

- God Allows U-Turns: Teens!

  www.godallowsuturns.com/teenlinks.htm

- Ray Whiting Mandalas

  www.raywhiting.com/mandala

- Sacred Texts

  www.sacred-texts.com/index.htm

- Science & Spirit

  www.sciencespirit.org/webextras/teensclique.htm

SAFE SPORTS

- Moms Team

  www.momsteam.com
- Teams of Angels

  www.TeamsofAngels.com

SUBSTANCE ABUSE

- Freevibe

  www.freevibe.com
- National Council on Alcoholism and Drug Dependence

  (800) 622-2255

  www.ncadd.org

SUICIDE

- American Foundation for Suicide Prevention

  (800) SUICIDE

  (800) 784-2433

  www.yellowribbon.org

TEEN SITES

- Blue Moon

  www.bluemoon.com
- CyberTeens

  www.cyberteens.com
- Teen Central

  www.teencentral.net
- Teen Voices

  www.teenvoices.com
- Teenwire

  www.teenwire.com

VIOLENCE

- National Campaign Against Youth Violence

  www.ncayv.org
- National Domestic Violence Hotline

  (800) 799-7233

  (800) 787-3224 (TDD)
- National Organization for Victim Assistance

  (800) 879-6682

- National Sexual Violence Resource Center
  (877) 739-3895
  www.nsvrc.org
  www.teenpcar.com
- Center for the Prevention of School Violence
  (800) 299-6054
  www.ncsu.edu/cpsv
- National Alliance for Safe Schools
  (301) 654-2774
  www.safeschools.org
- Don't Laugh at Me (DLAM)
  www.dontlaugh.org

VOLUNTEERING
- Servenet
  www.servenet.org

WEB SITES FOR GIRLS
- Girl Power
  www.girlpower.com
- Girl Scouts
  www.girlscouts.org
- Girl Site
  www.girlsite.com
- Girl Tech
  www.girltech.com
- Girl Zone
  www.girlzone.com
- Girl's Life
  www.girlslife.com
- Gurl
  www.gurl.com

WOMEN'S ISSUES

- Endometriosis Association
  (800) 992-3636 (Recording)
- National Osteoporosis Foundation
  (800) 223-9994
- National Women's Health Information Center
  (800) 994-9662
- PMS Access
  (800) 222-4767 (Recording)
- Women's Health America Group
  (800) 558-7046 (Recording)
- Women's Sports Foundation
  (800) 227-3988

YOGA

- Yoga.com
  www.Yoga.com
- Yoga Journal
  www.YogaJournal.com
- Yoga Directory
  www.YogaDirectory.com

YOUTH ORGANIZATIONS (SPIRITUAL)

- Focus
  www.infocus.org
- North American Interfaith Network
  www.nain.org/library/youthorg.htm
- Young Life
  www.YoungLife.org

Books for Teens
Fiction

COMING OF AGE

- Anderson, Laurie Halse. *Speak*. New York: Penguin, 2002.
- Enger, Leif. *Peace Like a River*. Berkeley, CA: Atlantic Monthly Press, 2001.
- Frank, Ann. *Ann Frank: The Diary of a Young Girl*. New York: Bantam, 1993.
- Kidd, Sue Monk. *The Secret Life of Bees*. Penguin, 2003.
- Lee, Harper. *To Kill a Mockingbird*. Little Brown, reissue: 1988.
- Potok, Chaim. *The Chosen*. New York: Simon & Schuster, 1967.
- Salinger, J.D., *The Catcher in the Rye*. Boston: Little Brown & Company, 1991.
- Twain, Mark. *The Adventures of Tom Sawyer*. University of California Press, 2002.

DIVERSITY

- Anaya, Rudolfo. *Bless Me, Ultima*. Berkeley: TQS, 1972.
- Asher, Sandy. *With All My Heart, With All My Mind: Thirteen Stories About Growing Up Jewish*. New York: Simon & Schuster, 1999.
- Craven, Margaret. *I Heard the Owl Call My Name*. New York: Dell, 1973.
- Kingsolver, Barbara. *The Poisonwood Bible: A Novel*. New York: Harper Perennial, 1999.
- Levitin, Sonia. *The Return*. New York: Fawcett Juniper, 1978.
- Marshall, James Vance. *Walkabout*. Littleton, MA: Sundance Publishing, 1959.

FANTASY

- Carroll, Lewis. *Alice in Wonderland*. New York: Ace Books, 1980.
- L'Engle, Madeleine. *A Wrinkle in Time*. New York: Yearling Books, 1973.
- Service, Pamela F. *The Reluctant God*. New York: Atheneum Books, 1988.
- Bach, Richard. *Jonathan Livingston Seagull: A Story*. New York: William & Morrow Co, 1973.
- Coatsworth, Elizabeth. *The Cat Who Went to Heaven*. New York: Aladdin/Macmillan, 1990.
- Highwater, Jamake. *Anpao: An American Indian Odyssey*. New York: Lippincott, 1977.
- Saint-Exupéry, Antoine de. *The Little Prince*. New York: Harcourt Young Classics, 1968.
- Swift, Jonathan. *Gulliver's Travels*. Los Angeles: Price Stern Sloan, 1947.

FRIENDSHIP

- Farley, Carol. *Ms. Isabelle Cornell, Herself*. New York: Simon & Schuster Children's, 1980.

RELATIONSHIPS

- Paterson, Katherine. *Jacob Have I Loved*. New York: Harper Trophy, 1980.
- Rylant, Cynthia. *Missing May*. New York: Dell Yearling, 1992.
- Staples, Suzanne Fisher. *Shabanu: Daughter of the Wind*. New York: Knopf/Borzoi Sprinters, 1989.
- Maclean, Norman. *A River Runs Through It and Other Stories*. Chicago: University of Chicago Press (Trd), 2001.

SCHOOL

- Kerr, M.E. *Is That You, Miss Blue?* New York: Dell, 1975.

SCIENCE FICTION

- Dyer, Wayne W. *Gifts from Kykis*. New York: Pocket Books, 1984.

SELF DISCOVERY

- Hesse, Hermann. *Siddhartha*. New York: New Directions, 1951.
- Newbery, Linda. *The Shell House*. London: David Fickling Books, 2002.
- Paulsen, Gary. *The Island*. New York: Dell, 1988.
- Rylant, Cynthia. *A Fine White Dust*. New York: Dell Yearling, 1986.
- Voltaire, Francois-Marie Arouet. *Candide*. London: Oxford University Press, 1968.

Nonfiction

ANGER
- Nhat Hanh, Thich. *Anger: Wisdom for Cooling the Flames.* New York: Riverhead Books, 2002.

ANIMALS
- Chernak McElroy, Susan. *Animals as Guides for the Soul.* New York: Ballantine Books, 1999.
- Goodall, Jane & Bekoff, Mark. *The Ten Trusts: What We Must Do to Care for the Animals We Love.* New York, HarperSanFrancisco, 2002.
- Mitman, Gregg. *Reel Nature: America's Romance with Wildlife on Film,* Cambridge, MA: Harvard University Press, 1999.

AIDS AND HIV
- Byars, Betsy. *The Eighteenth Emergency.* New York: Viking, 1973.
- Shilts, Randy. *And the Band Played On: Politics, People And the AIDS Epidemic.* New York: Viking Penguin, 1987.

ARTS AND ENTERTAINMENT
- Teague, Raymond. *Reel Spirit: A Guide to Movies That Inspire, Explore and Empower.* Unity Village, MO: Unity House, 2000.

ASTROLOGY AND DREAMS
- Abadie, M. J. *Teen Astrology: The Ultimate Guide to Making Your Life Your Own.* Rochester, VT: Bindu Books, 2001.
- Garfield, Patricia, Ph.D. *The Dream Book: A Young Person's Guide to Understanding Dreams.* Plattsburgh, NY: Tundra Books, 2002.

CONFLICT RESOLUTION
- Beekman, Susan and Jeanne Holmes. *Battles, Hassles, Tantrums & Tears: Strategies for Coping with Conflict and Making Peace at Home.* New York: Hearst Books, 1993.
- Trujillo, Michelle L. *Why Can't We Talk: What Teens Would Share If Parents Would Listen.* Deerfield Beach, FL: Health Communications, Inc., 2000.

ENVIRONMENTAL ISSUES
- Butterfly Hill, Julia. *The Legacy of Luna, The Story of a Tree, a Woman and The Struggle To Save the Redwoods.* New York: HarperSanFrancisco, 2000.
- Goodall, Jane. *Reason for Hope: A Spiritual Journey.* New York: Warner Books, 2000.
- Leeds, Joshua. *The Power of Sound: How to Manage Your Personal Soundscape for a Vital, Productive, and Healthy Life.* Inner Traditions Intl Ltd, 2001.

INSPIRATIONAL

- Allenbaugh, Kay, ed. *Chocolate for a Teen's Soul: Life-Changing Stories for Young Women About Growing Wise and Growing Strong.* New York: Simon & Schuster, 2000.
- Cotner, June. *Teen Sunshine Reflections: Words for the Heart and Soul.* New York: Harper Trophy, 2002.
- Dyer, Wayne. *What do you Really Want for your Children?* Quill, 1981.
- Gawain, Shakti, *Creative Visualization.* New World Library, 2002.
- Holtz, Lou. *A Teen's Game Plan for Life.* Notre Dame, IN: Sorin Books, 2002.
- Jarvis, F. Washington. *With Love and Prayers: A Headmaster Speaks to the Next Generation.* Boston, MA: David R. Godine Pubishler, 2000.
- Wade-Gayles, Gloria. *My Soul is a Witness: African-American Women's Spirituality.* Beacon Press, 1995.
- Orloff, Judith. *Positive Energy: 10 Extraordinary Prescriptions for Transforming Fatigue, Stress, and Fear into Violence, Strength and Love.* Harmony Books, 2004.
- Scovel-Shinn, Florence. *The Game of Life and How to Play It.* The C.W. Daniel Company Ltd, 1999.

INTERPERSONAL RELATIONSHIPS

- Paul, Anthea. *Girlosophy 2: The Love Survival Kit (Girlosophy).* London: Allen & Unwin, 2002.

INTUITION

- Orloff, Judith. *Intuitive Healing.* Random House, New York, 2000.
- Robinson, Lynn A. *Compass of the Soul.* Andrews McMeel Publishing, Kansas City, 2003.

MEDITATION

- Piver, Susan. *Joyful Mind.* New York, New York, 2002.

MIRACLES

- Mary Ellen, *Expect Miracles.* Berkeley, CA: Conari Press, 1999.

NUTRITION

- Melina, Vesanto. Brenda Davis, and Victoria Harrison. *Becoming Vegetarian: The Complete Guide to Adopting a Healthy Vegetarian Diet.* Summertown, TN: Book Publishing Co., 2000.
- Schlosser, Eric. *Fast Food Nation.* Perennial, 2002.

ORGANIZATION

- Morgenstern, Julie. *Organizing from the Inside Out for Teenagers: The Foolproof System for Organizing Your Room, Your Time, and Your Life.* New York: Owl Books, 2002.

PEACE

- Hepner, Lisa. *Peaceful Earth.* New York: Hold the Vision, 2003.

POETRY

- Banks, Coleman. *The Illuminated Rumi*. New York: Broadway Books, 1997.
- Ladinsky, Daniel. *Love Poems From God: Twelve Sacred Voices from the East and West*. Penguin Compass, 2002.

PRAYER

- Roth, Gabrielle. *Sweat your Prayers: Movement as Spiritual Practice*. New York: Jeremy P. Tarcher, 1997.
- Straus, Celia. *Prayers on my Pillow*. New York: Ballantine Books, 1998.
- Sweeney, Jon. *Praying with Our Hands*. Woodstock, VT: SkyLight Paths Publishing, 2002.

RAISING DAUGHTERS

- Pipher, Mary. *Reviving Ophelia: Saving the Selves of our Adolescent Girls*. Ballantine Books, 1995.

SELF-HELP: MOTIVATIONAL

- Carlson, Richard PhD. *Don't Sweat the Small Stuff for Teens: Simple Ways to Keep Your Cool in Stressful Times*. New York: Hyperion, 2000.
- Covey, Sean. *The 7 Habits of Highly Effective Teens: The Ultimate Teenage Success Guide*. New York: Simon & Schuster, 1998.
- Covey, Sean. *The 7 Habits of Highly Effective Teens Workbook* New York: Franklin Covey Publishing, 1999.
- Covey, Sean. *Daily Reflections for Highly Effective Teens*. New York: Simon & Schuster, 1998.
- Covey, Sean, and Debra Harris. *The 7 Habits of Highly Effective Teens Journal*. New York: Franklin Covey Publishing, 1999.
- Frankl, Viktor. *Man's Serach for Meaning*. Washington Square Press, 1997.
- Holtz, Lou. *A Teen's Game Plan for Life*. Notre Dame, IN: Sorin Books, 2002.
- Kushner, Harold. *When Bad Things Happen to Good People*. Avon, 1983.
- McGraw, Jay. *Life Strategies for Teens*. New York: Fireside, 2000.
- Peyser, Randy. *Crappy to Happy: Small Steps to Big Happiness NOW!* Boston, MA: Red Wheel/Weiser, 2002.

SERVICE PROJECTS AND SOCIAL ACTION

- Bell, Derric. *Ethical Ambition: Living a Life of Meaning and Worth*. New York, Bloomsbury, 2002.
- Boyers, Sara Jane, *Teen Power Politics: Make Yourself Heard*. Millbrook Press, 2000.
- Lewis, Barbara A. and Espeland, Pamela. *The Kid's Guide to Service Projects: Over 500 Service Ideas for Young People Who Want to Make a Difference*. Minneapolis, MN: Free Spirit Publishing, 1995.
- Lewis, Barbara A. et al. *The Kid's Guide to Social Action: How to Solve the Social Problems You Choose and Turn Creative Thinking into Positive Action*. Minneapolis, MN: Free Spirit Publishing, 1998.

SPIRITUAL

- Abadie, M. J. *The Goddess in Every Girl: Develop Your Teen Feminine Power.* Rochester, VT: Bindu Books, 2002.
- Anderhub, Werner and Roth, Hans. *Crop Circles: Exploring the Designs & Mysteries.* New York: Lark Books, 2002.
- Finley, Mitch. *Prayer for People Who Think Too Much.* Woodstock, VT: SkyLight Paths Publishing, 1999.
- Kornfield, Jack. *A Path with Heart.* Bantam, 1993.
- Martin, William. *The Parent Tao Te Ching.* Marlowe & Company, 1999.
- Morrell, Mary. *Angels in High-Top Sneakers: And Other Stories to Stir the Soul.* Chicago: Loyola Press, 2000.
- Nicholi, Armand. *The Question of God: C.S. Lewis and Sigmund Freud Debate God, Love, Sex, and the Meaning of Life.* Free Press, 2003.
- Paul, Anthea and Chris L. Jones. *Girlosophy: A Soul Survival Kit.* London: Allen & Unwin, 2001.
- Ruiz, Don Miguel. *The Four Agreements.* Amber-Allen Publishing, 1997.
- Singer, Marilyn. *I Believe in Water: Twelve Brushes with Religion.* HarperCollins, 2000.
- Sweeney, Jon M., ed. *God Within: Our Spiritual Future—As Told by Today's New Adults.* Woodstock, VT: SkyLight Paths Publishing, 2001.
- Tallard Johnson, Julie. *The Thundering Years: Rituals and Sacred Wisdom for Teens.* Rochester, VT: Bindu Books, 2001.
- Teasdale, Wayne. *The Mystic Heart: Discovering a Universal Spirituality in the World's Religions.* New World Library, 2001.
- Walsch, Neale Donald. *Conversations with God for Teens.* Hampton Roads, 2001.
- Winner, Lauren F. *Girl Meets God.* Random House, 2002.
- Zuck, Colleen, Elaine Meyer, and Laurie Daven. *Daily Word for Teens: Discovering What's Sacred in You.* Emmaus, PA: Rodale Press, 2002.

SUBSTANCE ABUSE

- Coombs, Robert H. *Cool Parents, Drug-Free Kids: A Family Survival Guide.* Boston: Allyn and Bacon, 2002.
- Gray, Michael. *Drug Crazy: How We Got Into This Mess and How We Can Get Out.* Random House, 1998.
- Hawkins, J. David, et. al. *Preparing for the Drug-Free Years: A Family Activity Book.* Seattle: Developmental Research and Programs, 1998.

SWEARING

- O'Connor, James V. *Cuss Control: The Complete Book on How to Curb Your Cursing.* New York: Three Rivers Press, 2000.

WRITING

- Cameron, Julie. *The Artist Way.* J. P. Tarcher, 2002.
- Lamott, Anne. *Bird by Bird.* Anchor, 1995.

MISCELLANEOUS

- King, Ross. *Michelangelo and the Pope's Ceiling.* Penguin, 2003.

Index

About the Author

Mimi Doe is a nationally acclaimed parenting expert and author of *Busy but Balanced: Practical and Inspirational Ways to Create a Calmer, Closer Family* and *10 Principles for Spiritual Parenting,* which won a coveted Parents' Choice Seal and was honored as a finalist for the Books for a Better Life Award. She also coauthored *Drawing Angles Near.*

Mimi is the founder of www.SpiritualParenting.com, a Web site dedicated to providing parents with information and support in raising kind, honorable children who remain connected to their spirits and their families. Doe's popular online newsletter, *Spiritual Parenting Thought for the Week,* has fifty thousand subscribers, and parents from around the globe are gathering in Spiritual Parenting Groups to focus on the principles and tools in Doe's books.

Doe is featured weekly on *New Morning* on the Hallmark Channel, and has made many other national television and radio appearances including *The Oprah Winfrey Show* and *The CBS Early Show. Ladies' Home Journal* called her a "parenting guru" and Doe's work has been covered in numerous publications including *Child, Parenting, McCall's, Family Cir-*

cle, Redbook, Reader's Digest, Publishers Weekly, USA Today, The London Independent and *The Washington Post.*

Mimi's workshops and seminars cross all cultural and religious lines and have changed the way thousands of parents interact with the children in their lives.

Doe performs consultations for corporations and nonprofit institutions in their outreach and communication to moms.

Mimi holds a master's degree in Education from Harvard University and lives in Concord, Massachusetts, with her husband and two children, ages thirteen and sixteen.

For more information on Mimi Doe's Spiritual Parenting newsletter, Reel Appeal Movie Guides, Soulful Homes products, upcoming appearances, and Spiritual Parenting Groups around the world, please visit:

www.SpiritualParenting.com.